a little girl called *Squeaks*

a story of hope

Biography of **Laura Gilbert**

Debbie Maddigan

authorHOUSE®

AuthorHouse™
1663 Liberty Drive
Bloomington, IN 47403
www.authorhouse.com
Phone: 1-800-839-8640

© 2011 Debbie Maddigan. All rights reserved.

No part of this book may be reproduced, stored in a retrieval system, or
transmitted by any means without the written permission of the author.

First published by AuthorHouse 5/10/2011

ISBN: 978-1-4567-5405-1 (sc)
ISBN: 978-1-4567-5406-8 (hc)
ISBN: 978-1-4567-5407-5 (e)

Library of Congress Control Number: 2011905427

Printed in the United States of America

Any people depicted in stock imagery provided by Thinkstock are models,
and such images are being used for illustrative purposes only.
Certain stock imagery © Thinkstock.

This book is printed on acid-free paper.

Because of the dynamic nature of the Internet, any web addresses or links contained in
this book may have changed since publication and may no longer be valid. The views
expressed in this work are solely those of the author and do not necessarily reflect the
views of the publisher, and the publisher hereby disclaims any responsibility for them.

Note to the Reader

This is Laura's story. Her mother was an addict and extremely abusive to her growing up. Raised in the poorest section of Vancouver BC it is a miracle she is alive today.

Some readers may find some of the content and language offensive. However, because this is a true story it needs to be told with authenticity. The greatest miracle about Laura's story is she never allowed her past to define her future. It's a story of hope.

Some of the names and places have been changed to protect the innocent.

Acknowledgements

A big "Thank-you," goes to all those who helped in the writing of this book. A special thanks to those who edited, investigated and took pictures; your part was invaluable.

To Mark, I have learned a great deal from you and really appreciated all your input. To Diane, thank you for sharing not only your artistic talents but your friendship.

To all my kids, thank you for your support and prayers. I can't imagine life without you.

And lastly I'd like to thank my husband Shaun who watched me plug away on my laptop for hours, he's my greatest fan!

Index

Part One
Life with Mom

"Rock-a-bye baby, in the tree top. When the wind blows, the cradle will rock. When the bough breaks, the cradle will fall. And down will come baby, cradle and all." When my bough broke, I had no one to catch me because my mother was a drug addicted alcoholic.

I was born in November of 1961. The first home I ever lived in was a place in Vancouver where the nuns looked after children whose mothers didn't know if they wanted to keep them or adopt them out. It took two months for my mother to decide, but in the end, I went home with her. Was it for the best? I'll let you decide.

According to the hospital records I saw as an adult, Social Services monitored us regularly. One of my earliest memories is when I was around four or five years old crying, "Mommy, I have an earache," or scratching myself until I bled from what I learned later on was a yeast infection.

"Quit your damned complaining," Mom hollered as her hand hit the back of my head.

My memories from those early years are like broken flashes, or maybe like little pieces of a nightmare you can't fully remember. They come back to me when I smell something, or hear a certain song. A lot of the music I heard back then I can't even listen to now without some sad memory attached to it.

During the 1960s the slums where we lived on the east side of Vancouver were gentler than they are today. The crime rate wasn't as high and there were fewer gangs.

There were plenty of drugs, though. The drug of choice was heroin because it was cheap and easy to get. The addicts shot up in private, never in the back alleys; they didn't want to draw any attention from the cops. If you weren't a heroin user but wanted a high, you smoked weed or hash.

There were always drunks hanging around outside on the streets, but I never knew what they drank because their booze was usually wrapped in a paper bag.

They were always so friendly. "Hey sweetie, what you doing out here all by yourself," they'd yell as I passed by.

"Nothin," I'd yell back as I hurried away from them. For some reason I never felt afraid because I felt like there was someone looking over me, keeping me safe.

Unlike today you hardly ever saw a drunk sleeping outside, because the police were quick to gather them up and put them in jail for the night.

Some things in the slums haven't changed. You can still see the hookers waiting for a car to pull up and offer them some work, the back alleys are still overflowing with garbage and the rats are busy trying to find their daily food supply.

Time on the skids is the same too because day and night are interchangeable. Sleep happens when you pass out regardless of the time of day. People randomly wander around twenty-four hours of the day, seven days a week and one day simply runs into another.

Really, for most it's a sad existence, but for some reason the slums attracted my mother; she was stuck to them like tar on pavement. It was the only place on earth she felt comfortable, and she lived in the slums no matter where she went, and I had to go with her.

I thought my mother was beautiful. She had black wavy hair, beautiful dark brown eyes, and smooth olive skin. She wore bright red lipstick, and I can't remember her wearing clothing any other color than black, especially when she went out. Black slacks or skirt, scarf, shoes, pantyhose and sunglasses--the only color on her was the red of her lipstick. If I had to pick a color to describe her, it would be black.

When she walked down the street heads turned, men gawked. It was always important for her to look her best, because she enjoyed the lingering looks and the whistles directed towards her. When we were at home, she usually wore a big shirt and nothing else. No underwear or pants just a big sloppy shirt.

I didn't get the dark wavy hair or olive skin. My hair was straight and blonde; my skin was fair and my eyes blue.

I remember one day taking a long drink of something in a cup left on the dresser because I was thirsty. I gulped and gulped and when I was done I had a little wet moustache above my lip. I let out a little burp and gave my mother a huge grin.

"You know Laura, you might not be so damned ugly if you didn't have those buck teeth hanging out of your mouth!" she said. It was the first time I'd ever thought about my own beauty, and her words defined me: I was ugly.

After that I became so self-conscious about my teeth. I seemed to have my hand permanently attached to the front of my mouth. I'd try to stretch my lips over my teeth, careful not to smile or laugh because they might slip out. Maybe if people couldn't see my teeth they might see the blondeness of my hair or the blueness of my eyes. Maybe I looked more like my dad, whoever he was.

I seldom saw Mom smile or laugh, especially where I was concerned, and when she did look at me, it was usually with disgust. She was either drunk or stoned most of the time, and slept any time during the day or night. I think even her dreams were nightmarish because when she woke up she always looked tired and miserable.

"Get out of my way, stupid. You're nothing but a pain in the ass." That is her voice. I hear it whenever I try to do anything. I never once heard her say she loved me and even if she had, her actions said something very different. She never fed me or kept me clean. She never held me or sang softly in my ear when I was sick. She never read me a book or played games with me when we were together. It was easy to pretend we were strangers.

Like many of the people on skid row, we were on social assistance and couldn't afford a nice place to live. The buildings we lived in were old and run down. The rats and the garbage that lined the streets also made their way into the buildings, making them smell awful.

I remember the big thick doors to each room. They were hard for me to open because they were so heavy. They were full of scratches and dents from all the kicks they'd gotten over the years and I'm sure each of them could have told some sad stories.

A whole floor shared one dirty bathroom, and the smell of urine was always strong because the toilets never were cleaned. The bathtub was one of those old clawfoots, and had a constant ring or two around it. I always thought its four feet were trying to hold it up off the dirty floor.

Mom never used that bathroom. Instead, she peed in the sink in our room. She was too drunk to make the trek down the hall and the sink was handier. Maybe, that's why she never wore any underwear. It was one less hassle.

The rooms were old and the paint was cracked on all the walls. They usually had a greyish brown braided rug that smelled like stale booze, cigarettes, and mildew, and people there didn't have very much furniture. Most rooms had a sink, a dresser, and a double mattress on a metal frame that made a terrible creak when you moved.

The inside of our room was always dark. Mom never opened up the windows, curtains, or turned the lights on because she was so sensitive to the light. Sometimes, if I thought she was asleep, I'd creep to the window to look at what was going on outside.

"Shut that damn curtain!" she'd snarl. I'd close the curtain as fast as I could for fear she'd come after me with her fists. The moment I heard her voice I ran to the nearest corner and put my hands over my head.

Cleanliness was not on the top of Mom's list either. She never killed the cockroaches that scurried across the dirty floor or washed the sink after she peed in it. Not to mention the ants that were always busy trying to find any kind of crumb they could take home. There were tons of spider webs in the corners and dust on the ledges and she seldom washed our clothes. We lived in filth, but of course I didn't know that. I was five and everyone we knew lived like we did.

One thing I learned when I was five: when people are drunk, they go from best friends to worst enemies within a matter of minutes. Their laughter turns to yelling and they are no longer buddies.

Most of the time I ignored the fights because they didn't last long, and no one was badly hurt. Drunks in general have a hard time standing up, let alone aiming their fists at one another, but every once in awhile the fights got ugly.

I remember one time Mom was partying with a bunch of men, and I was sitting on the bed playing with an old pocket watch I'd found somewhere. I loved the feeling of the long metal chain as it slid from one finger to the next, and the sound of the constant ticking noise when I put it to my ear. It was a good distraction from the party noise.

Tick-tock, tick-tock, tick-tock. I don't know why, but something about that rhythm soothed me.

My Aunt's ex-fiancé, Ovey, who was also a friend of Mom's, was over for this particular party, and somehow everyone ended up in the hall. Even though they were cursing and yelling at one another, I never thought much of it until I could hear glass hitting the walls.

"What the hell are you doing?" I heard Mom yell.

I quietly got off the bed, and peeked into the hallway. My mother was trying to break up a fight between Ovey and another man. There was a huge struggle until the man I didn't recognize took a beer bottle, and smashed it up against one of the huge wooden doorframes. The glass went flying everywhere, but the top part of the bottle the man was holding looked like shark's teeth. To my horror, he shoved the jagged part right into Ovey's mouth. Ovey screamed in pain, and put his hands to his face. Blood streamed through his fingers, down his neck, and onto the carpet, and the world started to spin. There was blood squirting everywhere, and I felt like I couldn't move. I started to sob, and force myself to take small steps back to the bed.

The noise and commotion out in the hallway suddenly quieted down, and I could hear Mom yelling, "Ovey, are you okay? Talk to me!"

I could hear a gurgling sound as Ovey tried to spit glass out of his mouth. I grabbed the old pocket watch, placed it to my ear, and held it there until its constant ticking lulled me into a deep sleep.

I have no idea what happened to Ovey or the other man. No one ever stayed the whole night so I never saw them again. When I woke the next morning, Mom was sleeping beside me, and there were no other sounds besides her snoring. It was like the night before had never happened. All I wanted to do was get out of the room before Mom woke up, so I quietly got off the bed, and opened the door. Scattered across the floor I could still see the blood and the shattered glass all mixed together. I carefully walked around the mess, and went to the Hudson Bay. As soon as I entered the big sunny store, I forgot about the fight, and headed towards the Malt shop.

I loved the malts they made at the Bay, and so did everyone else by the looks on their faces.

When the woman who worked there saw me come in she said, "Hello sweetie, would you like a malt?"

I nodded. She never once asked me for any money. I think she knew by the way I looked that I didn't have any. Mom seldom combed my hair and I was usually dressed in her clothes and wore her shoes, which were way too big for me. I'm not sure if she ever washed my face, but I could tell by the other kids in the shop I was different. Their clothes were clean and fit them and their hair was nicely combed. Maybe that is why the lady was so nice to me. She felt sorry for me because my mother didn't look after me like the other mothers did. Every time she gave me a malt both our eyes sparkled; when she handed me my malt, mine sparkled because she gave me a treat, and hers sparkled because I think she pitied me.

After my malt, I headed over to Woodward's for something more to eat. Other than the odd free malt, I ate very little because Mom never fed me. Usually I stole food from Woodward's downtown, or the nearest corner store. I used to go into the store and act like I was looking for my mother. Really I was deciding on what I wanted to steal and because I wasn't very tall, I took whatever I could reach.

When I saw what I wanted, I'd quickly take it off the shelf and hide it in my coat or under my shirt and take off.

Today was no different. I went into the store, found my favourite candy that was always on the bottom shelf, and hid it in my coat. I don't know why they had to wrap that candy in crinkly wrapping, it made a noise when I walked and it was a terrifying experience. By the time I got outside, my heart was pounding like a set of drums. I was so afraid that someone might catch me that my mouth dried out from all the nervous tension. I always had a hard time tasting or swallowing the food I'd stolen, because I'd eat it so fast I'd forget to chew. Then when I did swallow, it hurt my throat and the food sat like a rock in my stomach causing a huge stomach ache, but it was better than being hungry.

The fact I never got caught, made me think there really was someone watching over me who cared whether I lived or died.

We received food stamps once a month, and my favourite place to eat was the "White Lunch." It was so amazing because it was buffet style, and I could choose whatever I wanted! Hamburgers, fries, spaghetti, mashed potatoes---the minute we walked into the restaurant, my mouth started watering, and I'd pile as much spaghetti as I could on my plate. Spaghetti was my favourite and I'd eat it until I was so full I couldn't swallow another bite. Mom, unlike me, put very little on her plate.

We always sat on the stools at the counter, and it seemed like it took hours for her to eat. She always chose a curried rice dish, and for some reason she'd eat with her hands, even though they had forks. She played with her food and took little tiny bites. She'd move her rice from one side of her plate to the other, getting her hands all dirty.

Then *bang*--she'd pass out from all the drugs and alcohol, and her face was in her plate! I hated looking at her with her face and hair all stuck together with the rice. As I looked around the restaurant, everyone was looking at us, staring, whispering and shaking their heads. It was embarrassing.

"Wake up, Mom, we need to go home," I said in my quietest voice. "Mom, you need to wake up!"

I'd shake her until finally her head wobbled up from her plate and she sat up in her chair. I'd brush the rice off her face and pick it out of her hair as she looked at me with her hollow, glassy eyes.

"Come on we need to go home. Just hang onto me and I'll help you, okay?" I helped her stand up. She always put her arm around me and used me to keep her balance. It wasn't easy because she was heavy, but somehow I managed.

"Don't forget your Jell-O," the waitress said as we headed out the door. She gave it to me in a cup so it was easier to carry.

"Thank-you."

"You're welcome."

Then she smiled at me. I knew she saw me and not just my drunken mother. It was good memories like that, which kept me going when things got bad.

Mom and I staggered down the sidewalk with me balancing her in one hand, and my Jell-O in the other. I didn't want to drop her or my treat on the pavement. As soon as we got home, I laid her on the bed, and ate my treat. I took little tiny bites and licks to make it last as long as possible, and I loved the sound it made when I squished it through my teeth.

Mom was a restless soul, always looking for something she couldn't find, so we never stayed in one place for long, making it hard for me to make any friends. However, there were lots of pigeons no matter where we lived in Vancouver, and they became my constant companions.

On my way to the fountain to visit the pigeons, I loved to look at how the outside world changed over time. During the winter, everything looked cold, even the trees. They'd lost their leaves leaving them naked and I used to feel sorry for them.

Because it rained most of the time I felt chilled to the bone anytime I was outside. I didn't have any coat or boots to keep me warm and between the wind and the rain it was hard to keep my teeth from chattering.

The pigeons didn't have any warm clothes either, but they didn't mind because the rain never stuck to them like it did to me for some reason. Sometimes I'd watch them for hours as they splashed in the puddles. They never seemed to mind the weather.

In the spring the trees got new leaves. The daffodils were as yellow as the sun, tulips in every colour stretched from yard to yard, and crocuses grew all over the place. I loved playing in the blossoms the Cherry Trees dropped on the sidewalk. Everything was new and fresh, and all the pigeons cooed, and ran around the park with a lot more energy.

"Wait for me," I'd yell, but they never slowed down. They were always in a hurry.

During the summer it was warm and the pigeons were constantly looking for something to eat. I loved sitting by the fountain to cool off. The spray tickled me and made me giggle. I'd watch the pigeons as they scurried from one crumb to another. Sometimes when the pigeons needed a rest they came and sat on my lap to cool off and we'd visit.

"How are you doing today Miss Pigeon?" I said softly. "Did you know you are my best friend in all the world?"

When the fall came, and the Maple trees turned colour, the air was cool, and I worried about the pigeons because I didn't want them to be cold. They were my only friends, and I was afraid if they got too cold they might go away, but they never did.

Unlike the changing seasons, my little pigeon friends always looked the same. Their soft grey backs, and the bright green ring around their necks, mixed in with their purple eyes looked like little rainbows strutting across the grass. They were fun to watch because when they walked they bobbed their heads out of rhythm with their feet. They looked like uncoordinated robots unsure of where they were going, and they made me laugh.

Every day I visited them, they'd cock their heads to the side as if to say, "Come here Laura, come and play," and I always went with them. When it was time for me to go home, they followed me. Their presence made me feel loved, and I liked that I could see them whenever I wanted. They were so faithful and I praise God to this day for creating those little birds.

Mom and I often slept late in the mornings. There was no routine and very little food so there wasn't anything to get up for. When I did get up, I'd try to find something to eat, or I'd head for the park. The only time Mom really came alive was after the sun went down so she never knew where I was anytime during the day. When it got dark outside I'd head home.

Our room was always full of men, and she'd be drunk. She loved to party and before the evening was over she often invited some man to stay the night. I'm not sure how she decided who'd get to stay, but as far as I was concerned, they were all bad.

One night I was trying to stay out of everyone's way when I heard a man say to my Mother, "Now, isn't she a pretty little thing. You never told me about her."

He wasn't the first man to say those words, and he wasn't the last, either. Although I liked the fact someone called me pretty I knew Mom didn't like anyone paying any attention to me. I put my head down, hoping he'd go away but he didn't.

He walked over to me and said so sweetly, "Don't be afraid little one, I won't hurt you." The minute I heard that line, the blood in my body ran cold.

"Go away!" I yelled as my heart pounded in my chest.

"Oh, now you don't really mean that."

Then like all the men before him, he moved closer and closer to me until his hands were running up and down my whole body. A part of me liked what he was doing because I liked the attention and the soft touch felt nice. But mostly I was scared.

"Mommy?" I said softly. "Mommy?" I trembled. I was only five and I didn't understand what was going on. I wanted Mom to help me, but she just watched and never said anything. She stood

11

there, drunk out of her mind and then eventually she'd coax the man onto the bed where he started to touch her the same way. Once again I felt like someone was protecting me even though I couldn't see them.

"Get under the bed and shut-up," she snapped. "I don't want to see your ugly face again until morning, you hear me!" I never had a blanket or a pillow to sleep with; she just wanted me out of her way.

Before I crawled under the bed, I always grabbed my one eyed panda that a Salvation Army lady gave me. The pigeons weren't allowed in the house so my Panda was my best friend. When I crawled under the bed, mumbling how much I hated her friends, my Panda was both my protector and pillow. As I squeezed him, I'd start to calm down and relax. My bear was my safety blanket during those times; I could whisper to him knowing all my secrets were safe. When I wasn't busy with my panda, I drew pictures in the dust that had collected on the floor.

It was hard to get to sleep because the metal bed frame creaked and groaned as my mother and her friends moved rhythmically above me. Sometimes I was afraid the springs were going to break and crush me, but they never did. Eventually the noise stopped, and everyone fell asleep. Although it may have been dirty and cold under the bed, it was the safest place to be when Mom had company.

Occasionally, when Mom didn't have her friends stay the night she allowed me to sleep in the bed with her. I was always careful to stay on my own side because if I happened to do something she didn't like, she'd backhand me. I never knew what might make her mad, so I constantly lived in fear and was so nervous I cringed the moment she moved towards me.

Some nights she woke me up making funny noises next to me. When I opened my eyes to see what she was doing, I could only see her shadow because it was so dark. I could see her touching herself, and I could never figure out what she was doing. I quickly closed my eyes because I didn't want her to see me looking at her. After awhile she got quiet and fell asleep. I was happy when I knew she was sleeping because that meant I could sleep too; it was safe.

The only good thing about the bed was it wasn't as hard as the floor, and I had a pillow and blanket to keep me warm, but to tell you the truth, I liked it under the bed better, because it was quieter, and away from my mother's fists.

Many nights I left the room during the parties, and walked around Granville Street. I was only five, but I never felt afraid. It felt safer outside than inside.

The moon looked like it was resting on the tops of the mountains making the snow glisten. The stars twinkled in the night sky, and I loved trying to see the pictures they made. There was a sense of calmness and order outside that was absent inside our home and I know now the calmness I felt was God's love wrapped around me.

One of my favourite spots to go was the fountain on Georgia Street. I loved the way it looked like two umbrellas when the water squirted out, and when it was warm enough, I'd get right inside, and splash in the water. I'd be soaked by the time I got out, but it was so much fun! People threw their money in the fountain, and I thought they did that for me, so I'd gather up whatever I could find, and go shopping at the Bay.

On the second floor of the Bay, I purchased swans, frogs, and turtle bath toys. I held my toys in one hand and all the coins from the fountain in another as I rushed to the till.

"Oh my," the lady at the counter said as she helped me put my money and toys on the counter. "Looks to me like someone is going to have lots of fun in the tub!"

"Yup," I replied with a huge grin on my face. "Do I have enough money?"

"Let's see, each toy is ten cents." She counted out the change on the counter and I held my breath hoping I had enough. "You have more than enough my dear. Here you can take this money back and use it another time." she replied as she put my toys into a bag.

"Oh thank you," I squealed, and the moment she handed me the bag I rushed home, locked myself in the bathroom at the end of the hall, and poured myself a bath.

The bathroom was just as old and rundown as the rest of the hotel. The paint on the walls was a yellowy brownish colour stained from urine and cigarette smoke. The sink, and bathtub's porcelain was so worn that the black under the white paint was beginning to show through the cracks, and even though the tub was old, and rough, but I loved it, rings and all. I'd run the water as full as I could, and then I'd take all my clothes off, and slide down the side. I loved the feel of the warm water, and the way the water splashed when I hit the bottom. It was like having my own water slide.

"Wahoo," I yelled as I hit the bottom of the tub. Sometimes I spent up to three hours being a little girl who was lost in another world. A safe place away from the rage of my mother, and the men who abused me. The only time I left this imaginary place was when someone was rude enough to be banging on the door.

"Get the hell out of there, I need to use the bathroom," they yelled.

"Go away, I'm not finished yet!" The bathroom was mine, and I was not about to share it with anyone.

"Get out before I beat this door down," was usually the next thing out of their mouths, but when they figured out I wasn't coming out, the banging quit, and I'd go back to my imaginary world.

By the time I got out of the tub, my skin was all bumpy and

wrinkly like an old woman, but the smile I wore reached from ear to ear. Life was good when it was tub time.

Once a month Mom received her welfare cheque and we went shopping. I liked to watch her when she got herself ready; she was so pretty.

"What are you looking at?" I remember her saying to me. Then she put her lipstick on and said, "Stay behind me, and don't smile. I don't want anyone looking at those ugly teeth."

I put my hand over my mouth, walked behind her like she asked, and wished I were at the park with the pigeons.

I used to watch her as she walked in front of me. She looked so elegant. She was tall and thin and had a pretty figure. I wanted to be just like her. The sad part was we really were alike in many ways; few things brought smiles to our faces, and both of us were lost, lonely souls whose lives had no meaning.

We walked to the store and our grocery list was always the same: bread, sandwich spread, liverwurst, hamburger, three packages of Player's Plain cigarettes, a large bottle of cough syrup with codeine, a bottle of 222's and booze.

"Is that all?" The lady behind the counter asked.

"Yes," Mom snapped.

Then the lady put everything in a bag and said, "That will be fifteen dollars and ten cents."

Mom took her cheque out of her purse, wrote something on the back and then the lady gave her some money back. It was the same every month.

We didn't have a fridge, so Mom placed the food on the windowsill to keep it cool. In the winter, it worked fine, but during the summer, most of it went bad. I never liked any of the food she bought anyway. I thought the bread was great for the pigeons, and as for the sandwich spread and liverwurst, they were gross tasting and really stunk!

We didn't have a stove either, so Mom ate the hamburger raw, and that was really disgusting! I may have been hungry, but I could steal something much better to eat than what she bought, so that's what I did to survive.

There was a float shop near-by and one day as I walked by, I peeked inside to see what it looked like. There was a big picture of a long glass, full of ice cream and orange pop, and the minute I saw that picture I knew I needed one. I didn't have any money, so I made sure I sat on the stool nearest the door for a quick escape.

The waitress came over to my stool and said, "Hi sugar pie what would you like?"

"I'd like one of those like what's in the picture." I told her.

"One orange float coming up," she said and off she went. It seemed to take forever before she came back, but the minute I saw her coming with my float, my mouth started to water. Even though I was in a hurry to eat it, I couldn't help but look at the way the orange pop sparkled in the tall glass, and the ice cream sat in the middle like a cloud.

I put my mouth on the straw and sucked up the pop. Every sip from the straw tingled in my mouth, and each swallow was better than the one before.

"This is really good," I said to the waitress. She smiled at me and I took my time slowly sucking the float up the straw until it was all gone. Then I licked out the cup, careful not to leave one drop of orange pop or ice cream. The waitress walked by me on her way to help the other people in the shop, and I smiled at her every time because I didn't want her to get suspicious.

When I was finished my float and it was time to pay, I waited until the waitress had her back to me. Then I took off like a mean dog was chasing me. I never looked back determined to get out of the shop before she could catch me.

The mere fact I left that way tipped her off, and she came running after me; it wasn't a big deal because I knew I could outrun her, and all was going as planned until I ran into a Police Officer! I was not very tall and he looked like a giant compared to me. I am quite sure the orange was still stuck around my mouth, and my tongue for sure was the wrong colour, a dead give-away, not to mention the crazy yelling waitress.

"Stop that kid," she yelled all out of breath, "she didn't pay for her float."

The Police Officer grabbed me and said, "Where do you think you're going in such a hurry?"

I remember how deep his voice was, and how big he looked, which made my legs suddenly feel like rubber. I never talked much, but in my world, a lie well told was better than the truth, and I knew I was in trouble.

"My mommy told me not to talk to strangers," I said in my bravest voice.

"She needs to pay for her float," the waitress persisted.

The policeman told the waitress to go back to her shop and he'd come and talk to her later.

"Where do you live?" The Police officer asked.

I started kicking and screaming hoping to get away from him because the last place I wanted to go was home. Eventually I had to tell him where I lived and he marched me down the sidewalk.

When we arrived at the hotel, he knocked on the door, and I just wanted to die. Mom opened the door and the Police Officer said, "Is this your little girl?"

"Yes," my mother replied as she tried smoothing down her hair.

"She was caught stealing," he said as he took a quick look around, "I am going to let her go this time, but you need to keep a better eye on her in the future."

The more he spoke the colder my mother's eyes got. The

last thing she needed in her life was someone butting into our business.

"Thank you for bringing her home. I'll take care of it," then she grabbed me and slammed the door in the Police Officer's face.

I knew I was in big trouble. She slapped me across the face and said in a hushed voice, "You little pig, what were you doing stealing food?" She hit me so hard I fell to the floor and started to cry.

"Shut up and be quiet or I'll give you a real beating," she hissed.

I grabbed my one eyed Panda, ran to the bed and sobbed quietly. I wasn't thankful for the Police Officer because he'd spoiled my get away and gotten me into big trouble. Good thing the orange float was worth it.

One day simply led to another, and I was always the nearest and most vulnerable whenever Mom needed to throw her fists around. Her words hurt as much as her fists did, and I never understood why she hated me so much.

She was so restless that we were continually on the move from hotel to hotel, taking her addictions with us. No matter where we lived, our room was full of men, booze, and parties, and she loved it.

I remember one time, when I was six, Mom invited some of her men friends over for a few drinks, and the drunker they got the friendlier they became. I didn't like the way one of the men was smiling at me because he looked creepy, so I pretended not to notice him.

Eventually he came over and sat beside me. It had been awhile since one of her friends had come near me, so even though I felt scared, in a way I liked the attention.

"You are as pretty as your mother, or maybe even prettier," he whispered into my ear, "but don't tell her that." Then he smiled and winked at me.

No one had ever told me I was prettier than my mother was. He seemed so sincere I wasn't afraid of him until he put his hands under my clothes and started to touch me in my private parts.

"What are you doing?" I said as I started to shake.

"Do you like it?" he asked.

"I want you to stop, you're scaring me." I sobbed.

"Oh, I'm not hurting you, I love you and that's why I am being so gentle with you. When someone touches you like this, it means they love you." Then he stopped and walked over to my mother. She never told him to quit, and because she didn't, I believed for a long time that he loved me.

I loved my Gramma because she was the only one who ever spent any time with me. It was hard to believe she raised my mother because they were so different. One thing they both did share was their good looks. Gramma was beautiful too.

She was an older looking woman with white shoulder length wavy hair and loving eyes. She liked to wear nicely coloured clothes when she visited, and I loved all the bright colours she wore. I absolutely adored her.

Once a month Gramma rented a nice hotel room downtown and we spent the night together, just the two of us. I loved the rooms she picked because they always had a TV, a bathroom, and a big, comfy bed.

She always gave me a bath, washed and combed my hair, and dressed me in some new, clean clothes. I'll never forget the dress, hat and little purse she brought me once; I felt so grown up and pretty when I wore them.

When I was with Gramma, I couldn't help but smile. She was so much fun to be around, and she brightened my world. When I put my hands to my face to hide my teeth, she said, "Oh Laura, I love your smile. You don't have to cover your mouth when we're together." Then she smiled and I took my hand away from my mouth.

When we went out together, we held hands, and walked side-by-side down the street. She told me all about her Siamese cats, and we laughed about the silly things they did.

"How is your mother, Laura?" Gramma asked. I could tell she was worried about her because she always went from being happy to being sad.

"She's the same," I said.

"And how are you doing? Is your Mom treating you okay?" She knew the answer, but she always asked.

"I'm hungry, Gramma. Where are we going to eat?" hoping to change the subject. I didn't want to ruin our time by telling her how my mother treated me. Our dinner times were too special and I didn't want to think about my mother.

We always went to a nice restaurant and I could order anything I wanted, but I always ordered spaghetti. I loved the way I could slurp the long pieces into my mouth. Sometimes they were so long the noodle hit me in the forehead and made Gramma laugh. I loved to make her happy.

Often when we were eating I'd catch Gramma looking at me and wondered what she was thinking. When our eyes met, she gave me a big smile, and then she'd continue to eat her dinner.

After we ate, we went back to the hotel room and watched either "Mutual of Omaha's Wild Kingdom" or Walter Cronkite" on TV. I sat down on the floor in front of her as she stroked my hair. Then with a twinkle in her eye, and a smile on her face, she said, "Laura why don't you smell my feet, they won't stink, this time."

I always smelled her feet and said, "Holy Smokes, your feet really stink tonight." It was a game we played every time we were together.

"No they don't," she always replied, and then we'd laugh until we cried, never growing tired of playing our silly little game. To make the evening even better, we played "Go Fish," and then it was time for bed.

Before we turned the lights out one night I asked, "Gramma, what's wrong with my mother? Why is she always so mad at me? Am I doing something wrong?"

She got quiet and then she said, "Laura, your mother has always had a restless side to her, even when she was a little girl. She tried, I know she did, but as hard as she tried nothing made her happy. Did you know that she was married, and you have a brother named Darryl?"

I shook my head no and she went on.

"I thought when she got married it might take her sadness away, but it didn't. She was married to a man from eastern Canada. Darryl was only three years old when your mother ended the marriage, and Darryl and his dad moved back to Montreal." Then she choked back her tears and said, "I miss Darryl, he was such a sweet little guy, and in some ways you remind me of him."

"Why did she make them leave? Didn't she love them either?" I asked as I wiped a tear from my eye.

Gramma just looked at me with her tender eyes, and shrugged her shoulders. I guess neither one of us knew the answer to that question.

"Gramma, mommy hits me all the time and I don't know what to do to make her happy."

She looked me in the eye, stoked my hair and said softly, "Laura, your mother is a very sick lady, and that is why she eats the pills and drinks the things she does. She's sad inside, and doesn't know any other way to take her sadness away." Then she paused and took my hand.

I felt upset when she told me that, because if my mother would have let me, I could have made her happy. I wanted to show her I loved her, but she'd never let me come close to her. I don't remember one time she ever gave me a hug. The only time she touched me was when she slapped me across the face or hit me with whatever was in her hand at the time.

21

"Gramma," I asked, "why did she have me if she didn't want her little boy?"

"Well, sometimes Laura, things happen in life we aren't expecting and you were one of them."

So I was an accident. She never wanted me. No wonder she blamed me for everything. If I hadn't come along, she'd have been free to do what she wanted without having me tagging along.

I started to cry and Gramma wrapped her arms around me and held me so tight I could hear her heart beating. She always knew what to do when I felt sad.

"Laura, look at me. Your Mom may not have been expecting you, but I am so thankful you are here," she said. "I don't know what I would do without you." She wiped the tears from my eyes, kissed me on the cheek, and I fell asleep in her arms.

Life was safe with Gramma and I felt loved and wanted when I was around her. I cried every time I had to go home; she didn't cry but I knew by the look on her face she hated taking me back to my mother. I often wondered why she didn't take me home with her. I know now that Grandpa didn't want me around and that's why she always came by herself. Once again, a God I never knew was protecting me from an evil far greater than my mother.

We didn't see Ovey again for a few years after the fight in the hallway, until one day he showed up at the hotel. He knocked on the door and I can still see the smile Mom had when she opened it.

He had a bottle of something and they started drinking and talking. I sat on the bed and played with my Panda until I heard Ovey stutter, "H-h-h-hey, I gotta good i-i-idea for us, w-w-wanna hear it?"

I remember Mom slurring back at him, "Of course, you idiot! I want to hear it! What ya thinkin about?"

"I gotta job in Penticton and was thinking it would be k-kkinda nice to have you and Laura around." He smiled at Mom and she smiled back.

Then before I knew it she squealed and said, "That's the best offer I've had all day, let's go," and she slapped a big wet kiss on the top of Ovey's forehead. He was so happy he started to dance around the room. I wasn't even sure where Penticton was, but I knew it must be an exciting place the way Mom and Ovey were acting.

Ovey was a short little man with a round face and wore thick-rimmed brown glasses. When he stuttered I felt sorry for him because it took him so long to get out a word. I didn't think he was handsome, but he had a nice smile and he treated me well. I liked him too.

His new job was cleaning the only theatre in Penticton, and I thought maybe our lives might be different because we'd be a family.

We moved the very next day and I loved all the open fields as we drove down the highway. There were no big buildings to hide the sun's warmth. I hummed all the way hoping I might get to go to school and meet some friends.

"H-h-here we are," Ovey said as we drove into this little tiny town.

"Not much here, is there Ovey?" Mom said.

"Oh d-d-don't you worry angel. I'll take g-g-good care of you." He drove into a driveway and said, "We're home."

We lived in a small little place with one bedroom so I slept on the couch. That in itself was an improvement from having to be in the same room at night as my mother.

"Hey, Squeaks," Ovey said, using his nickname for me as he hauled our things into the house, "m-maybe you'll get l-lucky and s-s-see Ogopogo in the l-lake."

I never knew why he called me Squeaks, but it stuck and all Mom's friends called me Squeaks instead of Laura.

"Who's Ogopogo?" I asked.

"H-he's a m-m-monster that lives in the l-lake."

"A monster! A real monster?" I asked excitedly.

"That's w-what they say." He smiled at me and I couldn't wait to get to the lake and find that monster.

I was seven when we moved to Penticton and I loved the lake and the peace that came over me when I skipped the rocks over the water, watching the ripples reach further and further out into the lake. There weren't as many pigeons there, but there were ducks and ducklings and the geese wandered around as if they owned the place.

"Here Ogopogo," I'd call, trying to coax the monster out of the lake. "You can come out, I won't hurt you." I could just imagine a big scaly creature with a dragon's head and snake's body surfacing out of the deep. As hard as I tried to find him, I never did, but it was fun to look anyway.

Penticton wasn't very big so when we went to do our shopping at the corner store it didn't take the people long to figure out my mother was a drunk. Mom never tried to get along with anyone and was even rude to the nice lady at the store.

"How are you today?" The lady asked Mom as she put our groceries into a bag.

"That's really none of your damn business," she barked back. I felt sorry for the lady because she was just trying to be nice and I think my Mom embarrassed her because she went all red in the face.

After that when we visited the store the lady never asked Mom how she was doing, but she always smiled at me.

Thanks to Ovey, my dream of going to school actually came true. I never went to school when I was six so I was a year behind the other kids my age. Thankfully, I was small so everyone assumed I was supposed to be in grade one.

On one hand, I was looking forward to going, but on the other, I was afraid the kids might not like me. I was so shy that I had a hard time talking to anyone, and I was more self-conscious than ever of my buckteeth, thanks to my mother.

I'd hoped the first day of school would be like some of the shows I'd watched on TV where the kids got new clothes, and their mothers combed their child's hair, gave them a special breakfast and packed them a special lunch. Some shows the mothers even walked their kids to school and met the teacher.

My first day was nothing like the TV shows. I went to school on an empty stomach, and when Mom put my hair into pigtails, she pulled so hard I started to cry.

"Quit your bawling or I'll cut your hair off," she growled, and I made sure I kept all my sobs inside. She was mean enough to cut my hair off and I liked my hair.

My clothes were always too big for me and I don't remember her washing my face. She never walked me to school, and thinking back, I don't know how I found the school in the first place. The only thing she did do was make me a lunch, and I was thrilled when she handed me the bag. I left the house thankful to be on my way even though I was scared.

Once I arrived at school, the knot in my stomach slowly went away and I was excited to be with the other kids. The morning went by quickly. We found our desks and the teacher told us the classroom rules. Everyone seemed excited and I was looking forward to recess.

Sadly, recess wasn't as much fun as I thought it might be. Many of the kids knew each other and didn't want to include someone new. I noticed them laughing, and pointing at me. I was hoping they were making fun of someone else, but I secretly knew they weren't.

"She sure has big teeth hey." I heard one little girl say. "She kind of looks like a rabbit, or a beaver, and look at those clothes! They look like her mother's!" Then all I heard was their laughter, so I put my hand over my mouth and went inside.

After recess, we did our lessons until lunchtime. My tummy was growling and I was looking forward to having my favourite sandwich, which was cheese with Miracle Whip. When the lunch bell rang and the teacher told us to get our lunches, I bolted out of my desk as quickly as I could.

When we lived in Vancouver, we never had anything good to eat in our house, but since we'd moved in with Ovey that changed. He made sure we had groceries because he liked to eat as much as I did, and he always bought cheese and Miracle Whip because he knew they were my favourite.

I couldn't wait to sink my teeth into my favourite sandwich. My mouth was watering, and I'd waited all morning for this very moment.

"Oh no!" I whispered as I took the sandwich out of the bag, "this has to be a mistake."

Mom had made me a bacon grease sandwich, knowing my favourite was cheese and Miracle Whip. She used to make these kinds of sandwiches when we lived in Vancouver. She'd take the cold grease drippings from the bacon and spread it like butter between two pieces of bread. They were the most disgusting sandwiches in the world! They stunk and made the bread all slimy.

I was so upset and disappointed, not to mention embarrassed, that I quietly placed the sandwich back in my bag. It was hard to look around the classroom and see all the wonderful things the other kids were eating. I was so hungry! I laid my head down on my arms until it was time to go outside to play, because I didn't want to stare at the other kids' lunches.

The afternoon seemed to drag on forever. My stomach was growling and I was afraid the others were going to notice the noise. I couldn't concentrate on what the teacher was saying; the only thing I could think of was that I needed to get home so I could get something to eat.

The moment the bell rang, I ran all the way home. When I got there, I burst through the door and headed right for the fridge. About the time I was going to grab something to eat, Mom came around the corner, "What are you doing in the fridge?"

"I'm hungry because I didn't have any lunch," I said as I grabbed for a piece of cheese.

"What do you mean you didn't have any lunch? I made you a sandwich you ungrateful little shit. Where is it? "

Then she grabbed my arm, slammed the fridge door and marched me over to my lunch bag. She sat me down at the table and made me eat the whole slimy sandwich!

"Please mommy, I don't like this sandwich it makes my tummy hurt," I said as I tried to choke down a bite.

"Keep eating!" she said, slapping me across the back of the head. I chocked and gagged as the soggy, slimy, stinky thing slid down my throat and into my stomach. Before I finished, I felt sick.

The whole time Mom just looked at me with a smirk on her face. Once I finished the sandwich, I laid down on the couch and hugged my panda. The only good thing I could think of was Ovey loved to eat as much as I did, and hopefully I'd be feeling better by dinnertime.

School was difficult for me. I was no sooner in the door most mornings than the kids started to make fun of me.

"Hey Bucky, Bucky beaver teeth," they teased and I wondered if any of them even knew my first name. I tried to keep my hand over my mouth, but that never stopped their snide and unkind remarks. I never understood the saying, "Sticks and stones may break my bones, but words will never hurt me." Such a lie! A punch was easier to take than the awful things the kids called me. At least if someone hits you, eventually you forget about the pain, but when you get hurt with words, they're in your head and heart forever.

Every recess the girls played the game Swiss Skip and I stood and watched them. One day they were short a player so one of the girls hollered, "Hey you, do you want to play with us today?"

"Sure," I said excitedly. I was so afraid I might make a mistake that I concentrated on the game so hard I gave myself a headache. It turned out I was really good at Swiss Skip and the girls liked having me on their team because I helped them win. That game made recess a lot more fun.

One day during class, the little girl who sat behind me asked me to pass a note to the girl in front of me.

"What does the note say?" I asked.

"I just want to know if she wants you to be on our team during recess,"she whispered.

"Okay."

The moment I passed the note to the girl in front of me she hollered, "Mrs. Brown, Laura passed me a note just now."

"Give me the note."

She gave the note to the teacher and I ended up meeting the principal that day.

"Come with me Laura, " she said in her angry voice.

When the teacher took my hand and led me to the principal's office, the hallway seemed to stretch for miles. I was so scared my feet felt like they were stuck in cement.

"I promise Mrs. Brown, I'll never do that again," I pleaded as she marched me to the Principal's office.

"It's too late for that now Laura, you should have thought of that before you passed the note." Then she waited outside the office.

When I got into the office, I could feel my heart beating faster. The principal started to explain to me why I was getting the strap, and honestly, it didn't help, it only prolonged the agony.

"Laura, you know it is against the rules to pass notes during school time so now you have to be punished. Hopefully, you won't do it again."

I was so scared I couldn't think of one word to say to him.

When he removed the strap from his bottom drawer and told me to hold out my hands I started to cry.

"Please, I promise I won't do it again, please don't hit me," I pleaded.

"The rules are the rules," was all he said.

When the strap hit my little hands, it stung and made me scream. I couldn't stop the tears from flowing down my face and when I looked at my hands, they were all red from where the strap had hit them. I never dreamed that passing a note during class was so serious. I felt like nobody liked me, even if I could help them to win.

The girls never asked me to play again after I passed the note and recess became a type of torture. A playground can be a very lonely place when you are watching everyone else have a good time without you.

After a few weeks of being by myself during recess, I was thankful Mom rarely woke up in time for me to go to school.

When she did send me, I tried to keep to myself because one of the older girls was always trying to pick a fight with me. She'd follow me around and call me all kinds of mean names. I think her mission in life was to see how badly she could abuse me using words, fists or whatever else she could find to throw at me.

I was heading home one day when she threw a rock at my mouth, cut my gums and loosened a few teeth. I hadn't done anything to her and never could figure out why she hated me. I started to cry as I choked on the blood that was running down my throat. The worst part though, was the way she laughed at me when I started to cry. Everywhere I went someone was hitting me.

"What a big bawl baby, maybe you should stay home with your mommy!" she sneered.

The other kids laughed too, but not as much as she did, and I'm not sure what hurt more, my mouth or my feelings. I ran home as the blood squished through my fingers and when I came into the house crying, Mom just looked at me with her cold dark eyes.

"Mommy a girl at school threw a rock at me for no reason," I cried.

She just shook her head and never said a word. I never could figure out why she didn't care about me. All I wanted was for her to give me a hug and ask me what happened, but once again she left me standing by myself. I took care of myself, and she went to the kitchen for another drink.

When I look back to those years, I don't think she was capable of having any kind of feeling towards anyone. She was drunk all the time and the pills she took made her like a zombie.

One good memory I have about Penticton was the little church I found not far from where we lived.

I remember the first time I went inside. One of the ladies that was putting flowers in the front turned around and said sweetly, "Hello, what's your name?"

"Laura," I said shyly.

She stopped fixing the flowers and came down to shake my hand.

"Welcome Laura, I think it is time for a break, would you like some cookies and milk?" she asked.

Her eyes kind of twinkled when she talked and I loved cookies and milk so I nodded my head yes, and she led me to the kitchen.

"Do you live around here?"

"Yup, just down the street," I answered with my mouth full of cookie.

"Looks to me like you could use another cookie," she said and then she put a whole stack of them on my plate. I was so excited, I'd never been given that many cookies before in my whole life!

The lady came and sat beside me while I ate my cookies and

I told her all about my Mom and Ovey. She was so easy to talk to and I knew she cared because she listened to me. By the time I was done eating all those cookies I had a tummy ache, but it was a good one.

"Laura, before you leave I have some clothes that might fit you, would you like to take them with you?" She dug into a box full of clothing and pulled out some clothes she thought might fit me.

"Sure, I love getting new clothes."

She put a sweater and some other items in the bag, gave me a hug and said, "You are always welcome here, sweetie. Remember that, okay?"

I nodded my head and left holding the bag she'd given to me. I loved going there to visit when I felt sad. Everyone seemed so nice and I felt safe when I was with these people. When I was with them, I felt that same feeling I felt when I was younger; like there was someone I couldn't see watching over me. Not to mention I always got something to eat and more clothing before I left.

One Sunday I went to Sunday school by myself and it was the first time I'd ever heard about a God who made me and loved me just the way I was. It made me wonder if that someone I felt watching over me sometimes was God. If it was God I was thrilled to hear that God didn't make a mistake when he made me because God can't make mistakes. I wasn't an accident after all. I so badly wanted to believe what they said was true, but the fact my mother didn't love me made me feel unwanted. However knowing a loving God watched over me made me feel safer.

After a few months of attending school every so often, I managed to make a few friends. Sometimes I'd invite one of them over to play at our house, but I think my Mom scared them.

She'd walk around the house drunk wearing only her big shirt and was rude to my friends when they came. Her favourite line was, "What the hell are you doing here? Don't you have your own home to go to?"

Usually after she said that, they left, and I'd be so mad at her I wanted to punch her.

"Why do you always have to be so mean," I yelled, "You're nothing but a big bad witch and I hate you!"

"Don't you talk to me that way!" And then she'd slap me across the face before she went into the kitchen to get another drink. Anytime I sassed her back she'd slap me across the face or smirk at me and walk away. It just depended on her mood at the time.

It worked best anyway if I went to my friends' houses to play because their mothers were nicer than mine, and sometimes they even gave us snacks to eat while we played.

After I played at the other kids' houses, I realized that my mother was not the same as theirs. The other mothers loved their kids and they all had nice clothes and lots to eat. Their mothers didn't wander around in a big shirt or stagger around the house. You know, if I could have had one wish, I'd have wished my mother could be like my friends' mothers were; but somehow I knew that would never happen.

It's sort of funny what a person remembers. Occasionally during the school year, the school had raffles where the winner won a cake or some other little prize. I never won, but I did notice how popular the person was who did. I was always on the lookout for ways to make a friend, so I decided to have my own raffle and make sure the right person won.

I thought I was so smart when I came up with a plan. I stole money from Mom's purse, went to the bakery, bought a cake and then raffled it during recess. I didn't charge anyone for a ticket, because the raffle was rigged and I didn't think that would be fair.

"Anyone want a ticket to win a cake?" I asked. It didn't take long before all the tickets had been handed out. Those tickets had different numbers on them, but the numbers in the basket were all the same.

As the kids stood around me with their tickets in their hands, I felt excited.

"Okay everyone," I said, "the winning number is…ten."

Then I heard a little girl scream, "I win, I have number ten." She raced over to me and gave me a big hug. I felt so special.

"Do you want to share my cake with me?" she asked.

"You bet," I said excitedly. My little plan worked and it was fun to be popular even if it only lasted as long as the cake did.

It worked so well the first time I thought I'd try it again. Unfortunately, one of the kids caught on to my little secret and stabbed my foot with a pencil; I still have the mark to prove it. I never did that again, no matter how lonely I felt.

Even though I did have a few friends most of the kids bullied me, and as hard as I tried, I couldn't get them to like me.

The boys were especially mean, and one in particular was continually calling me ugly and stupid and hitting me whenever he got a chance. One day I'd finally had enough. I was so mad at him my mouth started to spout off before I had time to think.

"If you think you're so smart how about we meet after school and we'll see who the stupid one is!" I said in my meanest voice. I'd watched Mom fight lots so I figured if she could win a fight, I could too.

As I walked out to the meeting place, I saw him and a bunch of other kids waiting for me. Suddenly my mind kicked into gear, and I knew there was no way I was going to win. He was way bigger and a lot stronger and the closer I got to him the more I began to shake. He was waiting for me and had a grin on his face like one of those scary, smiling clowns.

"Come over hear you little chicken and I'll beat the crap out of you." He laughed and I hated him more than I'd ever hated anyone before! I was so tired of being called mean names and being picked on that my adrenaline kicked in and I was ready.

I was never one to back down, so when I looked up at his smiling freckled face, hate filled my heart. I shut my eyes and started swinging. He was so much bigger and stronger I knew he was going to beat me to death, so with my courage in my back pocket I ran home. The crazy thing is, the next day I noticed I had given him a black eye.

I never wanted to fight with anyone, I just wanted to have some friends. Even though the kids quit bullying me, it didn't help. In fact, it made matters worse because they stayed away from me. When I walked up to some of the girls at recess, or after school, they ran away and once again I was lonely.

Thank goodness for Ovey. I always looked forward to seeing him after he came home from work because I'd have someone to talk to.

"H-how was your day Squeaks?" he'd ask as he messed up my hair.

"Same," I answered, because most days I didn't get to school.

"And h-how's my lovely Joan?" he'd say, smiling as he went to give Mom a kiss.

Sometimes Mom let him kiss her and other times she'd just give him a disgusted look.

I knew he loved Mom, but he also had a healthy fear of her. He'd seen her slap me for no reason and he knew she'd slap him too if he didn't behave himself.

If Mom kissed Ovey we knew everything was okay, but if she didn't we knew she was going to have a tantrum.

When she had one of her tantrums, we stayed out of her way because she'd throw things and say awful things and we were afraid she might hit us with something. It was as if she was possessed and had no control over the demon inside her.

After she calmed down she was so worn out she usually went to the bedroom. Ovey and I were thankful she left because we could get something to eat.

"Squeaks, you r-ready to eat?"

"Yup," I'd whisper.

He'd make us something to eat and when Mom showed up I went to her bedroom until Ovey moved me to the couch.

During the wintertime, I always had lots of ear infections.

"Mommy, my ears are aching and there's blood and guck coming out," I cried, but her usual response was a grunt and then she'd walk away from me unless I complained too much, and then she'd give me one of her 222's.

Ovey's little black rabbit, Peter Cotton Tail, let me lay on his back when my ears ached. Peter's soft black fur, and the warmth from his body always made me feel better. The rabbit seemed to sense I needed him because he let me cuddle him like that for hours. I was sure God was making him stay still until the pain went away.

"Thank you Peter," I'd say. "I love you." We played for hours at a time, and like the pigeons, I knew Peter Cotton Tail liked me too.

If I wasn't battling an earache, I was itchy from a yeast infection. I didn't know until years later when I saw a doctor that's what it was, all I remember is I'd be so itchy I'd scratch myself until I bled. Nothing seemed to take that horrible itch away for very long, not even a bath. There were times I felt like I was going to go crazy.

"Mommy, I can't stand this, I am so itchy," I complained hoping she'd help me, but she was in her own lost world and in that world, I didn't exist.

Ovey also had some cats I played with and some days they never left my side. They purred when I pet their backs and rubbed their bellies and they'd rub their soft fur on my legs. They loved me to hold them and they cuddled me too, it was nice to feel wanted. My best friends were the pigeons in Vancouver, Peter Cotton Tail, and Ovey's cats.

"Here kitty, kitty," I called after one of the cats. "Here kitty, kitty," instead of the cat coming over like she usually did she ran the other way. I was furious, and started to run after her until I had her in my hand. As much as I loved that cat, I started acting like my Mom did when she didn't get her own way. I felt like I was going nuts because every time the cat didn't do what I wanted, I hurt it hoping the next time it would listen.

I hated the fact I hurt that kitty and I cried and cried and cried because that little cat was a lot like me.

"I'm sorry, I'm so sorry," I'd say to her, hoping she could understand. She had no control over what I did to her, just as I had no control over what my mother did to me. We simply took the abuse and prayed we'd live to see another day.

Those were some of the darkest days of my life because I saw how hurtful I could be. I loved animals and I promised myself that I'd never hurt another animal again, no matter how frustrated I felt. I didn't want to be like my mother.

When they say, "Misery loves company" Ovey and my mother were great company. They both loved to drink until they were miserable. If they could've quit at one drink they'd have been fine, but that was never the case.

We'd been living with Ovey for close to a year and I noticed they were fighting more.

One particular evening they started drinking and it wasn't

long before they were yelling at one another. I knew things were getting out of hand, so I jumped onto the couch.

Whenever I felt stressed, I'd rock back and forth on a couch or chair as if I were in a rocking chair. It made me feel safe and the rocking motion took my mind off what was going on around me. The louder the yelling and cursing got, the faster I rocked back and forth, back and forth. For some reason the rocking irritated Mom and she started swearing at me.

"Quit your bloody rocking! You're driving me crazy." I just looked at her and kept rocking because I didn't know what else to do.

"Oh l-l-leave her alone, she's not hurting anyone," Ovey said. I guess he was feeling brave that night; alcohol will do that to a person.

Mom was furious with him, "Who the hell do you think you are? She's my daughter and I'll tell her whatever the hell I want to." By the time she was finished talking she had her face pushed up against Ovey.

"N-now just calm down honey, I wasn't trying to get in the w-w-way," he said, backing away from her.

As the fight progressed and the yelling got louder, it changed from words to fists.

Ovey finally had enough and punched mom in the face.

"You stupid son of a bitch," Mom screamed when Ovey hit her. A two-by-four with a nail sticking out of its end seemed to materialize out of nowhere, and Mom picked it up and ran after him. When she caught up to him, she smashed the nail into his head.

"Ahhh," Ovey screamed as the blood came gushing out like a volcano and ran down his face. "I can't believe you did that," he cried.

I'd never seen a man cry before, and the harder he cried, the faster I rocked myself on the couch; back and forth, back and forth as I kept my eyes on Mom. She just stood there with a blank look on her face and never took her eyes off Ovey.

37

Mom dropped the board, Ovey staggered to the bathroom and I ran into the bedroom and crawled under the bed.

The next morning I noticed Ovey had stitches in his head. I'm not sure if my mother went with him to the hospital or he went by himself. All I know is I blamed myself for what happened. If he hadn't stuck up for me, she would've hit me and gotten over it. He, on the other hand, was going to wear the scars of that fight for a lifetime.

Mom always spoiled a good thing. Ovey asked us to move out of his house, and although I didn't want to go, I understood why we had to leave. What made me the saddest was no longer having Peter Cottontail's soft, warm fur the next time I had an earache.

Jack was one of the men Mom met through Ovey and we went right from Ovey's place to Jack's.

Jack was a short heavyset man with gray hair about ten years older than my mother was, and he called me "Squeaks" too. He was nice.

He must have made a decent living as a cook, because he lived in one of the nicer hotels in Penticton. It had a kitchen and a TV in the living room, and like Ovey's, it had a bedroom with a door and a bathroom. I slept on the couch and once again I was thankful I didn't have to share a room with my mother and Jack.

"So Squeaks, do you like your new home?" he asked.

"Yes," I said quietly, "it's really nice here."

"Well you just make yourself at home and I'll show your mother her new room." Then he smiled, took my mother's hand, went into the bedroom, and closed the door.

I decided I'd watch some TV and I'm not sure how long it took for Jack and Mom to return but I watched more than a few shows.

"Anyone hungry?" Jack asked, "because I'm starving!"

"I am," I said.

"Okay then I am going to make you my famous spaghetti sauce. I hope you like spaghetti?" he said teasingly.

"I love spaghetti, it's my favourite, right Mom?"

"How the hell would I know what your favourite dish is."

Then she cuddled up to Jack, gave him a big kiss and helped him make dinner. I'd never seen her make dinner and it made me happy to see her so happy. Maybe she'd changed.

Jack was right, he did make the best spaghetti I'd ever eaten. I ate so much I thought I was going to burst!

"This is sooooo good, Jack," I said after my third plate. "I think you are the best cook in the whole wide world." I gave him my biggest smile.

"Cover your mouth," Mom yelled.

I quickly covered my mouth and headed for the couch to watch TV, smacking my lips as I went.

The next morning after we'd had breakfast we went for a ride in Jack's Volkswagen bug.

"Wow, this is the coolest car! It really looks like a bug," I said. "See its headlights are the eyes, and the mouth is the top part, and the ears are the mirrors."

I was going to go on, but Mom butted in. "Get in the back and be quiet."

I crawled into the back seat and didn't care if Mom was going to be nice or not. I was on an adventure.

Jack loved my mother and I could see the feeling was mutual. It was the first time in my life I saw Mom try to make a relationship work. I think for the first time she felt like she had something worth changing for, and I was happy for her.

She was still addicted to the pills and cough syrup, but she stopped drinking and even started to cook. I wasn't sure where this woman had come from because it wasn't the mother I knew. Even our relationship wasn't as explosive, and the odd time I felt like she might even like me.

I remember the day I turned eight years old. Most years my birthday was just another day, but Jack made this birthday special.

When he came home after work, he had something unusual under one arm and lots of groceries in the other.

"Hey, I think today is a special day isn't it?" he said as he smiled at me.

"Yup, it's my eighth birthday today? How did you know?"

"Oh, a little birdie told me," he said, as he kissed Mom on the cheek. She always smiled when Jack kissed her; I think for once in her life she was happy.

"Well you can't have a birthday party without cake and presents," he said.

I guess Mom forgot to tell him we never celebrated birthdays, or any other occasion for that matter. Even though there were no other kids at my party, I was over the moon with excitement.

"No, no you can't have a party without a cake and presents. Did you bring some with you?" I asked, not sure if I was allowed to be excited or not.

"Come over here, Squeaks, and take a look in this bag."

I went over to him, took the bag out from under his arm, and couldn't believe my eyes.

"New stuffed animals! For me? Are they really for me?"

"Yes, they're for you, and don't forget the birthday cake."

He took the most beautiful cake I'd ever seen out of a box. It had roses on it and some words I tried to sound out.

"Does this say Happy Birthday?"

"It sure does." Jack winked at me and we ate the cake. I couldn't believe I actually had a birthday party. I'd never tasted a cake that good before in my whole life. I thought once I must be dreaming until I let one of the roses melt on my tongue, even my imagination wasn't that good!

As Jack and Mom cleaned up the dishes I went and sat on the

couch to play with my presents. They were so soft I kept burying my face in them, and I loved the way they smelled so new. It was a great day, and it didn't end with the cake and presents! Jack gave me a dime so I could go and get some coke out of the coke machine.

"Thanks, Jack! This has been the best day of my life!"

Had I hit the jackpot or what! I loved the way the pop bubbled in my mouth and I drank it so fast it gave me a brain freeze. I felt special that day, which was a new feeling. It was a wonderful party and I will remember it for the rest of my life. I think my mother enjoyed it too, because I saw her smiling a few times. That, all by itself, was a gift to me, maybe even the best one.

It was in the fall when Jack was transferred to Princeton. He had a job cooking at a camp and Mom and I went with him.

We lived in a little house on Old Hedly Road, and I needed to take a school bus to school. I still only went to school about three times a week, but it was more than when we lived in Penticton.

Memories, especially bad ones, have a way of sneaking up on us when we least expect them. I was riding the bus to school in Princeton one morning, and saw a woman pruning her rose bushes. Seeing her took me back to when we lived in Penticton and one of the guys followed me home from school. I guess he thought it might be fun to throw me into a pile of pruned rose bushes.

"Hey Beaver teeth, want to munch on some wood?" he said sarcastically. Then he grabbed me and threw me into the thorns. They dug into my skin and every time I moved pain shot through my body.

"Mommy, mommy," I screamed. "I need some help!" I sobbed. When Mom came outside, the bully ran away and in between sobs I yelled, "You big chicken, I hate you!"

I hurt all over, and Mom never did anything gently. She

grabbed me with the thorns still attached to my skin and dragged me into the house. I was crying so hard I could hardly breathe and it didn't help she was yelling, "Now what did you do, you stupid kid?"

She literally yanked each prickle out with some scissors and I knew she felt like it was my fault the boy hurt me.

I'll never forget thinking as she jerked out the thorns that they acted like a plug because the moment she pulled a prickle out I'd start to bleed. After the last one was out of my skin, she went into the bedroom and I cried myself to sleep on the couch.

As I thought back to that day, I was glad to be in another town, going to different school, and riding in the safety of a school bus.

My best friend in Princeton was Sally, a little girl who lived down the road from us, and we loved spending time together. She had Barbie dolls to play with, and I'd never played with a Barbie before. We had so much fun with those dolls. We loved to dress them up and pretend they were going somewhere special.

In a way, Sally taught me how to play like most little girls my age. We laughed a lot together and she never once made fun of my buckteeth like the other kids did. Time went faster when I was with her, and I was always welcome at their house, which meant more to me than words could ever express.

I can still remember the day Sally said, "Laura you can take this Barbie home if you want to."

"Really? Are you sure it's okay if I take it home?" I wasn't sure I'd heard her right.

"Yup, I have lots to play with, so you can have that one." She handed me the doll. Not only was this my first Barbie doll, but my first doll, period. I gave Sally a huge hug and sang all the way home.

We used to ride the school bus together and she made sure she saved a seat for me. None of the other kids wanted to sit with me, but Sally did. When she didn't go to school, I knew it was going to be a bad day. She always looked after me wherever we went and was the big sister I never had. I loved her with all my heart.

Sally's grandparents lived on the same farm as her family and her Grandfather liked to spoil us. He took Sally and me into town in his old red Ford pickup, and then he'd give us each two bits to buy French fries and milkshakes. Pretty cheap compared to today.

Grampa Coyne was always so kind to me and never told me to get lost like my mother did. He let me help him when he worked in the garden, "Laura," he'd say, "you ever planted a garden before?"

"Nope.".

"Well," he said, out of breath, "I'm plantin potatoes. Do you want to help me?"

"I don't know what to do," I said shyly.

"I tell ya what, I'll dig the hole and drop the potato and you fill the hole in with dirt. Think you can do that?" He smiled.

"Yup, I can do that." I was surprised he'd asked me to help him and was really dirty and happy by the time we were finished. He always made me feel useful and I never felt like I was in his way.

One day after I got off the school bus I ran home only to find the house empty. I had no idea where Mom was and by the time it got dark, Jack hadn't come home either. Mom and Ovey took off sometimes for a few days and left me alone, but this was the first time she and Jack hadn't come home.

I was so afraid I finally couldn't stand it anymore and ran over to Sally's house. Stubbs, their dog, came running towards me and I gave him a quick pat on the back before I knocked on the door.

Mrs. Coyne answered the door and the moment she opened it a crack, I flew inside almost knocking her over.

"Mom and Jack have gone somewhere and I'm afraid to stay by myself. Do you think I could stay here until they get home? I promise I won't be any trouble," I begged. Tears started to make puddles in my eyes. I knew by the look on Mr. and Mrs. Coyne's faces they couldn't believe any mother would leave an eight-year-old by themselves over night.

"Where did they go?" Mr. Coyne asked.

"I don't know, but I'm afraid to stay by myself in the dark." I sobbed.

Mrs. Coyne came over and put her arm around me. She always smelled like strawberries .

"Don't worry honey, you can stay here for as long as you like. Now go with Sally and she'll give you some pyjamas. It's bedtime."

I was thankful I had a place to go, and to tell the truth, sometimes I didn't mind it when Mom took off, because it meant I could go to Sally's house where there was a warm bed, lots of food and a wonderful friend. I loved every-thing about Sally's house. Her Mom and Dad were so sweet, and I'd never met anyone before who cared so much about me, other than my Gramma. Sometimes it was hard for me to understand why they cared when my own mother didn't. Looking back I can see how God was providing for me. He put me near the Coyne family and they made my life worth living.

When Mom eventually came home, I left Sally's house and went back to Mom. The Coyne's never wanted me to go, but I felt like I needed to take care of my mother even if she didn't want my help.

As soon as I walked through the door I asked, "Where did you go? I was worried about you."

"It's none of your damned business where I go or what I do," then she pushed me aside and said, " get the hell out of my way."

Then everything went back to our normal. I sat on the couch, Mom went to bed and Jack left for work. Nothing ever really changed.

Princeton's winters started in late October and lasted until March. I didn't have any warm clothes, and it wasn't uncommon for the weather to stay below freezing for days. I don't know how I survived sometimes because I spent a lot of time outside in one of Mom's sweaters and a pair of her shoes.

One day after school, I went over to see Sally and I was so cold when I got there, I couldn't keep my teeth from chattering. After a few hours, I was warm and ready to go home.

"Okay," Sally said, "but just a minute before you go. I'll be right back."

I wasn't sure what she was doing until she arrived with a brand new winter coat and a pair of winter boots in her arms.

"Here Laura, I have another coat and pair of boots and these will keep you warm. You can have these forever." She smiled and helped me put on the coat and boots.

They both were a little big, but I'll never forget how warm I felt when I put them on.

"Thank you Sally," I said in disbelief.

I ran home all excited about my new coat and boots and the moment I opened the door I yelled, "Hey Mom, look what Sally gave me!"

I was hoping Mom would be excited for me, but she never even looked at me. She turned her back and walked into her bedroom. I tried to convince myself that I didn't care if she noticed or not, but I did. The only consolation was I was going to be nice and warm all winter, and that alone had to be enough. I thanked God every day for that warm coat and boots, they were truly gifts from Heaven.

When Sally and I were tired of playing with the Barbie dolls, we went outside and played with her dog Stubbs. He was a Blue Healer and known around the neighbourhood for his big bark and bite. Sally told me that one time Stubbs bit a man so bad he needed stitches, but he liked Sally and me.

We went for long walks through the bush and Stubbs led the way. Sometimes he'd run ahead of us and then he'd wait patiently for us to arrive. When he saw us coming, he ran towards us and licked us all over our faces.

"Stubbs," Sally yelled, "Get down!"

I never minded him licking me all over my face because it tickled. We'd play outside until it got dark, and then Stubbs always walked me home first before he and Sally went home.

December arrived, and although we were making Christmas ornaments at school, I never dreamed I'd have anywhere to put them. We never celebrated Christmas, so when Jack showed up that day with a real Christmas tree, I could hardly believe my eyes!

"What's that, Jack?" I asked hoping it was what I thought it was.

"Well, Squeaks, you can't have Christmas without a Christmas tree, now can you?"

"Really? We are going to have Christmas this year? Do you think Santa Claus will remember me this time?" I asked with anticipation.

"I'm sure he will," Jack said.

"I can't believe this! We made Christmas ornaments today in school and now I have a place to hang them." I rushed to get the ornaments.

Mom helped us decorate the tree and I even saw her smile every once in awhile. I really believed our lives were perfect. I'd had my first birthday party and now we were going to celebrate our first Christmas. I was glad Mom had hooked up with Jack; he made our lives so much better.

I wanted so badly to stay awake all night Christmas Eve in case Santa Claus came. He'd never found me before so I was worried he might not know where Princeton was. I must have fallen asleep because when I woke up I was afraid to open my eyes for fear Santa Claus hadn't come.

I tip-toed over to the tree and squealed, "Mom, Jack, get up! Santa Claus came last night, get up, get up!" I ran to their bedroom and banged on their door.

"Please Mom, get up!"

Eventually they came out and Jack looked happy, but Mom looked grouchy.

"Well, look at this," Jack said as he grabbed a present from under the tree. "This one says, To Squeaks from Santa."

I grabbed the present out of his hands and Mom left the room.

"Where's Mom going, Jack?" I asked as I tore at the wrapping paper.

"Don't worry, she's just tired," he said. "What did Santa bring?"

"Oh look! A play ironing board and iron! I love it!" I started to pretend I was ironing something.

I guess I'd been a good girl because Santa showed up and it was the best Christmas ever! Life was wonderful, I had a great new friend, a roof over my head, food in my stomach, a warm coat and a pair of winter boots. I even liked going to school. I wasn't sure it could get any better.

We'd been living with Jack for almost a year when I noticed a difference in Mom. The sparkle in her eyes was beginning to fade and her temper had returned. The party girl inside her was trying to claw her way out, and that party girl was hard to keep under control. She started drinking again, and I knew it wasn't going to be long before the real Mom surfaced and things were going to change. I guess Mom could only pretend for so long before her need for alcohol took over. It had happened with Ovey and now it was going to be Jack's turn.

Jack must have wondered what was going on when all of a sudden she stopped cooking for us, and wasn't as happy. He'd never seen this side of her before and I knew he was in for a big shock!

She started drinking throughout the day and when she started, she couldn't stop. By the time Jack got home from work, she was drunk, and the drunker she got the nastier she became.

Soon our house turned into a party house, and Jack seemed to enjoy the parties as much as Mom did. As the parties became more frequent, I spent more time outside or in the bedroom. I knew the ugly side of my mother, and to survive I needed to stay out of her way.

It's a good thing I had the winter coat and boots Sally gave me because unlike Vancouver, the snow in Princeton stayed. I liked to make snow angels, snowmen, and slide down the hills. I even liked the coolness of the air because I could see my breath and my mouth tingled from the cold.

When I went hiking through the woods at night, Stubbs became my best friend. The walks with the dog were quiet and kept me away from all the noise and commotion of the parties. When I got tired, Stubbs walked me home and stayed there until Sally's Grandpa came to get him. Once Stubbs left, I quietly snuck into my Mom's bedroom until Jack moved me to the couch.

Mom's drinking was out of control. It was as if the moment she placed the liquor to her lips it unleashed an evil spirit. I don't think she ever entertained the thought that she could stop after one or two drinks. She was like a wild woman once she'd drunk too much, and always wanted to pick a fight with someone.

Eventually she'd be punched or shoved out of the way only

making her madder. She continually wore bruises all over her body and was miserable.

I felt like we had gone back in time to when we lived in Vancouver. I wasn't getting to school because Mom was drunk all the time, and our home went from a peaceful place to a place full of drunks looking for a fight.

I'd never seen Jack be physically or verbally abusive to my Mom until they started drinking. The more they drank the more they fought. I knew from the past that we were in trouble and it wasn't going to be much longer before something awful was going to happen, and I was right.

Mom, in a drunken rage kicked a coffee table at Jack and he lost it. From where I was sitting on the couch, for the first time, I saw him lose control.

"You bitch! Who the hell do you think you are?" he shouted. He grabbed my Mom's head by the hair, dragged her over to the stove and started to bash her head as hard as he could into the big knobs.

"Stop it, stop it you bastard, you're going to kill me!" she screamed as she tried to pull herself away. He kept bashing her head until she eventually quit yelling and dropped to the floor. There was blood everywhere. Her face started to swell up and she didn't even look like my mother. When she hit the floor, the room went quiet. I was sure she was dead.

I started screaming, "Mommy, mommy! W-wake up! Wake up mommy!" I sobbed as I rocked harder and harder on the couch, afraid to move. I thought Jack had killed her and wondered what he was going to do with me. He just stood over her as if he couldn't believe what he'd done, and she wasn't moving.

He finally turned to me and said, "Get into the bedroom and close the door."

I ran as quickly as I could because for the first time ever, I was afraid of Jack. The moment I got into the bedroom, I closed the door and hid under the bed. I may not have liked my mother, but I did love her.

It seemed like forever before I heard Mom whimpering and Jack trying to calm her down. I quietly snuck into the living room and saw Jack talking softly to her.

"It's okay, Joan, it's okay," he said to her over and over. He had his arm wrapped around her, and a towel on her head. I knew he was sorry for what he'd done by the way he was cuddling her.

I was relieved he hadn't killed her, but she had bruises all over her body and both her eyes were black and swollen. Jack looked heartbroken, I really think he loved Mom and never saw himself hurting her, but the booze turned them both into different people. I quietly went back into the bedroom and didn't come out until the next morning.

After that, their relationship was tense, and although I knew they still loved one another, Jack asked us to leave. It was one of the saddest days of my life. I would be moving away from Sally, Stubbs, Grampa Coyne, and all the comforts of what I considered a real home.

It was still winter when we moved to an old trailer that reminded me of the hotels we lived in when we were in Vancouver, dirty and ugly, and I was full of bitterness.

I no longer had any routine in my life and started to wander around town just to kill time. I missed Sally and Stubbs and very seldom got to school because Mom was too hung over to get me up in the morning. Every time our lives seemed to be good, Mom somehow found a way to ruin it. First Ovey asked us to leave because of Mom and now Jack.

There was a really sweet lady that lived near our trailer who had a little boy that I could play with. I liked her and called her "Nice Lady," because I didn't know her real name. I think she must have liked the name I gave her because she never corrected me. She always had time for me and made me feel like it was okay to visit.

I liked playing with her little boy and it was easy to tell "Nice Lady" really loved her son because she took care of him by feeding him good food, and making him take a nap. Sometimes, when I was there at naptime, I laid down on the top bunk. I wasn't tired, I just wanted to be part of a family and she always put a blanket over me and kissed me on the forehead.

As time went on, she started to question why I didn't go to school. I trusted her, so I told her about my mother and I could tell by the look on her face she wasn't very happy.

"Laura," she said, "I think it's time your mother and I had a little chat!" She had a little spunk and was in no way afraid of my Mom like some people were, so she took it upon herself to try to help me.

She stormed over to my house, with me running behind her, banged on the door, and the moment Mom appeared she started yelling.

"What kind of mother are you? Don't you realize how important it is for you daughter to go to school and get an education? If you don't smarten up I am going to take Laura home with me and she'll be my daughter, not yours. You better sober up and start acting like a real mother instead of a stupid drunk!" Then she took a breath and said, "You're pathetic."

I don't think Mom knew what hit her at first.

"Go to hell! This is none of your business." She screeched , but "Nice Lady" was not about to back down.

"If you don't start sending her to school and looking after her properly I'll take her and you'll never see her again. I'm not kidding. Do you understand?"

I hid quietly in the closet as the yelling and threats bounced off the walls. Although there was a part of me that wanted to live with "Nice Lady" another part of me felt like I needed to take care

51

of my mother. Mom had fought to keep me so maybe she did love me, and just didn't know how to show it.

It wasn't long after Mom and the "Nice Lady" fought we moved into a little cabin up the hill from the pub. I think Mom thought "Nice Lady" was spying on us.

The cabin had an oil tank for heat, and because Mom spent all her money on pills and booze every month, we were hungry and cold most of the time. The colder it got outside, the colder it was inside and Mom was getting extremely sick. I was worried about her because she spent most of her days in her bedroom under the blankets and I was afraid she was going to die. Spring was still a few months away and if I hadn't gotten my coat and boots from Sally, I likely would have frozen to death. I loved it when Mom actually had money to pay the guy who brought the oil, because that meant heat, and I could take my coat off in the house!

I remember a man who was a hunter brought us some moose, deer and bear meat, powdered milk and some bread and syrup. I have no idea how he knew about us or why he came, but if he hadn't brought that food I would have starved.

The bread and syrup were my favourites. I loved dipping my bread into the syrup, and letting the sweetness linger on my tongue. We never cooked any of the meat because Mom was too sick to cook. I'm not sure I saw Mom eat anything while we lived at the cabin, not even the bread or syrup.

Even though we no longer lived with Jack, he often popped by and took Mom out for a date. She was so sick I was surprised sometimes that she went with him, but she did. Sometimes they'd take off for a few days just like they'd done when we lived on Old Hedley Road. It was then I hated the fact we'd moved away from Sally. At least if we'd still been there I could have gone to her house while they were gone, instead of having to stay alone.

While Mom was away, I went to school more often, because

the kids shared their lunches with me. It was the only time I'd eat all day, and I appreciated every little bit of food the kids gave me.

After school, I'd go home to an empty house and play with the two stray kittens I picked up on one of my journeys. I didn't like the night times all by myself and rarely slept because I was scared.

Mom's addictions weren't cheap, and many times she'd sell what little food we did have around the house, and some of my things, so she could support her habits. She may not have needed to eat, but I hated being hungry.

When she finally came home, she brought some food with her that Jack gave her. I was so ecstatic; I grabbed the bags out of her hands and started to unpack the treasures.

"Wow, look at this Mom," I squealed.

"Put them away," was all she said then she went into her bedroom and closed the door. She didn't seem to notice the cats, and that was good, because they were a little wild and very pregnant.

I ended up with eleven kittens and two mama cats. I gave them some of the powdered milk and bread the hunter brought and sometimes they ate and I didn't, because there wasn't enough to go around.

As the kittens grew, they started to cause some problems. They pooped and peed wherever they wanted and the smell was gross. I am sure it wasn't very healthy for Mom or me. The other problem was I couldn't throw them outside even if I wanted to because they were so wild I couldn't catch them.

Mom eventually became so sick while we lived in the cabin that someone called an ambulance and she ended up in the hospital. The neighbour lady saw the ambulance and came over to see what was going on.

"Is everything alright?" she asked.

"I don't know," I cried. "My Mom is really sick and they are taking her to the hospital."

"Who's looking after you while she is away?" the lady asked. I looked at her afraid to say anything until she finally said, "Why don't you come and stay with us until your mother gets home from the hospital."

Then she took my hand and led me over to my new home. I was overjoyed because I didn't want to stay by myself and was sure she had heat and food at her house.

Her name was Mrs. Wilson and she had two boys and a little Chihuahua. I was so thankful to have somewhere to go where it was warm and I'd eat on a regular basis. Not to mention, I was sweet on the oldest boy, but the feeling wasn't mutual. The only time he wanted anything to do with me was when he wanted to play the hyperventilating game.

"Hey Laura, you want to play a game with me?" he asked.

I was surprised he asked me, "Sure, what kind of game is it?"

"Well, you have to stand against the wall and then I am going to use a towel and press it against your throat until you pass out. It is really cool, you're gonna like the feeling, I promise," he said with a big grin on his face.

"Okay, if you say it will be fun then I'll play." Really, I was scared half to death, but I wanted him to like me, so I stood against the wall like he asked.

As he pressed the towel tighter and tighter around my neck, the room started to spin and I loved the feeling until suddenly I hit the floor. Luckily, I never banged my head on anything on the way down. When the room quit spinning and I could see how much fun he was having I told him we should do that again.

"You're right," he said, "we should."

There was something scary and exhilarating about this game, even though I know now it was very dangerous, and to think we did it more than a few times that day. It's a miracle he never killed me. God was looking after me once again.

Mrs. Wilson made sure I went to school everyday with a lunch and that in itself made it a great week. Then to top it off, our school was preparing for its sport's day and I was actually there to participate.

My favourite events were the high jump and running races. I was good at both of them, which brought lots of praise and helped me to make some new friends. Let's face it; everyone loves a winner! I was so good at running and doing the high jump that the school wanted me to represent them at the Regional track meet. I couldn't believe they chose me to go, and was all excited until I found out you needed money. I didn't have any and was disappointed, but it was a good feeling to know I was good at something.

When I got home from school Mrs. Wilson said, "I have a surprise for you Laura: someone dropped off enough money for you to go to the track meet. Wasn't that nice of them?"

"Really, you mean I get to go?" I said, jumping up and down.

"Yup, you get to go. Here's your money. Now put it away so you don't lose it." Then she handed me my money and gently touched my cheek.

Only two more sleeps and I'd be off to the track meet. I was so excited because for me to go anywhere was huge, but the best thing of all was they chose me to go.

I was afraid I'd lose my money, so I asked Mrs. Wilson's boyfriend, "Willy, will you look after my money for me so I don't lose it?"

"No problem," he said, "I'll take care of it for you."

"Thanks."

The day before the track meet, Mrs. Wilson, her boys, the dog and I went on a fishing trip. I'd never been fishing before so it was a real learning experience. Who knew that it was a good idea to use grasshoppers for bait because that's what the trout liked?

In one way, I didn't like the idea of putting a hook through the poor grasshoppers, but when I realized they were dead it made it easier.

I loved being outside and I liked the feeling of the fishing rod in my hand as the water caught the line and carried it away. I loved the smell of the water, and the way the wind blew through my hair. The only noise was the sound of the river, the birds and the odd quiet conversation.

As I carefully cast my rod, I began to feel a tug on the end of the line. I was thrilled. I reeled in my line slowly so I could see what I'd caught, and there was a little trout hanging off my hook. I 'd like to say it was three feet long, but in reality, it might have been six inches. At that point, the size didn't matter; the fact I'd caught my first fish was all I could think about.

I laid the fish on the rocks while I ran to get the others. It should have been okay except I'd forgotten about the dog! Apparently, he loved fish and he ate mine before the others could see my big catch. I was so upset I cried and cried and cried. It seemed like it was the worst thing that had ever happened in my whole life, as strange as that sounds.

"Don't worry, honey," Mrs. Wilson said as she hugged me close, "you'll catch another one."

That was easier said than done, and as hard as I tried, I never caught another fish. Soon it was time to go back to the Wilson's and although I'd lost my big catch I had the track meet to look forward to.

I hardly slept the night before the big day. When I saw Mrs. Wilsons' boyfriend I ran up to him and asked, "Can I have the money I gave you for the track meet, please."

"I have no idea what you're talking about," he replied with a blank look on his face.

I was confused, because I knew I'd given him my money, so why wouldn't he give it back to me? His lie made me feel so angry I wanted to burst inside. I couldn't understand why he'd lie to me. Didn't he understand how important the track meet was?

"You're nothing but a big fat liar, and I hate you!" I yelled.

"Laura," Mrs. Wilson said kindly, "you must have misplaced it. Willy would never lie to you."

"He took my money and now I can't go to the track meet," I sobbed as I ran to my room.

My tears didn't make him give me my money back, and Mrs. Wilson must have thought I'd lost the money because I didn't get to go. I had been stupid enough to give my money to a total stranger instead of Mrs. Wilson, and it was just one more disappointment to add to the growing pile. A seed of bitterness took root in my heart and I hated that man for keeping my money. I knew, from then on that the only one that was going to look after me was me. Most of the adults I met, especially the men, were liars, thieves and perverts. I was so bitter about missing the track meet I became disrespectful, and couldn't wait until Mom got home.

Jack checked the cabin before he picked Mom up from the hospital and that was not a good thing for me. The cats looked after themselves while we were gone and left a terrible mess.

He knocked on the door and when Mrs. Wilson answered he said, "Hi, I am Laura's mother's boyfriend and I'm here to take her home."

"Oh, how is her mother?" Mrs. Wilson asked.

"Her Mom is getting out of the hospital today." Jack said flatly.

"That's wonderful news. I'll get Laura for you."

"Thanks for looking after her," he said like a robot.

"Oh it was a pleasure," Mrs. Wilson said. "Laura, grab your things, Jack is here to take you home."

I was still mad at Willy for stealing my money so I grabbed my things and ran to the door as fast as I could.

"Hi Jack, how's Mom?"

"Good," he muttered.

"You look after yourself Laura, okay, and come visit soon."

"Okay, I will," I said as I put my coat on.

The minute we left the house, I could tell by the look on Jack's face he was mad about something.

"Where the hell did all the cats come from Squeaks? I'll bet your mother doesn't know about them, does she?"

"Well, actually," I started to explain, but he cut me off.

"What the hell were you thinking when you brought them home? Sometimes I think you are as stupid as your mother says you are. When we get to the cabin you need to clean up the mess those damn cats made before your mother gets home."

"I don't have to listen to you." I said with a scowl.

Then he hit me and called me a bunch of awful names. I started to cry because I felt helpless and confused. Our house was never clean and the stench was there long before my mother went into the hospital. I had no idea how I was going to clean up the mess because we never had any kind of cleaner. I ended up just using some warm water and a rag. It was easy to pick up the cat poop, but the pee had stained the carpet, and as hard as I tried, I couldn't get the smell out of the rug.

I never meant to leave a mess. As hard as I tried, I knew it wasn't going to make any difference. My tears soaked into the carpet and became invisible, just like I was to everyone around me, especially my mother.

As I cleaned up the mess, it dawned on me that those poor cats hadn't eaten for a week. The poor little things must have been starving- not that anyone besides me cared.

Jack had an awful time catching the cats, and I was glad they got a few good swipes in because I knew he was going to take them away and I'd never see them again.

"You keep at this mess and I'm going to get rid of these bloody cats and pick your mother up." I was glad when he left because he scared me.

When Jack and Mom arrived home the cabin looked better

than before I'd started cleaning, but the smell of cat pee was still lingering in the air.

Mom walked into the cabin and didn't say anything, so I thought I was home free.

"Hi Mom, are you feeling better?" I asked cheerfully. She never even acknowledged me, so I went and sat on the couch.

Jack made us his famous spaghetti for dinner and I ate five big plates. My stomach was so full it looked like I'd swallowed a basketball. I made sure to get good and full because I wasn't sure when I'd get to eat again.

Jack was still in love with Mom and convinced her to move back to Penticton with him because he had another job. He didn't want us to live with him, but he wanted Mom to be close. I didn't want to move back to Penticton because the last time we lived there the kids bullied me, but my opinion never mattered, so we moved. I was ten years old.

In Penticton, Mom and I moved into a rooming house that the locals called "The Dirty Dozen." It was a dump, we rarely had any food and Mom was back drinking and popping pills. When she wasn't with Jack, she was miserable, and I was starting to hate her.

They may have liked their little arrangement, but I detested it because they started taking off again and leaving me all by myself for days on end. I never knew where they went or when they'd be coming home and I hated being alone at night.

One day after they had left, I went to school and was playing with my friend Theresa when she asked, "What's the matter Laura? You seem kinda quiet today?"

After a few seconds I whispered, "My Mom is missing."

"What do you mean she is missing?"

"I don't know where she went and I'm afraid to stay alone."

I no sooner had the words out of my mouth when she said,

"I got an idea; you can come home with me until your Mom gets home okay?"

"Okay," I said hoping her parents would agree to our little plan.

After school, I went home with her and when she explained to her mother that my Mom was missing, she was obviously shocked. I'm sure I must have looked like an orphan by the way I was dressed, which is why her mother never asked me any questions. I knew she was concerned about my situation, but like most, wasn't sure what she should do about it. Like the Coyne's they opened up their hearts and home to me and I fell instantly in love with them.

I'll never forget the macaroni mixed with tomato soup that Theresa's Mom made every day for lunch. God always seemed to have someone available to help me out when I needed it the most.

For some reason I'd check everyday to see if Mom was home. Even though I liked it at Theresa's house, I worried about my mother. Sometimes I wished she'd stay away forever, but she always came back like one of my ear aches. When I found out she'd arrived back home I thanked Theresa's Mom for everything and went home, wishing home was somewhere else.

When I opened the door to our room, her eyes narrowed the moment she saw me, and she grunted, "What are you doing here?"

"Well," I said, "I couldn't stay at Theresa's forever, so I came home."

"Too bad," was her reply.

"You got that right," I said sarcastically.

"You are not going to talk to me like that! Who do you think you are, you little brat?" I was sure Mom was going to backhand me but instead she said, "I have a good mind to put you into a

detention home. Maybe you'd learn how lucky you really are!"
She slammed her bedroom door in my face.

Mom and I fought a lot after that and she started to feel like
she couldn't handle me anymore. When I was younger, she could
catch me and beat the hell out of me, but now I was faster and
could throw a punch better than she could and I'd learned how
to protect myself from her.

All I wanted was for her to love me like she loved Jack. She
never wanted to get rid of him even if he bashed her head into
a stove. What was wrong with me that she hated me so much?
What did Jack have that made her love him so easily? Was it
because he looked after her? I'd been looking after her for years
so it couldn't be that. I longed for her to smile and look tenderly
at me the way she looked at him, but she never did.

The only thing I could think of that Jack did differently from
me was he gave her nice things. I knew she loved sweets so I
decided I'd bake an easy bake chocolate cake for her that Sally
had given to me. I'd been keeping it for something special, maybe
this was the right time.

I'd watched Mom light the gas stove a few times and although
I'd never lit it myself, it looked easy enough. I turned on the gas,
but I couldn't get the match lit. I could smell the gas stinking up
the room but never thought anything of it. After a few more tries
I lit the match, bent closer to the burner and when I touched the
match to the stove the flames flew into the air. I didn't get out
of the way until the fire licked my hair, eyelashes and the hair
off my arms, quicker than I could have licked the chocolate off
a beater.

My arms were so sore from the burns that I wrapped them
in a cold wet towel to ease the pain. I never cried out or made a
noise because I knew that Mom would go crazy. It was better to

quietly clean up the mess and go to bed. Once again I'd failed. Mom was right. I was stupid.

After the disaster with the cake, I decided to visit the church I'd visited the last time we lived in Penticton. The minute I got through the door I felt like the chaotic world I lived in couldn't touch me, and I was safe from all life's hurt and broken promises.

As I entered, one of the ladies exclaimed, "Laura, how have you been? We've missed you." Then she gave me the biggest hug I'd gotten in a long time. It was such a wonderful feeling to know that someone actually missed me.

"We moved away for a few months," I said, "but we are back now for awhile."

"Well, we're glad you are back. Are you hungry?"

"Do you have any cookies?" I asked shyly.

"Yes, we sure do," she said, and she took my hand and we talked all the way to the kitchen. Before I left, they gave me some newer clothes and invited me to Sunday school. When I could, I went, because it was fun and we always got a snack.

I remember one time after Sunday school was over and we were eating our snack, I noticed a cross on the wall with a man hanging from it.

"Who's that man hanging on that cross?" I asked the teacher.

"His name is Jesus," she replied. "He's God's son and he died on the cross to pay for all the bad things you and I have done."

Why would Jesus have to die for the bad things I did? I can remember thinking about that all day and when night came, I started to cry because it was my fault Jesus died.

It was always my fault.

Penticton was never a good place for me. I ended up making friends with a bunch of kids as rebellious as I was and started smoking, stealing, and cutting school. I finally realized I couldn't make Mom happy, so I quit trying. I was sick and tired of always being the one blamed for things I had no control over, and the quiet little girl started to rebel.

These new friends liked me, as long as I did what they said. If I needed to do bad things to have friends, then so be it. I was sick of being alone and for a change it was time for me to worry about what I wanted, so, that's exactly what I did. If I felt like staying out all night, I did. I stole cigarettes and money from Mom and didn't give a damn about anyone but myself.

My best friend Bev was a screwed up as I was and what ever she wanted to do, we did. Maybe that's why we got along so well. She led and I followed.

I was on a walk one day when Bev caught up to me and hollered, "Hey Laura, want to roast some marshmallows."

"Where are we going to roast them?" I asked.

"I know of a good place on the top of the hill over there. Are you coming?"

"You bet." I never turned down good food.

"Let's go. I have everything we need," she said grabbing my hand.

As we climbed the hill we were giddy with excitement. Neither one of us could wait to stuff our mouths with marshmallows.

"I'll start the fire if you like?" I said. "What did you bring to start the fire with?"

"Matches." Bev replied.

"Well how are we going to start a fire if all we have is matches and no paper or wood?"

"I never thought of that. All I was thinking about was the marshmallows and the matches."

"Good thing I came along," I giggled as I started pulling some dead looking grass and putting it into a pile.

"Here I can help."

"Sure."

Before long we had a huge bunch of dry grass, and a few twigs.

"Here goes," I said as I lit the match.

Here goes alright. The moment the match hit the dry grass a soft wind came up and like magic, everything around us started to burn.

"Oh shit," I yelled, "now what are we going to do."

Bev immediately took off running towards some houses near by and I followed her.

"Help," Bev yelled, "there's a big fire on the hill! You need to call the firemen."

Lucky for us a lady heard us and called for help.

"You girls stay with me," she said with a worried look on her face. Then she looked at us and asked, "You girls didn't have anything to do with the fire, did you?"

"It was an accident," I blurted out before I had time to think.

I'd no sooner confessed when one of the firemen arrived and started asking questions.

"Anyone know how the fire started?" he asked the lady.

"Talk to the girls," she said.

"It was an accident," I said, "we were just going to roast a few marshmallows when the wind picked up and the whole field caught on fire!"

"Do you girls understand how disastrous this fire could have been? People could have lost their homes and everything they owned," the fireman said firmly.

He lectured us for what seemed like hours and although our faces looked serious, inside we were ticked off with him. We didn't mean to start the fire, so why was he getting after us so much?

Mom somehow found out about the fire and of course was furious with me; but to tell you the truth, I liked it when her buttons got pushed.

By the time I was eleven years old I had a very bad attitude and far too much freedom. Mom started to nag again about putting me into a detention center.

"You little bitch," she said, "you are not staying with me any longer. You have always been trouble and I'm sick and tired of having you around. I can't even stand the look of your ugly face. The best place for you is jail or a detention center where you might figure out how lucky you really are."

She had been a great role model in one way, she taught me how to stand my ground and I could yell, swear, and be just as mean and ugly as she was. I should have known better than to think I could ever win an argument with her, but I was always a positive thinker and wasn't afraid to try.

"I am not going to any detention center. I am staying here with you whether you like it or not! You're the bitch, not me." I said defiantly.

Before I knew what was happening, Mom grabbed my hand and started dragging me across the room. I thought she was just going to throw me out into the hallway, but that was not her plan.

"Mom, what are you doing? Stop, you're hurting me!" I shouted.

"Shut up," she yelled as she struggled to get me near the door.

The doors were solid wood and when she opened that enormous door and started to push me out into the hallway, I started to pull myself back into the room. She was still stronger than I was, so as hard as I tried, I couldn't get free from her grasp.

"Mom stop! Leave me alone," I screamed.

To this day, I don't know how she managed to get my hand onto the doorframe, but she did. Before she slammed the door, I somehow managed to get all my fingers out but one. When the door struck my finger, the pain shot through my body like an electric shock. I let out a horrible scream while I struggled to get free, but my finger was stuck in the door and there was no way I could get it out on my own. Every time I moved, the pain shot up my arm and Mom was holding onto my other hand so I couldn't reach the doorknob.

"You are a selfish little brat and I'll teach you a lesson if it's the last thing I do. No one back talks me, especially you!"

Between all the yelling and screaming, the manager came running up to see who was making all the noise.

"What's going on in there is everything all right?"

"Please open the door!" I cried.

The moment the door opened instant relief swept over me. My finger pounded with each heart beat and started to swell, but at least I was free. I was shaking and crying so hard I slumped onto the floor.

"I hate you, I wish you were dead!" I sobbed.

Between the pain in my hand and the one in my heart, I was numb. Did I really deserve what she'd done, or was Mom just being her mean self?

The manager was furious with her and proceeded to curse and yell at her, but it didn't do any good. She just stood there emotionless as if what she had done was the right thing to do, and the manager had no right to intrude. The manager on the other hand was outraged. He gently picked me up off the floor and hugged me tight until I quit crying. It was nice to know that someone cared.

"What in the hell is wrong with you?" he asked Mom. She always seemed to know how to twist things around.

"It was an accident, she's fine!"

"Are you okay?"

I nodded my head because I was afraid to say anything.

"If you need anything, come and get me." Then he left and I followed him out the door. There was no way I was going to stay alone with Mom. The only place I could think of that was safe was the church. I ran sobbing harder with each step hoping someone would be there to help me. The minute I got through the door one of the ladies came running towards me.

"Oh my goodness Laura. What happened?"

I showed her my finger and my whole body began to shake as I told her the story. She listened to every word, which helped ease the pain, and her hugs made me feel loved and lovable.

"I think we need to call the police," she said as she stroked my hair.

"No, please, please don't call the police. I'm okay, it was just an accident. "

"Laura maybe the police can help you so your Mother doesn't hurt you again."

"She won't hurt me again." I lied. "I gotta go. Thanks for being so nice to me, but I need to go home."

Once again I didn't want my Mother to get into trouble. Not to mention if she had tried to help me she may have ended up with stitches like Ovey did. It was better for her if she didn't try to save me from my mother.

When I arrived home, I quietly entered the room and Mom was snoring on the bed. I knew I couldn't stay with her any longer, so I stole four dollars and twenty cents out of her purse, and packed all I owned into a little bag, which wasn't much. Then I quietly left the room never looking back. The only place I knew I'd be safe was Gramma's I just needed to get there.

I ran as fast as I could to the Greyhound bus depot. My heart was pounding so hard I thought it was going to jump out of my chest by the time I got there. I asked a man which bus was going to Vancouver and he pointed me in the right direction. When I found the right bus, I slipped into a seat near the back. The bus driver hopped onto the bus and started talking to everyone.

Back then, you didn't have an actual ticket to show to the bus driver like you do today; you paid inside the terminal and if you were on the bus the drivers assumed you'd paid for a ticket.

"Hey little missy, did you buy a ticket?" asked the bus driver.

"I sure did."

He believed me, for which I was very thankful, because I had nowhere to go if he had kicked me off the bus.

After the bus left the terminal, I started wondering how I was going to get to Gramma's house. The bus only went as far as Vancouver and she lived in Richmond, which was too far for me to walk. The only way to get to her house was to hire a cab and I knew I didn't have enough money.

As I looked around at the passengers on the bus, I couldn't believe my good fortune. Sitting in the seat ahead of me was a woman who had trustingly set her purse under her seat and went to sleep. I quietly took her purse to the bathroom and took all the money she had out of her wallet. She was rich! I hadn't seen so much money in my life. I took her wallet, threw it into the garbage, and placed her purse under her seat where I'd found it. Thinking back, I wish I'd put her wallet back into her purse so she didn't have to replace all her cards. But I was eleven. What did I know?

Sleep came easy: I had money, no mother to beat me, and I was heading towards Gramma's house, hoping she'd let me stay.

Once the bus arrived in Vancouver, I grabbed my things, threw them into a locker, and ran outside as fast as I could to grab a cab. I was afraid the woman might notice her wallet was missing and figure out it was me who took it.

I went to the Hudson Bay, had some lunch, bought a T-shirt that said, "I love my Gramma", a brand new stuffed Panda with two eyes and a set of dishes for Gramma. I couldn't carry all my purchases with me because they were too heavy so they said they'd deliver them the next day.

Gramma lived in Richmond in a one bedroom little house with pear trees surrounding it. Just looking at it brought a huge smile to my face and a sense of relief. I knocked on the door and when she saw me, she was really surprised.

"Laura, what are you doing here?" she said as she ushered me through the door. "Where's your mother?"

When I told her how things were at home, and showed her my finger, she told me to wait and she'd be right back.

I heard her in the next room, "Please we can't send her back to her mother. She's sick! I promise you I'll take care of her and she won't be in the way."

"Oh I don't care," Grandpa grumbled, "just as long as she stays out of my way and behaves herself we'll give it a try."

This was Gramma's third marriage because her other two husbands had died. Her first husband was my aunt's dad, her second husband was my Mom's dad and this husband didn't have any children. My Mom never liked this new Grandpa and I was beginning to understand why.

"Thank you," Gramma said sincerely and then she grabbed me and gave me a big hug. "Welcome home Laura."

I was so excited I started to cry. Gramma's house was safe and maybe for once my life would be normal. I never went back to the locker to retrieve my stuff for fear Grandpa might change his mind while I was gone, so Gramma bought me some new clothes to wear that actually fit.

Gramma was surprised when the dishes and my new Panda arrived the next morning.

"Oh my Laura. How did you afford these?" she asked.

"I found a wallet and it had lots of money in it so I bought you a present," I said feeling very proud of myself. I was glad she didn't ask me anything else because I didn't want to lie to her anymore.

On the nineteenth of every month, it was Pension cheque day

for Gramma and my Family Allowance cheque usually arrived at her house around the same time. Usually she forwarded the Family Allowance cheque to Mom, but I beat Gramma to the mailbox and kept the big eight-dollar cheque without her knowing. I figured it was my money because I wasn't living with Mom anymore.

Gramma's tradition on Pension cheque day was to cash her cheque and then go for lunch at the mall. Now we could both cash our cheques and go for lunch. I just wasn't really sure how to cash a cheque so I knew I'd have to watch everything Gramma did if I was going to cash mine without her knowing.

We left for the mall and headed right for the bank. When we went to cash Gramma's cheque, I saw her scribble something on the back of the cheque and then the lady gave her some money. "Thank you very much," Gramma said as she put her money into her purse.

Once Gramma was ready to leave the bank it was time for lunch. We were heading towards the restaurant when I started to walk cross-legged pretending I needed to go to the bathroom.

"Gramma I need to go to the bathroom, so I'll meet you at the restaurant."

"I can go with you honey."

Feeling a little panicky I said, "No, Gramma, I'm a big girl, I'll meet you at the restaurant."

"Alright, the washroom is right there and the restaurant is just around that corner."

As soon as Gramma was out of sight, I went to the bank, scribbled on the back of the cheque and went to the same lady Gramma used.

"Hi, my Gramma forgot to give you this cheque. Could you please cash it for her?" I said trying to sound very grown up.

"Sure," she said and before I knew it, I had eight bucks in my hot little hands.

On my way to the restaurant, I stopped and bought Gramma a little leopard made of Blue Mountain Pottery that cost almost exactly eight dollars. I couldn't wait to get to the restaurant to give it to her. I loved making her happy!

When I arrived at the restaurant, I gave Gramma her present and I could tell she was puzzled.

"Oh Laura, you shouldn't have… but thank you."

"You're welcome Gramma. I love you."

"I know you do honey, and I love you too." She grabbed the menu and asked, "So what do you want to eat? Spaghetti?"

"Yup." I giggled. I always ordered spaghetti.

We ate our lunch and went home. I felt like the luckiest girl in the world.

I loved being at Gramma's house. I was never hungry or cold and she always made me feel special. Every morning I could smell the coffee- it always smelled so good-and milk and fresh baked buns and bread arrived at the door like magic, and I wondered how they got there.

"Good morning Laura, did you have a good sleep?"

Gramma greeted me every morning. I always went and gave her a big hug and then we usually ate toast or porridge for breakfast, and talked about what our day was going to look like. To me it was like being in Heaven! Gramma was a great cook and seemed to find pleasure in trying to fatten me up. The only bad things about Gramma's house were the sleeping arrangements and Grandpa.

The only bedroom consisted of two twin beds and Gramma insisted I sleep in hers.

"Gramma please, let me sleep on the couch. I don't want to take your bed." I begged but she wouldn't hear of it. She wanted to make sure I had a good sleep. I didn't like the idea of Grandpa and me alone in the same bedroom, but if Gramma said it was okay, I believed her because I knew she'd never knowingly let him hurt me.

She always seemed busy throughout the day. When she wasn't cooking, she was caring for her Siamese cats that were continually pregnant. She didn't breed them on purpose; they just weren't spayed so they were always having kittens.

One day after a new batch of kittens arrived Grandpa said, "Laura, you need to come with me and help me get rid of these kittens."

I wasn't sure why I had to go but I went anyway. When we got to the barn he took the kittens, put them into a plastic bag, tied a knot in the top and then headed towards a ditch full of water.

"What are you doing," I screamed at him.

"I'm killing these damn kittens," he said. Then he threw the bag into the water and used a stick to keep the bag from floating to the top.

"They'll drown," I cried, covering my ears so I couldn't hear their meows.

"Shut up! This is how it's done if I have to get rid of cats," he snarled.

I never said a word because he scared me. After a few minutes, Grandpa threw the stick into the water and went back to the house. As I stood by myself looking at the bag full of kittens drift down the ditch I started to cry. My sobs became louder and my heart felt like it was going to break. I had kept my promise never to hurt an animal again, and wanted Grandpa to do the same.

After I quit crying, and gathered up enough courage to enter the house, I went to the kitchen to be with Gramma. It was safe there.

Grandpa wasn't thrilled with me being around and didn't try to hide his feelings. He hardly spoke to me, which suited me fine; I liked it better when he ignored me.

He liked to chew snuff and peel apples in his big old rocking chair that no one was supposed to sit in but him. Little did he know that every time he went out, I was in that chair rocking to my hearts content. I think part of the reason I did it was to be cheeky, but the rocking motion did comfort me. I just needed to be sure I wasn't in the chair when he arrived home.

One time he caught me in his chair and it looked like his eyes were going to bulge right out of his head.

"Get the hell out of my chair," he yelled. I bolted so fast out of that chair it was amazing I didn't break a leg. The only other thing Grandpa really cared about were his dogs.

He raised puppies and sold them-none of them went into a ditch. They were Labrador dogs and the puppies were so cute. He sold them for five dollars a piece and every time one sold, it made me sad and I prayed they went to a good home.

One chore Grandpa gave me was to walk the dogs. I loved the way they licked me and wagged their tails. They made me feel loved and we always had lots of fun together.

While on a walk one afternoon, I met two girls. Julie who was eight and Amy who was fourteen; I was eleven, right in the middle. They were great friends. They never teased me about my teeth and always included me in whatever they were doing.

Amy and I spent the most time together, likely because Julie was three years younger than I was and wasn't allowed to do the things Amy and I could do. The nice thing about the three of us though, was if Julie was around, she was never left out.

There was an autobody shop behind Gramma's house named "Clives". It was an older building with bays where they worked on the cars and a little room in the back with an old rickety bed and pictures of naked women pinned to the wall. The only reason I knew about the room was Julie and I spied on Clive whenever we could.

He was the man who owned the shop. He had a thick German accent and told us he was thirty-six years old. He had black greasy hair slicked back with a little wave in the front and always smelled like car oil. His hands and nails were black and greasy and he had terrible yellow rotten teeth, but that didn't seem to stop him from smiling. Even though he wasn't anything to look at, we all liked him.

Amy told me that her and Clive were boyfriend and girlfriend and they were having sex. Sometimes I wasn't sure if all her stories were true or not, but at the time it really didn't matter.

Clive was always super nice to us girls. The moment we showed up at his shop he'd say, "Hey, here come the most beautiful girls in the world!" Then he'd grin at us and stop working. It didn't seem to matter how many cars needed to be worked on, he always made time for us and never shoved us aside.

"Ah Clive, you're just sayin that," I used to say to him.

"No I'm not! The truth is the truth, what more can I say?" When he said that it made me smile.

Amy spent most of her time after school hanging out at Clive's, so I was able to see her almost every day. I was looking forward to summer holidays so we could spend more time together. When I arrived at Gramma's it was too late to enrol me into school so I paced around the house waiting until school was over so I could meet up with the girls.

I wonder if I ever drove Gramma a bit crazy pacing around the house until my friends came along. I know I drove Grandpa insane because he really didn't want me there in the first place. If I had gone to school, at least I'd be away for six hours of the day. In some ways I kind of liked driving him nuts because I didn't like him.

Every day was the same. I'd watch for the girls to come home from school, and if I missed them for some reason, I'd go to Clive's and find them there.

One day I went over to Clive's place to visit Amy, but she was nowhere in sight. I was going to go home when Clive insisted I stay.

"Hey, what's the hurry, you may as well stay and visit me, what you gonna do at home?"

That was a good question because the fact was I didn't have anything else to do.

"Okay, I'll stay a little longer," I said.

"Great, want to see my special room?"

I already knew where the special room was and I'll never know what possessed me to go with him that day, but I'd grown to trust him, plus I was curious because maybe there were things in there we couldn't see from the window. That would be a great bit of news to share with Julie!

Between trust and curiosity, I followed behind him until we were inside the room, and he closed the door.

"Don't tell the other girls I said this, but I think you are the prettiest of any of them." Then he whispered, "Even Amy."

"Holy smokes," I said, "you really think I'm prettier than Amy?"

That thought had never crossed my mind before. He seemed so genuine I believed him. With each word, he slowly moved towards me and his voice got quieter with each step. I'd never seen him like this before.

"Why don't you sit on the bed, you will be more comfortable," he said smiling.

By this time, it was as if he had me under his spell. The friendship we had acquired over the past few weeks made me more than willing to do as he asked so I hopped up onto the bed.

"You know Laura, I know your life has been very hard, Amy told me all about your Mom," he said, "and I'd like to be your friend and help you feel better, if you'd like me to."

By this time, he was right beside me and I could smell the oil on his skin. It took me back to when my mother's boyfriends touched me, and suddenly I was afraid.

"I need to go home now Clive," I said in a matter of fact way. I stood up from the bed and ran out of the room.

He followed me and yelled, "Have a good day, see ya tomorrow."

The next day after school I went back to Clive's to see if Amy was there; for some reason she still hadn't shown up. I was so disappointed; I loved hanging out with her. Clive sensed my disappointment and was quick to invite me into the "special room" where we could talk and I agreed to go. The last time I followed him into that room I didn't notice how small it was and there was no windows, not to mention it stunk like the old hotel rooms in Vancouver.

As we walked into the room, he slid his hand through his hair and I liked all the attention he was giving me.

"Laura it looks to me like you could use a little fun in your life, what do you think?"

I wasn't really sure what to think but a little fun sounded like a good idea.

Then he went on, "You are so beautiful and it drives me crazy to see you so upset. I like you and I can't believe anyone would want to hurt you. Your mother doesn't know what a beautiful little girl she has. You deserve to be loved and I want to love you."

"You love me?" I said in disbelief.

"How could anyone not love you?"

Then he moved closer to me and I had no reason to be afraid of him anymore. He gently led me over to the bed and told me to lie down. I did what he said and at first, I wasn't sure what was going on, but before I knew it, he was lying on top of me.

Suddenly I found my mind wandering back to when I was a little girl and the men touched me. Somehow it seemed different because I knew and liked Clive. Sadly, I took his word when he said he loved me. Even though he was touching me inappropriately the fact he said he loved me made it okay in my mind. I know now that love is not just a sexual act, but back then it was the only way I felt loved. When he was finished he smiled and said, "Thanks Laura, have a nice day."

I wasn't sure what happened. I pulled my underwear and pants up and went home. I felt gross and wanted to take a bath, but I didn't feel like Clive or I had done anything wrong because he loved me.

Gramma was busy in the kitchen making cookies when I got home.

"Gramma would it be okay if I had a bath?" I asked.

"Sure you can, and when you're done come back down to the kitchen, there should be some fresh baked cookies by that time," she said as she put a pan into the oven.

As I sat in the nice warm water, my mind wandered back to when I was a little girl and how much I loved bath times. I stayed in the bathtub until the water got cold and wished I could see Amy. I missed her.

Amy showed up the next day and I told her what happened with Clive. She was furious. I decided I didn't want to go to Clive's with her that day, because she was really mad and I didn't want to be in the middle of a big fight.

When she saw Clive, she asked him if what I had said was true, and he denied it. I am not sure if Amy really believed him or me. All I know is I never saw her again, and that made me sad. I continued to spy on Clive for curiosity's sake, but never stopped to visit for long.

Thankfully, summer was almost over and I knew Gramma would be enrolling me in school. I was excited because I'd get to see Amy again and was ready to have some routine in my life. It was good-bye to August, and a big hello to September.

Unlike my mother, Gramma actually did enrol me in school and I was excited because now I had something to do during the day. Making friends over the summer made the first day easier.

I'm not sure what possessed me to do the things I did, but one day I went to the corner store near Gramma's house and asked "Could you please set up an account in my Gramma's name? Sometimes she likes me to pick things up for her after school."

"No problem," said the Chinese grocer. "I'll get one started right away."

Wow, I thought, *that was easy*. People were so trusting back then. The storeowner never even questioned me. He just set up an account.

I went to the corner store at recess and bought myself a treat almost everyday. I especially liked the Long Johns with the whip cream in the middle, and if I was really hungry, I'd buy two.

It wasn't until I'd racked up twenty dollars on my bill that Gramma found out what I'd done.

"Laura, did you start a charge account at the store in my name?" she asked.

I hung my head and said, "Yes."

"Why would you do that? The store called today, and I owe them twenty dollars. That's a lot of money. I never thought you'd steal from me," she said as if I'd broken her heart.

"I'm sorry Gramma. I never thought I was stealing from you. I just wanted to get a treat, that's all," I started to cry because I knew I'd disappointed her.

If I'd done that to my mother she'd given me a good beating. Maybe this time Gramma should have punished me, but the fact she was disappointed hurt more than any beating.

"I really am sorry, Gramma. I promise I'll never do that again. Please don't stop loving me," I sobbed.

She was very quite for a moment and then she came over and gave me a hug. "I forgive you Laura, but don't do anything like that again, it's wrong."

I honestly never thought that what I'd done was wrong; all I was thinking about was how good those Long John's were.

The next day I was just kicking around waiting for the girls to arrive when Grandpa showed up in the back yard.

"How about you make yourself useful and help me feed the dogs. Their dishes are in the shed," he said.

"Sure," I was surprised that he was talking to me, in the first place. I thought maybe he was actually starting to like me and wanted to spend some time with me.

As he started to fill the dog dishes with their food, he turned to me and said, "Straddle that dog and move, back and forth, you'll like it."

"I don't want to do that Grampa."

"Do it or I'll send you back to your mother!"

I started to cry, "Please, don't make me do that."

His eyes narrowed and he whispered, "Do it."

I straddled the dog and was so embarrassed and ashamed I felt sick to my stomach. He watched me and kept shouting orders. I was shaking with fear and couldn't wait for him to let me get off the dog and leave. I was afraid if I didn't do as he said he would make me go home. He was a pervert! He made me feel so dirty inside it was hard for me to think afterwards. I was so upset I couldn't walk the dogs for a few days because he'd taken all the fun out of it.

I tried to stay away from him, but it was hard especially when we had to sleep in the same room. I hated him. The worst part was I had to wear two masks, one when I was with him and another one when Gramma was around. No wonder I was so mixed up inside.

Within a few days of the dog incident, I was thinking about taking the dogs for a walk when Grandpa shouted, "Hey Laura, I want to show you something in the garage."

Even though I knew it wasn't going to be a good thing to go into the garage with him, he held my future in his hands, so I quietly followed him. I knew that if he made a big stink about me not listening to him he'd make Gramma send me back to my mother, and I didn't want to go back to her.

The moment he shut the door, I started to shake.

"What did you want to show me?" I whispered.

He came up behind me, wrapped his arms around me and started to touch me all over. He kept saying to me, "Does this feel good? Do you like this?"

At first I couldn't move because I was trying to block out the whole horrible event until eventually I broke away from him and cried, "Grandpa what are you doing?"

His replied sarcastically, "This is much better than the dogs isn't it?"

I wanted to puke. Grandfathers aren't supposed to fondle their granddaughters, are they? Maybe he made my mother do the same things and that's why she was the way she was.

This may have been his way to get me to leave, but I wasn't about to let him win! I ran out of the garage and stayed outside until it was dinnertime.

When I went into the house, Gramma was putting dinner on the table and Grandpa shot me a look that said, *Keep your mouth shut!* It was like I had to be two different people. One was scared all the time of what Grandpa might do next and the other had to look happy for Gramma's sake.

It was a quiet dinner and as soon as I finished helping Gramma clean the kitchen, I went to bed. I never slept much that night because I was afraid of what might happen to me if I did.

With Amy out of the picture, Julie and I spent a lot of time together. We hadn't seen Clive for a while so we decided to go and see how he was doing.

He was busy working on a car when we came around the corner and after we talked for a few minutes, he said, "Laura, you want to see the coffee room?"

I looked at Julie and although I knew what he was after it was okay because he loved me.

"Is that okay Julie? I won't be long," I said.

"Sure," she said, "I'll be here when you get back."

I left Julie outside and followed Clive into the coffee room.

"How about you lie down there on that couch. It could be fun," he said excitedly.

I didn't mind the last time we were together, but this time it was different. He kept trying to kiss me with his tongue and then he tried to push himself inside of me. He was hurting me and I couldn't figure out what he was doing because no one had ever treated me like this before. I was so confused and afraid that I pushed him off me and ran out of the room.

"I'm calling the cops Clive," I screamed.

"Go ahead," he said as he smiled with his yellow teeth, never dreaming I might actually do as I said.

It was difficult to run as my pants were down around my ankles and I couldn't see because my tears were clouding my vision. I was such an idiot sometimes. It was the first time I questioned whether Clive really loved me or was just using me.

By the time I reached Julie, I had my pants pulled up, but I was hysterical. All I knew was I needed some help. She was shocked when she saw me and kept asking me over and over again what was wrong.

"We need to find a phone and call the police," I told her. We raced as fast as we could to the nearest shop, and I told the people that someone had tried to hurt me. It took them a little while to calm me down before they called 911.

I told the 911 lady who I was and she kept asking me what the problem was, but I was afraid to tell her.

"Laura, if you want me to help you, you need to be honest and tell me what happened," said the lady on the other end.

I was so frustrated I blurted out, "Clive tried to fuck me, so I ran away." I was sobbing so hard by this time it took awhile before I could hear the lady on the other end of the phone.

"Calm down, you are safe now. I'll send a Police Officer right away. What's the address?" she said kindly.

"380 Charles Road, Richmond," I sobbed.

"They'll meet you at your house in a few minutes, okay?"

"Okay," I said, then Julie and I went to Gramma's house to wait for the police to arrive.

We arrived at the house the same time the Police Officers did. They were in plain clothes, so at first I didn't know who they were. They introduced themselves and we all went into the house.

Gramma and Grandpa looked confused and I could tell they were concerned. Grandpa looked a little pale as the Police Officer started to ask me questions about what had happened.

"So Laura, can you tell me what happened today?" he said in a concerned voice.

"Oh nothing really," I lied. "I was just afraid, that's all."

They knew there was more to the story so one of the Police Officers asked Julie to come outside with him and she told him the truth.

When they got the full story they told me I was never to go over to Clive's again, and if he scared me, I was to call the police right away.

"Okay, I will," I said.

There were lots of police cars around our neighbourhood the next day, which freaked Grandpa out for good reason. We were all looking out the window when Grandpa started yelling, "Look at all these police cars around here. I told you she was nothing but trouble! She needs to go back home. Get rid of her! And I mean it!"

"I am not going back to my mother," I screamed back at him, and before I knew it, I could feel the palm of his hand slap the back of my head as hard as he could. Gramma was horrified and began to cry. I know that she didn't want me to go back to Mom, but in her mind, she had no choice.

Grandpa was sure the Police Officers were out to get him, so he wanted me out of the house as soon as possible. Both Gramma and I were heartsick and we knew I had to go. I only went to school in Richmond for one month before they shipped me back to Penticton to be with my mother. I never told Gramma what

Grandpa did to me because in those days, there were some things you just didn't discuss.

While I was at Gramma's, Mom had moved to "The Valley Hotel" in Penticton. Wouldn't it be great if she came running, arms open wide and a big smile on her face to greet me? Well, in my world that only happened in the movies. She as usual, was not a bit happy to see me. I think she had really enjoyed my time away because there was less hassle with me gone. I'm not even sure she said "hi" when I entered the room.

There was a Chinese restaurant attached to the Valley hotel that had a jukebox. My favourite song was "She's A Lady," by Tom Jones. Music was always something I enjoyed, not only for the beat, but also for the words. It took me to a nicer place and I could listen for hours.

When I wasn't at the Chinese restaurant, I'd look for a place that had a TV. Most of the hotel lobbies and the furniture stores had them, and no one seemed to mind my sitting and watching the programs for hours. When the TV shows ended, I headed home and tried to get some sleep.

I started school again and found a few friends who were sisters. Sandra was sixteen and her sister Sue was the same age as I was, eleven. They didn't seem to worry about how I looked or where I came from, which was such a blessing.

One evening I could hear swearing, screaming and fighting outside our room and when I poked my head out of the window, I realized four girls were beating on my friend Sandra.

"Get off of her or I'll call the police," I yelled.

They must have believed me because they took off, leaving Sandra all battered up on the sidewalk. I grabbed some money out of the arm of my Panda and ran down the stairs as fast as I could, "Are you okay," I asked.

"Yeah, I think I'll be fine, but why didn't you come down and help me?" she asked angrily.

"I wanted to, but my Mom wouldn't let me out of the room." I lied. "I had to sneak out when she wasn't looking. At least I scared them off," I said hoping she knew I'd done my best. I suggested a peace offering.

"If you like, I could buy you something to eat if you're hungry?"

"Sure, that sounds great." Sandra said.

I helped her off the ground and together we found a booth in the restaurant.

My heart ached for her because I knew when you were beaten up, it hurt your body, and your feelings. I tried to make her feel comfortable, and as we were eating our food and enjoying the jukebox, I could tell she was slowly starting to feel better. I was so glad I was there for her, because it gave me a chance to make someone I knew feel better, and I longed to be needed.

I hated my mother in every sense of the word. I'm not even sure if hate covers the contempt and disgust I felt towards her. She was pathetic and I told Sue, Sandra's sister, I wished Mom were dead. I felt if she were out of the way, my life could be so much better. She seemed to screw up any good thing that came along including me.

I can't even remember how our fight started, but when Mom started beating me, I started hitting and kicking her back. She was relentless and kept coming at me, going on and on about how I was driving her crazy. All I could here was "Blah, Blah, Blah." Then suddenly time stood still and the next thing I remember I was standing outside the hotel with Sue.

The police showed up followed by the ambulance and Sue and I were curious as to what was happening until we saw Mom, unconscious, coming out of the hotel on a stretcher. When I saw her, my emotions were so confused. One minute I was crying and the next I was laughing.

I was in shock.

Sue just looked at me and gave me a big hug; she knew how hard it was for me to live with Mom.

I told Sue I needed to go back inside and get my Panda because it held all our money. On my way through the lobby, a Police Officer yelled, "Stop. Who are you and where do you think you're going?"

"My name is Laura" I said, "and that's my mother on the stretcher. I need to get into my room so I can get my Panda," I choked the words out between the tears.

"I'm sorry about your mother," he said. "Let me come with you."

He followed me to the room and once I had my panda, we went downstairs together. Mom had already left in the ambulance and suddenly I felt very alone and afraid.

The Police Officer told me he wanted to take me down to the Police Station for questioning, so I said good-bye to Sue and wondered what was going to happen to me.

We went into a small room with two chairs and one of the Police Officers said, "Laura, someone stabbed your mother, do you know who it was?"

I was shocked when they said someone had stabbed her. I'd stolen a knife from a souvenir shop that had a Canadian Mounted Police on the handle, with a blade about six inches long, but I didn't remember using it to stab my mother.

"I don't know who stabbed her," I exclaimed. "I just remember her hitting me, that's all I remember."

"You're sure you don't remember anything else?" The officer asked kindly.

I just shook my head; I didn't remember anything about a stabbing. I was as surprised as anyone that she'd been stabbed and I felt confused.

They called a Social Worker and she arranged for me to stay at a foster home until Mom was better.

"Okay Laura, it's time to go. It's been a tough day hasn't it," the Social worker said softly.

"Where am I going?" I asked her.

"Well, we've found a nice place for you to stay until your Mom gets better, okay?" She took my hand and we went to her car.

I felt a little relieved because I wouldn't be by myself, but I was worried about Mom and I couldn't figure out who could've stabbed her.

Once we arrived at my new home, the Social Worker talked to the lady, and then she left. The minute she left me at the foster home, the lady said, "Follow me Laura and I'll show you where you will be staying."

She sounded sort of scared so I thought maybe I was the first foster kid she'd ever had. She took me to a small bedroom with a single bed, and once I was inside the room, she left and locked the door behind her.

She actually locked me in the bedroom and I couldn't get out! I felt trapped. I decided the only way she'd likely open the door was if I had to go to the bathroom so I politely yelled, "I need to go pee." I was sure she didn't want me peeing on her rug and I was right.

The moment she unlocked the door, I bolted out of the house, squeezing my panda as I ran.

"Where do you think you're going?" The lady hollered after me.

"None of your business," I replied and ran back to Social Services. When the Social Worker saw me, she was shocked.

"Laura," she said, "What are you doing here?"

"That lady is crazy! She locked me in a room and the only way I got out was to tell her I had to pee. I'm not going back there-I don't care what you say!" And I stomped my foot for emphasis.

I guess they thought after all I had gone through they'd better place me in a different home, and my new foster home was much better. They had a few kids and two Lassie dogs. The family made sure to feed me and look after my basic needs, but they were very strict and I couldn't just take off whenever I wanted to.

I stayed with them for three weeks until Mom came home from the hospital, and in one way, I was looking forward to going home because I missed my freedom. At least when I lived with my mother I could do whatever I wanted, when I wanted.

Mom looked better physically than the last time I saw her, but she was as self-centered as ever.

"Where's the money?" were the first words out of her mouth. She wasn't concerned about who looked after me or how I was doing, but only where the money went.

"I have no idea," I lied. I'd spent the money, and didn't want her to know the truth. She didn't have the energy to fight with me, so our lives picked up from where they left off; she laid down on the bed, and I sat on a chair.

I hated Penticton and missed my Gramma, so when Mom decided to move back to Vancouver I was eager to go. She bought two bus tickets, loaded up all we owned into a few paper bags, and off we went.

Once we got on the bus, she started to act very strange. "Laura, there's someone on this bus that's going to kill me," she whispered. "Keep your eyes open."

I thought that maybe she'd gotten into a fight before we left Penticton, and someone really was after her. That thought scared me, and the longer we were on the bus the more agitated we both became. By the time we were near Mission, she was hysterical.

"I need to get off this son of a bitchin bus right now!" she screamed running down the aisle. She was so paranoid that I was sure her neck was going to snap off from looking around so quickly. Everyone on the bus got very quiet and I could tell they were scared too.

"Listen lady, calm down," replied the bus driver sternly. "As soon as we get to Mission, you can get off the bus, but I am not letting you off in the middle of nowhere."

He looked mad, and I couldn't wait until we could get off the bus. She had me so afraid and embarrassed for her that I was exhausted.

Once the bus arrived in Mission, Mom exited as fast as she could off the bus and I had a hard time keeping up with her. She grabbed our few belongings and headed to an old hotel. We stayed in Mission for two nights until Mom talked Aunty Kim into coming to get us.

There were very few words between my mother and my Aunt because they never got along and to be honest, I think Mom was surprised my aunt came to get us in the first place.

When we arrived in Vancouver, Aunty Kim dropped us off at a rundown hotel. At least this place was relatively clean. The man behind the counter used a white cane so I knew he was blind, but was amazed at how he moved around.

"We need a room," Mom said rudely.

"Okay, how many nights?" the man asked.

"I have no idea," she said.

"We have daily and monthly rates. Let me know what you want tomorrow and we'll get it figured out. It's late and I bet you are both tired," he said kindly.

"I'm tired and hungry," I blurted out.

"Shut up Laura," Mom hollered.

When she said that to me I could see the man was upset. "I bet a little girl like you would like a sucker."

I nodded my head and he dug into a big glass jar and pulled out a big lollipop.

"Here you are, and I want you to know you are welcome to watch TV anytime you like, okay?"

"Okay, what's your name?" I asked in between licks.

"My name is Joe."

"Can I call you Uncle Joe?" I asked.

"Sure ya can. I don't have any family so Uncle Joe sounds really nice." Then he turned to Mom and said, "Here's your key."

Mom grabbed the key, we went to our room and both fell fast asleep.

Uncle Joe was a good man, and treated me really well. Sometimes he'd take me for a walk, and we'd stop and get ice cream at a little Chinese café.

When I was at the hotel watching TV around dinnertime, he always gave me a TV dinner and we'd watch cartoons together. Sometimes I wondered how he could even watch TV when he was blind, but I never asked because I didn't want to hurt his feelings.

Social Services checked up on us and told Mom she needed to find a better place to live for her daughter; I bet that made her mad. There was someone out there looking after me, but not her. She liked where she was living, and for once she had to move whether she wanted to or not. The only bad thing was I really didn't want to move either because I loved Uncle Joe.

We moved to the Lily Hotel in Burnaby, but I still visited Uncle Joe about once a month. He eventually sold his hotel and bought a house close to the Canadian National Institute for the Blind where he could get some help when he needed it.

"Where do you think you're going?" Mom asked one day as I was heading over to Uncle Joe's.

"I'm going to see Uncle Joe," I replied.

"Well make yourself useful and ask him for some money." Mom was always on the lookout for money.

I left and walked over to Uncle Joe's, but every time I asked him for money, he said no. He didn't want to support Mom's habits. He was happy to feed me while I was with him, and give me some pocket change, but he was not at all interested in supporting my mother.

The last time I saw Uncle Joe I was under a lot of pressure.

"You need to get some money from him," said Mom.

"Can't you sell something?"

"I've sold everything we have already. Don't come home unless you get some money, you hear me!"

Her addictions were costing more and more, and mentally she was getting sicker and sicker. I was so afraid of her that I knew I didn't dare come home without any money for fear she'd beat me half to death.

When I arrived at Uncle Joe's, he asked, "What's the matter Laura? Something botherin you?"

I hung my head and mumbled, "Uncle Joe Mom told me I needed to get some money from you or she was going to hurt me. Please, can you just give me a little bit for her?"

"No Laura, I refuse to give that woman one cent! She's nothing but a drunk and drug addict and I am not going to support her bad habits. I'm sorry but that's the way it's going to be."

I felt so torn up inside because I didn't want to steal from my Uncle Joe, but I was too afraid to go home without any money.

"I need to go to the bathroom," I lied. "I'll be right back." The moment I started to riffle through the dresser drawers in his bedroom, he came around the corner. He may have been blind, but he wasn't deaf or stupid.

"What are you doing?" he yelled. "I thought you were different from your mother. Get out of here and don't ever come back!"

"I'm sorry Uncle Joe, but my Mom said I couldn't come home without money," I was shaking by this time but it didn't help.

When I looked at him, I could see he was disappointed in me, and that stung. I knew his anger was more about my mother than me, but the reality was I'd hurt the one who cared about me, not the one who used me to get what she wanted.

"Don't call me Uncle," he said.

The room at the Lily Hotel wasn't any cleaner than Uncle Joe's but it was much larger. It had its own bathroom separate bedroom a kitchen and a living room.

One perk for me was the TV. I rocked back and forth on the old brown couch and watched my shows for hours. The couch was soft and comfortable; the only thing I didn't like was the dust that came out whenever I moved.

One weekend I met a girl named Karin whose mother lived in the Lily Hotel too. Karin visited her on the weekends, but stayed in a group home during the week. Her mother lived a few doors down from us, so every weekend that Karin came we were inseparable. I loved it when she visited because I thought she was cool. She was eleven days older than I was, but she seemed so mature because she smoked, had a boyfriend, dressed stylishly and wore makeup. She was good to me too. She gave me some of her old clothes, showed me how to put make-up on and how to smoke; how cool is that when you're twelve? I idolized her and wanted to be just like her.

Unlike the other places we lived, there were lots of kids at the Lily Hotel. We all played together during the week because none of us ever got to school. I found them easy to be around because we all lived the same way, and were free to come and go as we pleased.

These new friends stole make-up from the store and played "Spin the Bottle," but when the bottle stopped at them, they took a piece of their clothing off instead of a quick kiss on the cheek. Even when I didn't want to participate in the stealing or the game, the word "no" might have meant the loss of a friend, and I wasn't about to take the risk. Even though I still thought of the pigeons as my friends, they weren't as fun as the kids.

There was a lady that lived behind the hotel named Mrs. Rodgers who had a nice husband and a couple kids. She always took the time to talk to me and when she smiled, it made me feel special.

"Anyone interested in a fresh baked apple turnover?" she hollered one day when our little gang was outside playing.

"I am. " Everyone answered and ran over to her house. We were all excited because good food in our world was hard to come by.

The moment she handed me mine, part of me wanted to eat it as quickly as I could, while another part of me wanted to make it last as long as possible. Those apple turnovers were amazing! The warm apples and flaky pastry melted in my mouth and it was like having a treasure resting on my tongue.

My weekday friends and I were not a good mix. We started stealing more, breaking and entering homes and trashing them for the fun of it. I was having a great old time until I decided to steal a bike from school and a teacher caught me.

The only good thing that came out of the whole mess was the school got involved and began asking the right questions for a change; like why wasn't I in school more often?

Mom was lying on the bed and I was busy playing with my panda when there was a knock on the door. I quickly got up, and was surprised to see a well-dressed lady standing there.

She smiled and said, "Hello, my name is Mrs. Reimer. Is your mother home?"

"Yup," I answered.

"May I come in?" she asked politely.

"Sure," I said. I liked her smile and her eyes twinkled. Mom quickly got off the bed and came to the door.

"Who did you say you were?" she asked as she tried to get herself awake.

"My name is Mrs. Reimer and the school has sent me to see how we could help your daughter with her schooling."

As she spoke, she was looking around the room and I knew she could see how bad our situation was. Mom was only wearing her big shirt, and I was dirty. The room we lived in was filthy and I'm sure it didn't smell very good.

"Laura's just fine," Mom yawned, "and you need to leave." Then Mom pushed Mrs. Reimer outside and slammed the door in her face-she was mad.

"What the hell have you been up to that we have a teacher at our door?"

I had lost all respect for her, so when she started hurling questions at me, I was quick to answer, "I don't have to tell you anything. You don't give a damn anyway."

She hit me across the face, and to my surprise, she started to cry. It was the first time I'd ever seen my mother cry after she'd hit me. For a brief moment, I thought maybe she really did love me. I felt sorry for her. I could see the pain in her eyes. Her life was such a mess.

Our eyes met for a brief moment, and then she went and lay down. I felt bad I'd talked to her the way I did because in all honesty, I never wanted to hurt her.

Mrs. Reimer visited shortly before my twelfth birthday and the odd thing was Mom bought me a new blue record player. She never said anything, so I wasn't sure if it was a birthday gift, or an "I'm sorry" gift, it was just sitting on the table when I got home.

"Thanks Mom, this is awesome!" I said, wishing I could give her a big hug.

She never said a word; she simply went into her room and closed the door.

The record player came with two albums, "Elvis" and the "The Best of Country Hits" and I spent hours listening to them as I rocked myself back and forth waiting for the weekend to arrive.

Our home life was getting more bizarre by the second. Mom was sure someone was out to kill her so she kept the couch pushed up to the door and put knives in the door jams. She was so paranoid by this point, she started to carry a knife around with her, and I was afraid she was going to stab me.

She quit eating and sleeping, and if I wanted to get out of the room, I had to climb through the window.

I was so afraid of her I caught a bus and ended up at Clive's place. I knew I needed some money and that Clive always had a stash.

When I arrived, Clive was working on one of his cars. "Well, well, well, if it isn't Laura! Long time no see." His eyes roamed my body.

"Clive, I need two hundred dollars. I'll do whatever you want me to do."

"Really? Come with me," he said as he wiped the grease from his hands. I was so desperate that I followed him hoping I could go through with whatever he had in mind.

"You want two hundred bucks? That's a lot of money." He went to a drawer and took out two hundred dollars.

"For two hundred bucks a guy should get whatever he wants, don't you think?" He handed me the money and I shoved it into my jacket pocket.

"I guess so," I replied. Panic took over and I was wishing I was somewhere else. I never should have gone to Clive in the first place. I knew what he was like, but I was desperate. Fear wrapped itself around me and yelled, *run, run*. But I couldn't make my legs work. I kept repeating over and over in my mind, *I need to do whatever he wants because I need the money.*

"Get on the bed," he ordered.

When I lay down, his big greasy hands started to unbutton my blouse and I started to shake all over.

"Get off me Clive, I can't do this," I cried, as I pushed him off me.

"What the hell do you mean you can't do this! You aren't gettin paid for nothing you little tramp!"

I'd never seen him so mad. My hands were shaking so bad it

was difficult to get the money he'd given me out of my pocket so I could throw it at him. Money flew everywhere and as he was trying to gather it up, I buttoned up my shirt and got out of there as quick as I could.

I was frantic. I had no money. I couldn't go to Gramma's and my mother was crazy. For the first time in my life I felt so desperately afraid I just wanted to die.

Mom was pacing around the house when I got home from Clive's. Her eyes were wild and her body was shaking. Every time she heard something, she'd point the knife where the noise came from and start to cry. She was terrified.

I was so afraid for her that I went down to the main desk and told the manager what was going on. He called the ambulance and they took her to the hospital, which meant I needed to go somewhere too.

The Social Worker who came to help was a nice lady and I asked her if I could go and stay with the Rodgers' family because I knew them and they lived close by. The Rodgers agreed to let me stay, and I was thrilled to be going to a place that had food, and was nice and clean. Not to mention she made the best apple turnovers in the world.

The Rodgers' had a boy and two girls of their own but their son was in foster care when I arrived. I heard he was really mean to the other kids and had to go for anger management classes. There was just us three girls, which was nice for me. Their two little girls were four and ten years old and I loved making the little one Mickey Mouse pancakes. We cuddled as we watched cartoons together on the couch, and I liked looking after her.

Mrs. Rodgers took me to a Doctor for the yeast infection I'd battled for years, and I also went to see a dentist for the first time in my life.

She made sure I went to school and always packed me a lunch.

It was the first time in my life I'd had any kind of routine that lasted more than a few days.

I especially loved school when Mrs. Reimer was there. She was the lady that came to check up on me; another one of those blessings God planted in my life. She made me feel good about myself and had a way about her that made me feel accepted. She always had lots of patience with me when I struggled with my schoolwork, and never made me feel stupid; she just continually encouraged me to try.

I can still hear her saying, "You can do this Laura. Just give it a try. Don't give up, you can do it."

The more time we spent together, the more I loved her. She always had time for my stories, and we became so close she started inviting me for dinner at her house.

I was so excited the first time she invited me. I tossed and turned all night long wondering what her house might look like. I was thrilled to be invited and nervous because I didn't want to do anything silly and make her not like me anymore.

When Mrs. Reimer picked me up, we drove out to her farm, and I could see the horses and cows in the pasture, and the dogs and cats were running around free as the wind.

When she introduced me to her husband I thought he was at least seven feet tall, and the kindest giant I'd ever met.

While Mrs. Reimer was making dinner, Mr. Reimer taught me how to ride a horse, and it was great! He had lots of patience and he made me laugh. When I was with him, it made me wonder if this was how a father was supposed to be. After we rode the horses, we went inside where Mrs. Reimer was busy making us dinner. We both loved music, and I could hear Rodger Whitaker playing on the record player as she cooked.

"Did you like riding the horses?" she asked.

"It was fantabulous!" I said.

"She's a great little rider," Mr. Reimer added. I couldn't wait until I might get to ride the horses again.

"Dinner is just about ready," Mrs. Reimer said with a smile. "Would you like to help me set the table, Laura?"

"Sure."

"Go wash up and you can help me." She pointed towards the bathroom and I skipped all the way there and back.

When we set the table, we used her good dishes and fine silverware and we even used wine glasses. I felt so grown up; I'd never drunk out of a real wine glass before.

We prayed before dinner and it made the meal seem even fancier because we'd invited God to come!

Sometimes they picked me up and took me to church. I loved every moment we spent together because she had a way about her that was warm and inviting. She was one person in the world, other than my Gramma, that I never wanted to disappoint. I was sure Mrs. Reimer was just like the God I learned about in Sunday school. They both loved me and wanted to keep me safe. More than anything, I wished the Reimer's would adopt me.

I'd been with the Rodgers for close to a year when everything started to fall apart. Their son returned home and he was still very angry. There were times he scared me because he had such a bad temper.

The Rodgers' had a hidden drinking problem too, and I say that because they weren't drunk all the time like my mother, but every second weekend was one big drunken party.

One party they had some friends over, and let their son and I get drunk. I was thirteen at the time, and it was the first time I'd tasted alcohol. I loved the feeling of being drunk and life was happy and fun. The adults laughed at us as we staggered around the house and made silly comments. It seemed like such a blast! For the first time I understood why my mother stayed drunk; no worries, no pain, just fun.

I was surprised to see how the alcohol affected Mrs. Rodgers.

She became downright miserable, and picked fights with Mr. Rodgers. When he didn't want to fight with her she started accusing me of having an affair with him.

That was ridiculous. He was a very honourable man and I never would have done such a thing. Not to mention I was only thirteen years old. I don't know if she thought; *like mother like daughter*, or if it was just the booze, but in the end, it didn't really matter.

She started calling Social Services with crazy excuses why I needed to leave. Although Social Services knew what she was saying wasn't true, for my safety they removed me from the house. It was a good time to move because her son started getting crazy ideas about touching me and I was not in favour of that at all.

Part Two

Foster Homes

It wasn't long after I left the Rodger's house that Social Services started legal proceedings to make me a ward of the court.

This meant I'd no longer be under my mother's care, but the government would take care of me until I was nineteen years old. They served Mom with legal papers so she could fight to keep me, but she never showed up.

Every time I went to the courthouse for my hearings, my eyes scanned the crowd hoping she might come and beg for me, but she never did.

Maybe she thought she was doing me a favour by not coming, but I felt like she'd abandoned me for good. She'd finally gotten her wish to have me out of her life and I was crushed inside. I continued to blame myself for all the bad things that went on in our lives, and thought maybe if I weren't around she'd be happier. It's a terrible feeling to know that your own mother doesn't love you, especially when you still love her.

When I officially became a ward of the court, my emotions for my mother went from love to hate. Maybe living without her would be the best for us both. The court said I could see her whenever I wanted to, but I was so hurt I didn't care if I ever saw her again. Two can play the game of abandonment, and I was so broken inside I couldn't even think of seeing her anytime soon.

For what felt like the thousandth time, I found myself in the middle of a situation I had no control over, and was placed in a Foster Home.

The Grahams were a nice couple with a little girl named Angie and a little boy they fostered named Lenny. Mrs. Graham was around nineteen or twenty and her husband was thirty-two. Social Services were a bit concerned with the age of Mrs. Graham, but foster parents were hard to find and she was willing.

She was a very nice looking woman even though she was a bit on the chunky side. The only thing I ever saw her wear were moo moos, which basically were a large chunk of material that fell loosely from the neck. She was as kind as she was big and I liked her a lot.

Their daughter was four years old and badly spoiled; I think she was used to having whatever she wanted, when she wanted, and that could be frustrating at times.

They lived in a rust-coloured rancher she kept neat and clean. Even the outside was neat. It wasn't uncommon to see her outside after a big rain, in her bare feet, with a box of salt in her hand, killing slugs on the sidewalk. Slugs were not welcome in her yard.

I appreciated all the Grahams did for me, so I offered to look after the little kids every Sunday so they could have a sleep-in day. She quickly accepted my offer and was extremely excited at the prospect of not having to jump out of bed as soon as the sun came out. I enjoyed helping her and she was thankful for the help.

Mrs. Graham had Certs, Coca-Cola and cigarettes with her everywhere she went. I thought she was cool because she was young and fun, and I could talk to her without fearing for my life.

We got along really well, and yet I was afraid she'd start to hate me if I stayed around too long. It seemed I was only lovable for a little while before I'd do something and people changed their minds about me, so I tried really hard to be on my best behaviour.

During my stay at the Grahams, Mrs. Reimer and the principal arranged for me to go Royal Oak, an alternate school for kids with learning disabilities. I was excited because maybe this time I could succeed in school. I knew in my heart that I wasn't stupid I just needed a little extra help.

Royal Oak concentrated less on academics and more on life skills. Through the week, we went for work-experience at the local stores and on Fridays we went bowling.

They modified our subjects allowing us to be successful for a change, and it was nice to go to school and not feel dumb.

One of my favourite places was the cafeteria at the school. When I did my work experience there, they gave me a free lunch, and I loved the frozen pizzas they sold. For the first time ever, I tried to do my best, and I went to school everyday. The teachers were caring and supportive.

I remember two teachers in particular. One was a math teacher from England, and the other was a Chinese lady.

The math teacher had the nicest accent, and I loved the way he rolled the vowels around in his mouth when he talked. He always had time for us kids, but for some reason he had to leave and return to England. We were all so upset that he was going because he was more than just a teacher; he really cared about us kids.

I planned a going away party for him so he'd know what a difference he'd made in our lives. He was so surprised when he arrived at his party, I think if he'd been a girl, he'd have cried. When we said good-bye to him, there were enough tears shed to start a small waterfall. Kids like us rarely found adults that could see through our problems to our potential as he could.

Another teacher I liked was a little Chinese lady, and most of the kids except for me were mean to her for some reason.

One night she took me to Chinatown for authentic Chinese Food. It was a little different from the Chinese Food I was used to, but it was delicious. Usually, I was quite shy around teachers, but she made me feel so comfortable around her I had no problem carrying on a conversation. I think I talked more than she did that night.

School was awesome for the first time in my life. I had teachers whom I liked and respected, and some good friends.

I met Charlie at school and I liked her, but quickly found out she was a glue sniffer. She told me it took her to a wonderful place where life was good and peaceful and anytime I wanted to try it she'd show me the ropes.

It hadn't been the best day at school; it was one of those days where everything seemed to go wrong. I saw Charlie after the last bell, and when she noticed me she invited me outside.

"Hey, you want to try a little glue? It will take your worries away." She smiled, then dug a bag and some glue out of her backpack.

"Sure, after the day I've had anything to make it better sounds good to me," I said.

We went behind the school and she showed me what to do. I took the bag filled with glue, put it over my mouth and nose and breathed in until I thought my lungs would break.

I was expecting a happy-go-lucky feeling like I did the time I got drunk, but instead it made my ears buzz and my head feel heavy. I didn't feel good, the smell stuck to me for hours, and I had a splitting headache.

"What do you think?" Charlie asked with a big smile on her face.

"This sucks!" I said as I tried to spit the glue out of my mouth.

"Oh, sorry about that," she said disappointingly.

"See ya tomorrow."

I left the schoolyard and walked home as fast as I could. When I got into the house, Mrs. Graham was washing the dishes.

"How was your day?" she asked.

"It sucked, but thanks for asking," I grumbled.

"What's the matter?" she asked genuinely concerned.

"Oh nothin really, I just have a really bad head ache."

"Well go and lay down for awhile. Maybe you'll feel better by suppertime."

I left the kitchen and went to my bedroom. Not only did I have a headache, but I couldn't get the smell of the glue to go away. So much for the idea that sniffing glue makes your troubles disappear. For me it just added a few more.

At the end of my first school year at Royal Oak, I won the Citizenship award. When they called my name, I felt like a movie star who had just won an Oscar. I was so surprised!

Most of the other kids' parents were there, but not mine. I remember strutting up to the stage feeling very proud of myself, and thinking the only thing that could have made the moment better would have been if Mom could've seen me. Maybe seeing me win an award would convince her I was a good daughter, and she'd want me to come home. Sadly, I knew that she never wanted me back no matter how good I might be.

I met Mom every second weekend at a Chinese restaurant. Other than the sounds of the other people talking, and the odd clinging of the dishes, it was quiet between us.

"I need money for cigarettes. Ya got any?" she'd ask.

"Nope."

Our conversation lasted a minute at the most. Our visits always left me messed up inside, like sniffing glue. I was moody and not a lot of fun to be around after our visits. Unfortunately, the Grahams were the recipients of my pent up anger towards my mother, and even though they knew the reason, it didn't make it any easier for them.

One night they threw a party, and I snuck into the liquor cabinet and got bombed. Booze made me brave, and any fear I had when I was sober got lost in the bottom of the bottle. By the end of the evening everyone knew I was drunk and no one appreciated my sense of humor.

Unfortunately for me, it got me kicked out of their house. Having to leave reinforced in my mind that my mother was right, I really was a nuisance.

The guilt I felt was overwhelming. Between my moodiness and getting drunk, I think they'd had enough after seven months.

A woman from Social Services arrived and drove me to a nearby group home. This particular home was for girls only, and talk about crazy.

Although I'd never been in a group home before I'd heard how awful the housemothers were and wondered where they found them. This particular one confirmed everything I'd heard, she was nuts. The other girls hated her too; bitch was a common adjective used to describe her. She was in it for the money, and that was easy to see.

After curfew, one of the girls came to my room and said, "We're all going out for a smoke. You want to come?"

"Sure," I said as I climbed out of bed.

"Follow me," she whispered.

We went into one of the other rooms, opened the window and blew our smoke outside.

When we were all finished our cigarettes, we threw the butts out the window and tip toed back to our rooms. I was almost asleep when I heard the housemother holler, "Everyone out of bed, right now!"

I don't know how she found the cigarette butts outside so soon, but she did.

"It's hard enough to be liked in this neighbourhood without you bunch of dead beats. I guess you don't really appreciate how embarrassed I get when you do stupid things. "

We were all just looking at her, hoping she'd let us go back to bed, but she wasn't nearly finished.

"Want to know how embarrassed I feel? Strip down and pick the butts up and throw them in the trash."

"What!" we all said at once,

"You heard me, strip down. Maybe next time you'll think twice before you do something to embarrass me!."

Thank Heaven it was dark and no one saw us. She managed to embarrass us, but to this day, I am not sure how that punishment fit the crime. I tossed and turned all night long waiting for the sun to pop into the sky so I could get back to Social Services and tell them what happened. I was so relieved when they said I didn't have to go back there, I literally jumped for joy.

They placed me into a receiving home until they could find me somewhere else to live and I loved the couple that ran it. They were so sweet. They prayed before each meal just like the Reimers' did and I liked that. Their acceptance of me as a person gave me hope, and I was disappointed when I had to leave.

"If you ever want to adopt someone," I said, "I would love to be your daughter."

"We'll keep that in mind," they said, then they hugged me and I was on my way once more. I was fourteen by this time and all I wanted was a place to call home.

The Social Worker in charge of my case thought it would be beneficial for me to be with other kids so I'd have some friends. As we drove up the driveway to my potential new home, my heart was pounding and my hands were sweaty.

"Laura," she said softly, "if you're not comfortable with this home after our interview, I promise you I'll try and find you a more suitable place, alright?"

I could tell by her eyes that she really wanted what was best for me, and at least this time I would have a say.

"Okay," I mumbled.

I hated the fact that I didn't have a place to call home or a mother who gave a damn about me. I also hated the fact that I was always the one who had to move from home to home. The fact is I hated life in general, so even though I was given a choice I was bitter.

When we arrived at the door, a very kind-looking woman answered.

"Hello, come in and welcome to our home," she said in a soft Irish accent.

She was an older woman who was very nice looking and well dressed. She was neat and clean and her hair was curled. She wore glasses and had sparkly green eyes. Even though my first impressions of her were good, I knew they were always nice when the Social Worker was around. I wasn't about to be talked into anything.

I quietly listened to the Social Worker and the woman talk. The woman said there were seven boys and one girl, and that if I stayed the other girl would have company, which would be nice for her. From my experience with boys, I was afraid they'd try to fondle me, and the thought of that made me sick. I completely shut down the idea of this being the place for me until I saw a young girl walking up the driveway.

When she came through the door, it was Karin, my friend from the Lily Hotel. My heart started to beat faster when I realized who it was. I couldn't believe my eyes and good luck.

"You know, I think this would be the perfect place for me to stay," I said with a huge grin on my face.

The housemother agreed, and I squealed with joy. Life was beginning to turn in my favour.

I loved my new foster home at the Shay's. It was clean and we were well fed, the atmosphere was warm and loving, completely opposite from my last group home. The house parents were awesome, and I loved listening to their thick Irish accents. Even the boys were okay.

I overheard them say that Social Services gave them two dollars a day per child for food. How they managed to stay within that budget was a miracle. One way the Shays stayed on budget was to buy their own food to eat. They never used our money to feed themselves.

We usually had porridge for breakfast, soup and a sandwich for lunch and either shake-n-bake chicken or meat loaf with lots of macaroni and cheese or potatoes for dinner. Our snack before bed was usually cinnamon toast and I was never hungry living there.

When special holidays like Christmas came, we had turkey with all the trimmings, and for dessert she made a trifle, which was my favourite. We loved the holidays especially the turkey sandwiches we had for lunch afterward.

Food was always important to me because for so many years I walked around half-starved. Sometimes when I looked at the wonderful dinner set before me, I thought of my mother, and wondered what she was eating. I never let that thought linger too long because it hurt too much. Besides, we all ate together in the kitchen, and there was lots of conversation and laughter. It was nice being part of a family.

The couple took the weekends off and their daughter, a registered nurse looked after us. She was strict and loving, something she'd learned from her parents.

We all had chores to do, and most of the time no one minded because every week we switched jobs. Our housemother gave us four dollars a week and we could spend it any way we wanted. Most of mine went towards cigarettes and entertainment, and it was the first time I had my own money to spend.

We looked forward to the weekends when we went to the teen night club. Our curfew was midnight on weekends and ten pm during the week. At fifteen, I thought the times were okay, and

I made sure I got home on time; otherwise, we got grounded for a week.

The night club was very plain on the outside, but inside it transformed into a disco haven. It had a big shiny ball that threw its colours across the room, light hitting the ground, the walls, and all the people, making everything sparkle. I loved to look at the lights, listen to the disco music and dance the night away.

Everyone seemed to dress up when we went to the club; it was a problem for me at first because I never had any nice clothes. Thankfully, as more girls arrived they'd lend me their clothes so I could get dressed up too. It was fun dressing up, and sometimes I'd catch myself thinking I was pretty until I heard my mother's voice in my head telling me otherwise.

Life was beginning to have some meaning and a quiet contentment was starting to make its home in my heart. I began to take school more seriously and attended regularly. The house parents made sure we all completed our school assignments, and often told us how important it was to get a good education.

My work experience at the school cafeteria was going so well they hired me, and that was a real bonus. It meant I could have a free frozen pizza for lunch every day I worked. I loved those cardboard pizzas.

One of the classes I took at Royal Oak was woodworking. Mrs. Reimer was still a part of my life, so in woodworking class I made her a cutting board in the shape of an apple, and three little wooden cats to hang on her wall. I couldn't wait to see her again so I could give her what I made.

One night the phone rang and it was for me.

"Laura, you're wanted on the phone love," Mrs. Shay said.

I was surprised someone was calling me because I usually didn't get any phone calls.

"Hello."

"Hi Laura, it's Mrs. Reimer. I was thinking it was time for you to come out to the farm for dinner. Are you busy tomorrow evening?"

"No, I'm free," I said before I'd even asked if I could go.

"That sounds great, I'll pick you up after school. See you then."

I could hardly contain my excitement because of the gift I made for her. It seemed to take forever before we got to her farm and I could give her the gift I'd made. I waited until we were inside.

"I have something for you Mrs. Reimer," I said as I dug the gifts out of a bag. "I hope you like it. I made it myself."

"Oh my goodness, they're beautiful! You did such a good job. You should be very proud of yourself." Then she went off to find a hammer and some nails.

She was so impressed with my work that she immediately hung the cats on the wall and used the cutting board to prepare dinner. It made me feel good to think she liked what I'd made her, and I knew she appreciated all my hard work.

When we sat down to eat that night she put a big piece of roast beef on each of our plates. After we said grace, I dug right into my dinner but Mrs. Reimer sat quietly looking at hers.

"What's the matter honey? Aren't you hungry?" Mr. Reimer asked.

"I'm having a little trouble eating Daisy," she said softly.

"Who's Daisy?" I asked. I couldn't figure out what she was talking about.

"Well," she paused, "the roast we're eating tonight used to be Daisy," she said. Then she looked up at me and said, "Oh I'm just being silly. Go ahead and enjoy."

I wasn't sure if I should tell her Daisy tasted good, bad or if I should stop eating Daisy all together, but I was hungry and Daisy was already half eaten on my plate.

Royal Oak went from grades eight to ten and then everyone went to a regular high school. I thought I would literally die if

I had to attend High School with my buckteeth. The teachers knew how stressed I was and eight of them wrote letters to Social Services convincing them I needed braces.

Because my teeth protruded out so far, I was going to have to wear headgear all day for three months, and that was a huge problem for me. I couldn't bear the thought of wearing headgear on the first day of High School.

"Please," I begged Social Services, "let me home school until I don't have to wear this headgear anymore. I can't go to high school looking like this; I already have a hard enough time getting along with the kids. Please, you have to let me stay home."

"I agree," Mrs. Shay said, "I'll be a helping her until the headgear comes off. Then she can go to school."

"I promise, I'll do all my work," I pleaded.

"Alright, as long as it's okay with Mrs. Shay that's what we'll do. You'll home school until the headgear comes off and then you'll attend school."

I was so relieved I gave them both a huge hug. I was determined to do my best. This was another time in my life where God seemed to appear and help me out in my time of need.

For three months I home schooled, and although I went to high school with only the train track braces it was no easier. The kids were in cliques, and I found it hard to make friends. Then to make things worse I never got the kind of help I needed in order to do the schoolwork. I started to feel stupid around the other kids, making it harder for me to fit in. I was lonely and I missed Royal Oak.

Thank heavens home was a good place to be because Karin was there. We were great friends and everyday I looked forward to seeing her. She was pretty, smart, and cool, plus she was popular with the boys. She always had a boyfriend and things always seemed to fall into place for her. I thought that if I hung around her enough, some of her good luck might rub off onto me.

Eventually I became part of Karin's little gang of friends. It was such a new feeling to be included that sometimes I acted giddy and immature.

Karin and Mark, one of the boys from our little gang started to date. He was such a great guy. You could tell by the way that he looked at her he was head over heels in love. They went out every weekend and as their relationship became more serious Karin began to throw the curfew rule out the window.

Mark had a cousin, Danny, whom Karin was sweet on too. I think she liked Mark because he was plain sweet, and Danny because he loved smoking pot as much as she did. The four of us spent the weekends together partying and hanging out.

I really liked Danny and eventually we started to date. He was my first real boyfriend, and let's face it-- when you are fifteen a boyfriend is very important.

What a pair we were! Danny suffered with bad acne, and I had braces, yet we both understood a person's heart was more important than their looks, so we never judged one another.

He had a cool Dodge Dart car with an "ahooga" horn. That's just what it sounded like when he blew it. *A-HOO-ga, a-HOO-ga.* It was a crazy sounding thing and it always made me laugh. When we drove in his car I was sure everyone on the streets was looking at us with envious eyes. Whether that was true or not I'll never know, but it was fun to think that someone might be envious of me.

I was so shy when I wasn't drunk or high that making conversation with Danny was like trying to pull a dandelion out of a garden. The only topic that was easy for us was Karin because we both adored her.

One night the four of us decided to use Danny's car and go to the drive-in theatre. As usual, we only had enough money between the four of us for two tickets, so two of us had to hide in the trunk until we got into the Drive-In.

"It's my car," Danny laughed, "so I guess Mark, and Karin ride in the trunk."

We stuffed Karin and Mark into the trunk and after we paid

we parked the car, popped the trunk and released the trunk dwellers. Whenever the four of us were together, life was a blast.

Danny and I dated for a short time until the topic of Karin became old. I was okay with it for a time, but after awhile it began to feel like he was taking me out just to stay close to Karin.

After he brought her name up for the millionth time I burst into tears.

"Why are you always asking me about Karin?" I asked. "She's all you want to talk about."

The poor guy didn't know what to do. It wasn't as if he'd said anything wrong or been mean, yet deep down I knew all these questions weren't about keeping a conversation going. They were about something deeper.

Danny told Karin that the reason he'd broken up with me was he thought I had too many problems. I have to admit when I was sober and could talk I was always sad, and crying about my life; but the real reason he broke up with me was because he liked Karin better than he liked me. Plain and simple.

I felt like I had screwed up our relationship because of my emotional state. Although I wanted desperately to hear Danny's *a-HOO-ga* horn out my bedroom window that never happened. His good-bye as a boyfriend was for good.

Much to my surprise life didn't end after Danny broke up with me, and even though I was no longer a part of the gang, I was determined to get on with my life because I was a survivor.

I'd been in the group home for about a year when Allison arrived. She was sixteen and had been working as a call girl.

She was a beautiful girl with long, thick, black hair that hung down her back and a body every girl envied. The reason she landed up in our group home was she accidentally got pregnant from one of her clients and had an abortion. Because of her age, Social Services gave her a place to stay until she got better.

Her boyfriend was her pimp and because she was so young and beautiful, she attracted a richer clientele making them both a lot of money. He was so concerned about the money he bought her a pager, and the moment that pager went off, she went to the nearest phone, and then took off to meet the client on the other end. I thought she was extremely brave because I knew how mean men could be.

Personally, I thought her boyfriend set her up from the beginning because he knew what he had. Her looks and personality were so beautiful he knew he could get a really good price selling her. Even though she said she loved him, I found that hard to understand.

Karin wasn't around much so Allison and I spent lots of time together. Bumpers on the border of New Westminster and Burnaby, was a night club for teens and was my favourite weekend hangout even though they didn't serve booze.

Allison and I were regulars at Bumpers, and every so often older men snuck in and invited us to go partying with them. Normally, we never went. However, one particular night, we decided to accept their invitation.

We left Bumpers and went over to one of the guy's apartments. It wasn't long before more people showed up and the party was on. There was lots of booze and I thought I'd died and gone to Heaven. The beer that night seemed especially yummy and I drank so much I had to be piggy backed to the bathroom. Everyone started laughing and making fun of me, even the guy who was piggy backing me, and I thought I was hilarious.

The more I drank the more flirtatious I became, so when it was time for my new friend to drive me home, he had one thing on his mind.

When he put his hand on my leg I yelled, "Get your damn hand off my leg! Didn't ya ever hear you should use two hands when you drive you moron!"

I wrecked his romantic moment, and because I missed curfew that night I was grounded for two weeks. I had the worst hangover in my life the next day, and felt really stupid about the way I'd acted. Maybe a couple of weeks at home would be a good thing; everyone might forget how stupid I'd been when I was drunk and invite me back to the next party.

Karin was home one weekend so Allison and I invited her to hang out with us. Bumpers was starting to become boring so the three of us decided to hit the night clubs downtown. Allison was the only one that had a fake ID and had gotten into an adult club before, but we were sure if we got dressed up we'd look old enough to get in without ID.

We were all dressed in Allison's clothes, and I thought we looked far older than sixteen. We thought we were so beautiful in our hooker outfits. Karin wore a gold outfit, I wore a silver outfit and Allison wore a sequined black outfit. We were all wearing five-inch heels and I'm not sure how we walked in those things without looking like we were drunk, but we did!

We left the house giddy, wondering what the evening might have in store for us. After all, a real club had to be a way better than Bumpers.

When we finally arrived, we walked up to the door and where devastated when the bouncer said, "Sorry girls, not tonight. Come back in a few years!" We were embarrassed and very disappointed, but we'd gotten all dressed up so we weren't about to let one *no* spoil our evening.

We ended up at Mr. Mike's restaurant, a huge let down from a club or party, but better than going home. It's really quite amazing that someone didn't try to hire us the way we were dressed! Another blessing in disguise.

It wasn't long before Allison left the group home and moved

in with her boyfriend. I worried about her because being a hooker could be dangerous and she was a sweet girl.

Karin started missing all the curfews at the group home and I knew it wasn't going to be long before they'd kick her out. I was right. That was one thing about this particular group home; you obeyed the rules or you left. It was as simple as that.

Karin moved back in with her mother, and believe me there were no rules in that house, which suited her fine.

The day she left was one of the darkest days of my life. I didn't care about anything anymore. I found myself getting drunk and missing curfews. I was becoming more and more difficult at school and at home. I missed Karin and every time they grounded me, it only made me more rebellious. I'd wrapped my whole life around one person. As unhealthy as that was, I couldn't shake the idea that Karin needed to be there for me. For some reason she held my identity in her hands, and I was so upset with life in general it wouldn't have taken much to end it all.

In my great wisdom, I ran away from the group home, quit going to school and talked Social Services into letting me move in with Karin and her mother. They lived off Broadway and 7th avenue in Vancouver in a social housing complex.

It was a small two-bedroom apartment with a galley kitchen, a dining room, and an attached living room. It had a small bathroom and although it wasn't fancy, it was home. One of the things I liked best about the place was that it looked out onto a park and I could see the pigeons strutting around acting as if they owned the place. Their presence always brought me a sense of comfort.

Karin loved to smoke pot and I thought if I wanted to be

like her, I needed to smoke it too. Acceptance had always been important to me, so I was a willing follower.

Karin and Mark were still dating, but he wasn't interested in doing drugs. He never smoked pot or cigarettes, but would have the odd drink. Danny on the other hand, loved smoking pot and getting drunk, so the three of us would get together when we needed a buzz.

Karin said that Mark was her boyfriend, yet she sure spent a lot of time with Danny. Many nights after she'd get home from a party, I'd be up waiting for her to fill me in on the night's events. She'd go on and on about what a wonderful evening she'd had, and how much she loved Mark-you know, girl talk-except she was the only one that had anything to say. I didn't even have one boy interested in me, and she had two. How fair was that?

It aggravated me that she had it so easy. It was as if she had a magic wand and could magically make things happen. If I had a wand, it was broken because there was nothing magical about my life.

After numerous nights of listening to her stories, I decided if anything was going to change I needed to do something. I got all dressed up one night after Karin left, and headed for Bumpers on my own. If I got lucky, maybe I'd have a story to tell by the end of the evening.

It was fun to be back in the night club scene with the disco ball throwing its rainbow colours across the room, and everyone dancing to the music. I loved just being around other people, and it was way more fun than sitting around at home with Karin's mother.

I was just about to leave when I heard, "Hey, beautiful. Do you need a ride home?"

He was a nice looking older man and very charming.

"Well," I said with a little giggle, "that depends on whether you're going my way or not."

"I'm sure that can be arranged," he said, and before I knew it I was in his car.

"You may not know this," he said with a grin on his face, "but I play the guitar and many of my friends think I sound just like Gordon Lightfoot."

"Holy smokes, you must be good!" I said naively. "I love Gordon Lightfoot."

"Would like to come over to my house for a drink?" His eyes sparkled when he spoke and I loved drinking so I was more than willing to go.

"Okay," I said, "that way you can prove to me you really sound like Gordon Lightfoot."

We both laughed and maybe if I got lucky I'd have a story to share with Karin when I got home. It was always about Karin.

When we got to his apartment, he gave me a drink of rum and coke and then took out his guitar. His apartment was clean, and very nice. There were a couple of guitars and amps hanging around and a great stereo sat in the corner.

He took out his guitar after he made our drinks and I was impressed with the way he could play. The more I drank the more he sounded like Gordon Lightfoot and I decided his other friends were right about him.

As time went on we had more to drink, and eventually he put his guitar down, put on some soft music, and sat beside me on the couch. I could smell his cologne and he smelled really good. He started to stroke my hair softly with his hand as he whispered how beautiful I was making me tingle all over. Before I knew it, we were making out on the couch and on our way to the bedroom.

Booze and I together were a bad combination. When I was drunk I had no thoughts of tomorrow, and what consequences my actions might bring. All that mattered was the here and now, and how much fun life was at this very moment.

"I love you Laura. Let's make love," he said gently.

"Okay," I whispered. "If you love me."

When it was finished, we got dressed, never spoke a word and went to the car.

I was confused and hurt when he didn't say anything on the way home, because I thought he loved me. All I could think was, "Is that it?"

After all the times Karin had spoken about how great sex was, I was disappointed. I lost my virginity that night to a man who lied about loving me and it hurt.

When I got out of the car, I never looked back. I knew it was good-bye to Gordon Lightfoot, but at least I had a story to tell Karin.

That night when she got home, I sat quietly with a little smirk on my face waiting for her to finish her night's stories so I could tell her about mine.

"So, what did you do tonight?" she asked likely thinking I'd say nothing.

"Well, I am not a virgin anymore."

That caught her interest and she wanted all the details. I filled her in leaving out the part that I didn't enjoy the sex, and that it had left me emptier than ever. I was only sixteen at the time, and had given myself to a complete stranger.

Every chance we had, Karin and I threw a party. After the one night stand with Gordon Lightfoot my self-esteem was at an all-time low. I felt like the only time anyone wanted to have me around was if they wanted to use me for something. Karin's mother was away, so we threw a party and I got super high that night.

I couldn't think straight and bizarre thoughts were whirling around in my brain like a cyclone. More than anything, I wanted to know if the people we were hanging out with really cared about me. Would they save me if I needed them to?

As I sat on the couch, a thought began to whisper into my ear.

Why don't you just jump out that window and then you will know, it said. *It's only three stories.*

At first, it was just a quiet whisper, but the longer I sat, and the higher I got, the louder the voice inside my head became.

Come on Laura, how will you ever know who your real friends are? Jump. Go ahead. It's the only way you'll ever know. It was shouting by now and I felt like I was in a trance and completely out of control.

I walked over to the window, opened it as far as it could go, and sat on the window ledge facing the crowd. When nobody noticed, I ventured a little further outside. The only thing anyone in the apartment could see of me was my feet and my hands as they clutched the window. Suddenly, I could hear the window ledge begin to crack and the sound made me panic. If it broke, I'd kill myself and that wasn't the goal.

At first, no one even noticed that I was hanging out the window until I started to scream.

"Help me someone, I'm falling!" I cried. Suddenly there were arms reaching out all around me grabbing and pulling me into the apartment. The ledge scraped and bruised my legs and I was bleeding.

I guess they do really care about you.

I had nearly killed myself, but that was secondary to having friends at that moment. I was so insecure and high I was willing to throw myself out a window to see if anyone cared. What was wrong with me?

Once I was back on the couch the reality of what had happened began to sink in. I think I thought if they saved me, I'd feel accepted as a person, but instead I felt ashamed.

The room suddenly became very quiet, and the staring eyes and contempt I felt were more than I could bear. I went to my bedroom realizing my cry for attention had backfired. Instead of it making me more popular, it made me freakish.

I could hear Karin as she settled everyone down,

"It's okay, she's just having a bad night that's all. Anyone ready for another drink?" And the party resumed without me.

Why couldn't I be like her? I buried my head in my pillow until I could no longer hear the noise. If I'd been younger, I'd have crawled under the bed, because it always felt safer there.

I became the babysitter for Karin's mother, Evelyn.

At first, we were like two old drinking pals, until she got drunk and wanted to pick a fight. The booze made me chatty, funny and affectionate and the last thing on my list of fun was a fist in the face.

As time passed, I began to resent the fact I had to look after Evelyn while Karin was off having a grand old time. How did I always end up being the caregiver of a drunk?

As I watched Evelyn, I couldn't help but think of my own mother. They were alike in so many ways. They hung around with seedy men, had wicked tempers, and often had the crap beaten out of them before the evening ended. Really, the only difference between the two was Evelyn had a relationship with her daughter and my mother didn't.

I started to realize I needed to find a different place to live because I'd stepped back in time. The drinking and fighting were getting out of control, and one night I tried to break a fight up between Evelyn and one of her boyfriends and the guy punched me in the face.

"What the hell!" I shouted.

I thought for sure he had broken my nose with the amount of blood that was shooting out of it. Evelyn had enough wits about her that night to call the police and they arrested him. By morning though, I had two black eyes, a swollen nose and a terrible attitude.

I didn't get it. I had fun when I drank. It was a release for me and life became worth living. I wasn't the angry drunk who picked fights so they could get their face beat in, and yet it happened to me more than once.

Because Evelyn had the man arrested, Social Services was informed and they were on the doorstep the next morning. They wanted Karin and I to go into another group home, but somehow we convinced them to let us live together in an apartment. The only rule they had was they needed to approve our new home.

We were only sixteen at the time, and for the life of me I don't know why they allowed us to live on our own. There's a good chance they knew we weren't going to stay in a group home long anyways, and perhaps they thought a good dose of reality was the only way we'd learn.

When we first started looking for an apartment, it was a big thrill-until we figured out we couldn't afford anything decent. We finally found a rooming house in Vancouver that had one small bedroom with a double bed, dresser and a hide-a-bed in the living room. The kitchen had a small table and three chairs and the bathroom had a pedestal sink and one of those old-fashioned bathtubs that reminded me of my childhood days.

We felt so grown up once we started living on our own. We were in charge of our own lives. There were no rules to keep, housemothers to worry about or curfews.

Although the apartment came with some furnishings, we didn't have the other basic things so thankfully Evelyn had extra pots, pans, plates, cutlery and linens to get us started.

Because we could only afford the necessities, the walls were bare and we wanted our home to look nice. We both hated living in an undecorated place, so one night we came up with the great idea we'd steal what we needed to make our place homey.

We waited until dark, smoked some weed for courage, and went from balcony to balcony and stole whatever we thought might fit the décor of our home. It was a real rush as we quietly choose a nicely decorated balcony and then took what we wanted.

"What about this?" I whispered to Karin, lifting a pottery vase.

"Ya, I like that, it will look great in our living room, don't you think?" she whispered back.

Really, it was like shopping at the big department stores, only we didn't need any money! We also picked up a few cats we liked and brought them home to keep us company.

We decorated our apartment with plants, wind chimes and little ornaments from our neighbours' balconies and were thankful they had the same taste in décor as we did. The only down side to all our stealing was we could never invite our neighbours to our parties, because we were afraid they might recognize what we'd stolen from them and want them back.

It was difficult to make ends meet. Even with Karin working. So when Sherry, one of Karin's friends wanted to move in with us we were all for it. With more money, we could buy booze for our parties and food for our bellies. Life was good.

When I first met Sherry, I thought she was nice. She seemed to have a good sense of humour and liked to party like the rest of us, so it seemed like a good fit.

Neither she nor I were working and Social Services were constantly after us to get a job. Finding a job for me wasn't easy because I was shy, could only read three or four letter words; plus my self-esteem was so low I doubted I could even wash dishes well enough. Regardless of how I felt I knew I needed to try, otherwise Social Services could place me back into a foster home, and I didn't want that to happen.

I decided I'd try getting a job at the racetrack because I loved animals and thought it was something I could do. Back then, if you wanted work you'd wait at the gate of the track until someone offered you a job. I snagged a job as a "hot walker." After the horses ran, I walked them around the track so they'd cool down, and then I'd put them in their stall. There was always lots of activity as jockeys raced their horses around the track, and trainers busied themselves from morning to night. I loved being with the horses and in general the people were good to work for.

For every horse I walked, they paid me a dollar. Most days I could only walk five or six horses because I had to catch a bus or hitch hike in order to get to work and back. Mornings were the hardest because the buses didn't run at 4:30am and trying to hitchhike at that time of the morning was a little difficult, the streets being so quiet.

The afternoons were easier as I could catch a bus home. However it cost me almost half the money I'd earned that day. The whole situation was less than ideal because I didn't make enough money, the hours sucked, and the commute was brutal.

I never was in the right place it seemed. Sherry got a job at the track the same day as I did, and got a higher paying job. They paid her one hundred dollars a week to clean out the stables and brush the horses. The difference in our wages only added to the feeling of being unworthy, and my measly forty–two bucks working seven days a week didn't go very far.

I hadn't been home very long before Sherry came through the door.

"So you got the low-paying job hey Laura?" she smirked.

I could tell she was trying to rub it in and I didn't appreciate her humour.

"Lay off," Karin said, "at least she has a job."

I never said a word because the more I got to know Sherry the less I liked her.

"Yeah," Sherry said, "I guess you're right." She threw her pack onto the couch and asked, "Anyone using the bedroom tonight?" She slept with anyone willing to crawl into the sac with her and I thought she was disgusting. I could never figure out why Karin liked her, but she did.

"Go ahead," Karin said, "I'll sleep on the couch with Laura tonight.

The only thing going through my mind was I hoped the guy

she brought home was nice because we usually all hung out for awhile before her and her new boyfriend retired for the night!

Eventually I quit the racetrack because it was too far away and the money was terrible. Social Services threatened to take my clothing allowance away if I didn't work which was ridiculous because I owned one pair of Chinese slippers, and the rest of my clothes were second hand.

Karin knew I didn't have the courage to fight with them, so she became my voice.

She called my Social Worker and explained to her my clothing situation. She could be very persuasive when she needed to be and thankfully, they believed her, and didn't take my clothing allowance away.

I tried looking for work, I really did, but honestly, I wasn't sure where to start. I had no formal training and I read very little. I certainly wasn't academic, which meant getting a job at a bank was totally out of the question-I couldn't even make change at a convenience store. The longer I thought about all the things I couldn't do the more defeated I felt.

My old companion Depression began to coil itself around me like a snake that was slowly choking the life out of me. The more I tried to find a job I could do, the more depressed I got, because in my way of thinking there weren't any. I felt dumb, stupid and worthless. Then throw loneliness into the mix and you have Laura reverting to rocking back and forth on the couch, listening to music and waiting.

It seemed like I was always waiting. Waiting for my mother to love me; waiting for kids to like me; waiting for food; waiting for Gramma to come; waiting for Prince Charming to sweep me off my feet. I was always waiting for something good to happen and my life to change but it never did.

I was tired of fighting and the only time I felt good was if I was drunk or high. Comparing myself to Karin and Sherry didn't help either. The constant struggle raging in my head wore me out, and I used to think it would be easier if I were dead. At least all the feelings I had about myself would be gone forever.

Although I put on a happy face when Sherry and Karin arrived home with their boyfriends, I'd given up inside. I'd given up on the idea that my life would be happy and was sure I was destined to a life of loneliness. I watched Karin juggle between Mark and Danny and wondered how she could be so lucky.

When I watched her, it seemed like everything she touched turned to gold. In my mind, she was always the person everyone loved and wanted to befriend. To me, her life was like a fairy tale that never ended, and I envied her.

As time dragged on my depression grew deeper, and as hard as I tried to fight it off, its weapons of mass destruction were winning. A person can only exist in a black hole for so long before their mind starts to think devilish thoughts.

I'd spent most of the night alone, when Karin and Sherry showed up with some of their friends. The once quiet apartment was now full of loud male voices, women laughing and so much conversation it sounded like a foreign language. I was pleased to see everyone and there was a lot to drink and the apartment smelled of weed. It felt good to be drunk and high, and although I knew the feeling wouldn't last, it was a good break.

Eventually the party ended and everyone went home. I looked at Karin and Sherry and said, "Hey girls, the evenings still young, you want another beer?"

"No thanks, I'm beat," Karin yawned.

"I'm tired too," Sherry said. "I'm going to hit the hay. See you in the morning."

I wasn't tired and couldn't understand why they had to go to bed so soon. All I wanted was some company, and it didn't seem very late.

" Aw come on," I begged, "just one more and we'll all go to bed." But they both just shook their heads and left the room.

I looked at the bottle of rye that was three quarters full sitting on the table. I grabbed the bottle, and poured it into my mouth until I needed to take a breath or drown. I was drinking it so fast it was pouring out the sides of my mouth and down my shirt and the more I drank, the worse I felt. I was obsessed with the booze because I was sure it was the only thing that could make me happy. I was out of control, and I knew it.

Well, some friends those two are, the depression mocked, *They don't even want to spend time with you. As soon as everyone goes home, they leave you all alone again. Great friends you have.* I grabbed the bottle and took another huge drink.

How's the job hunting going? You can't be very smart if you can't even deliver papers or wash dishes, it sneered.

I took another drink trying to get the voice in my head to quit, but it was relentless.

Let's face it, no one likes you, not even your mother, now that's really pathetic. You're a failure Laura. The reason everyone around you is unhappy is because you're such a screw up. Everything is your fault. Don't you think you'd be doing everyone a favour if you just killed yourself?

The ugly depression kept hounding me and the more I drank the more hopeless I felt.

I put the finished bottle down on the table and went into the bathroom. I opened up the medicine cabinet and looked for the pill bottle with the most pills. As I placed the pills to my lips I felt like I was finally in charge of my life, and no one could stop me. I downed all the pills in the bottle with a glass of water and stared at the hollow face in the mirror, and for a brief moment I saw my mother looking back at me.

I poured myself a bath, took off my clothes and slid down the side of the smooth finish on the tub. The warm water, pills and rye were starting to take effect and I went back to being that little girl enjoying her warm bath while innocently playing with her bath toys.

All at once, wild thoughts began racing through my brain, *Don't you think you should at least say good-bye to Karin, and tell her you love her? After all she's your best friend. How selfish are you?*

It took all I had to pull myself out of the tub and wrap a towel around myself. The room was spinning, and I tried to stand up, but I was too dizzy. I got on my hands and knees and crawled to Karin's room.

When I reached her, I pushed on her to wake her up. "Karin, I love you," I whispered. It was hard for her to understand me because I was having trouble forming words.

She sat up in her bed and asked, "What's the matter Laura?"

"I love you Karin," was all I could get out, and then everything went black.

When I finally came to, I was in the back of an ambulance with the nicest stranger I had ever met.

"Stay awake. Don't go to sleep." He said this over and over again. I was in and out of consciousness, and I don't remember much about the ride, yet something about that man made me think someone cared whether I lived or died, so I fought to live.

The next thing I remember, I was at Vancouver General Hospital and the nurses were running around frantically.

"What the hell are you doing?" I yelled as they tried shoving a tube down my throat and into my stomach. I started to gag, but they didn't stop until my stomach was completely pumped out. Then they took me up to the psychiatric ward.

I was tired, but I couldn't sleep because I was afraid of the people who were wandering the halls. All of a sudden, the reality of what I'd tried to do made me wonder if maybe I wasn't crazy after all.

"When can I go home?" I asked the nurse when she came in to check on me.

"I don't know Laura. You'll be here for a few days so the psychiatrist can try to help you." She smiled. "Try and get some sleep."

She left the room. I knew I was at the mercy of the psychiatrist and there was a part of me hoping that they'd figure out what was wrong with me.

The psychiatrist they assigned me was cold and distant. I felt like I was just a number rather than a person because of the way she treated me. I was sure she was thinking I was just another lost cause taking up her valuable time.

"So Laura, what brought you here?" she asked as she flipped through some papers in front of her.

"It was an accident," I replied.

"Really?" She looked up from her desk. "Pretty big accident, wouldn't you agree?"

I didn't want to talk to her. She was mean and she made me feel stupid. Too bad she wasn't like Mrs. Reimer. Mrs. Reimer could see everyone's potential and worth. Everyone was a person to her, and you knew she cared. No one was a number in her world.

After a few days of gruelling questions, the psychiatrist told me I could go home. She didn't help me. I still felt rattled inside, didn't like myself any better, and she didn't give me anything to help my depression. My guts were in a knot and I felt like I could puke at any moment. I also didn't want to go home because I was afraid of what Karin might say.

I went home praying she'd greet me with open arms and a big hug, but the moment I got into the apartment she started to yell at me.

"Why the hell did you try to kill yourself? Are you nuts?" She was extremely upset with what I'd done and I'll never forget her angry eyes and harsh words. Knowing I'd let her down seemed worse than trying to kill myself. Now how crazy is that?

When the rest of the gang showed up, I could tell they looked at me differently too. I knew I had been the main topic of discussion the past few days, and now that I was home, there was an uncomfortable feeling whenever I entered the room.

Why did I do such stupid things? Maybe the apple didn't fall far from the tree. Perhaps I was just as sick as my mother was; the thought of that reality terrified me, yet if it was true, then maybe she'd understand better than my friends did. I guess it's natural when you're hurting to seek out your mother.

I took the bus to the east side where Mom was living and as the bus moved from street to street, I enjoyed watching the people coming in and out of the bus.

There were mothers with small children, giggling and laughing as they spotted puppies and birds out the window, older people that looked like life had been tough and the bus was just a ride from one hurt to another, and teenagers like me skipping school. The bus looked to me like a quilt, with all of us making up part of a pattern with our different colours of clothes and skin.

I loved sitting, watching, and imagining where all these people were from, and where they were going. The people on the street all seemed to be in a hurry to get somewhere, except for the ones with their hands out asking for money. They stayed at their same corners year after year. The bus was a great distraction and I enjoyed the ride.

It took around an hour to get to Mom's bus stop, and I was the only one that got off there. It was an awful part of the city.

As I began to walk to Mom's, I noticed three men fighting. That by itself wasn't out of the ordinary, but the knife was. I stood motionless as two of the men grabbed the other one and threw him down.

"No, no, please, don't," the man screamed.

Ugly sounds flew through the air as they stabbed the man repeatedly, and I could hear him gasping for air. Then it was quiet and the stabbed man lay lifeless on the ground.

The other two men quickly dug through his pockets, took his wallet and a few other things, and ran down the alley throwing something in a nearby dumpster.

My heart was beating so fast I could feel it trying to thump its way out of my chest. As heavy as my legs felt I started to run as fast as I could towards Mom's place.

Then my imagination took over and I wondered if they had seen me watching, and were following me. As all these random thoughts were racing through my mind, I ran faster. When I reached Mom's door I started to bang on it as hard as I could.

"Mom, let me in! Hurry, let me in!"

I was screaming by this time and it took forever before she opened the door. Although she didn't recognize me at first, there was no way I was staying in the hallway so I pushed her aside and immediately locked the door. I was so afraid there were beads of sweat running down my face and I was trembling.

She looked at me with her empty eyes and kept nodding off as I tried to tell her what I'd seen. I knew she hadn't heard anything I'd said. However, it was good to get it off my chest.

I was too afraid to go home that night, so I spent the night on the floor curled up to the old-fashioned metal water heater to keep warm. I couldn't help think of what I'd witnessed and kept replaying the scene over and over in my head.

I never did get the chance to tell her why I'd come in the first place. I knew she was too out of it to identify with my trying to kill myself and I also knew if I told her, and she didn't respond the way I wanted her to, it would only make things worse. Maybe it was best I never got the chance.

The next morning when the sun peeped through the covered window, I got off the floor and left. Mom was still sleeping and

I knew she likely wouldn't even remember I'd been there for the night.

I needed to know whether what I witnessed the day before was true or just a figment of my imagination, so I went back to the alley. I stood motionless as I looked at the chalk outline of where the man had died. I wasn't crazy after all. I did witness a murder, and there were lots of policemen around to prove it.

One of them saw me watching and asked, "Did you happen to see anything suspicious here yesterday?"

I was so afraid, all I could do was shake my head no and head for the bus stop. I was too afraid to say anything to them for fear one of the killers saw me tell and I'd be next.

The people that got on and off the bus suddenly seemed to be looking at me suspiciously. Even the children seemed to be looking at me differently. By the time I got home, I had myself convinced that one of the men on the bus knew I'd witnessed the murder and had followed me home. It reminded me of Mom when she thought someone was trying to kill her on the bus. I wished I'd been more sympathetic towards her because it was a terrifying feeling.

Karin and Sherry were sitting around the table discussing their day when I burst through the door. I was crying and shaking so badly I had trouble locking the door behind me, but once it was locked I slid onto the floor and buried my face in my knees.

"Hey, what's wrong?" Karin asked as she came and sat down beside me. I was so terrified I had trouble talking. "It's okay Laura, what happened?" Karin stroked my hair and I could feel myself starting to calm down.

"I witnessed a murder on my way to Mom's house, and I was too afraid to tell the police because I think one of the guys who killed that man saw me and followed me home." I took a deep breath and Karin helped me stand up and sit on the couch.

"Oh brother, here we go again!" Sherry said disgustingly.

I'm not sure they believed me at first, but the more details I told the more interested they were. At least Karin was.

131

"Wow! That's quite the story Laura," Sherry mocked.

"Lay off," Karin said and shot a few daggers towards her. "Come on Laura, why don't you go lie down and get some rest. You look tired."

She took me by the hand and laid me on the bed. For a long time after that, I was paranoid, and was sure that someone was following me. My imagination took on a life of its own and had it not been for Mark who convinced me they'd caught the killers and they were in jail, I think I'd have ended up back in the Psychiatric ward.

Because I'd tried to kill myself Social Services was no longer concerned about my work status, but my mental health. They wanted me to take some time to get feeling better before I went back to work.

Boredom took over my days as I waited for Karin to get home. We didn't have a TV so I spent most of my days rocking on the couch and listening to the local radio station.

I was never invited to go out with the gang any more, because most of them were afraid of me. My mere presence put everyone on edge. They didn't know how to respond to me, so it was easier for everyone if I stayed away.

I wished with all my heart that they could see how I felt inside. I needed to know my life meant something to someone. I was so mixed up that most days I didn't know who I was or where I was going, and to be ignored and tossed aside only made things worse.

After a few weeks, everyone had forgotten about my suicide attempt, and showed up at the house. It was nice to be around people again, and the moment the party started and the booze started to take effect, life was good again.

The more I drank, the happier I became, and to laugh felt so good. As I was enjoying the party, I noticed a new girl sitting on the couch. When I was drunk, I had lots of confidence, so I wandered over and introduced myself.

"Hi, my name is Laura. What's yours?"

"My name is Lana. Pleased to meet you Laura." She giggled. She had the nicest smile and I immediately liked her. She didn't seem to be as wild as the other girls I knew, and her eyes were full of life. It wasn't long before we became good friends.

Lana's father died when she was little and because I never knew who my father was we had something in common right away.

Her mother ran a daycare and it was fun to watch Lana play with the kids. They loved her because she took time for them and made them laugh. I used to think she'd make a great mother someday.

Her mom's eyes brightened up the moment Lana entered the room, and you could tell she loved her more than anything else in the world. I wished my mother could see me the same way.

Lana and I enjoyed our times together; the only problem was we were both a little on the impulsive side, which got us into trouble more than once.

One night we were bored so we decided to take her Mom's car for a little drive around town. Neither one of us had a driver's license at the time, but that didn't concern us. After all how hard could it be to drive a car? People do it all the time.

"Do you know how to drive a car?" Lana asked.

"Well of course I do," I lied.

I got behind the driver's wheel, feeling very important I might add, and my unsuspecting friend got into the passenger's side. The minute I put the keys into the ignition I could feel the adrenaline as it rushed through my body. The whole idea was a recipe for disaster, but we never thought anything could go wrong.

When the car started, there was a quick bit of silence before we started killing ourselves with nervous laughter. That was one of the things I loved best about Lana-her laugh-and she used it often. When she started laughing she could make my worries melt away as fast as a popsicle melts on a hot day.

We didn't get very far before I hit a fence in the alley because I mistakenly hit the gas pedal instead of the brake. Oops! End of laughter, end of good adrenaline.

That whole fight or flight thing took over and we both opened our car doors and ran as fast as we could before anyone could see us. All we wanted to do was have a little fun. We never meant to hurt anyone or anything, yet somehow things never turned out as we thought they would.

We ran into her house to get her brother and some of his friends to help us. When the guys looked at me, they rolled their eyes and I could tell they thought this had been my idea, and that I was nothing but an idiot.

"Lana why do you hang out with this loser? She's nothing but trouble," one of them said.

I just stood there as they continued hurling their insults at me.

"Back off," Lana said. "It was my idea not hers. So are you going to help us or not!"

I was surprised, because normally no one stood up for me except Karin. It was then I realized how good a friend she really was.

Sherry, good old Sherry-the more I got to know her the more her true colours showed. When I first met her, I thought she was a rainbow full of sunshine and goodness, but sadly, she was as black as a starless night. When she wasn't the center of attention, she turned into the wicked witch, mean-spirited and spiteful.

After the car incident, I guess she figured Lana should be warned about being my friend. Most people can accept the truth about themselves, even if it hurts, but when someone spreads lies about you, that's a completely different story.

Lana wasn't like lots of the other girls we hung around with. She was good-hearted and kind. She came and asked me if what Sherry had said about me was true, and I was so shocked I couldn't speak. I felt like I'd had a stroke. Nothing Sherry had said was true; she lied. I didn't even know where to start. To this day, I will never know why I didn't stand up for myself. It took me a full week before I got enough nerve to tell Lana the truth and for her that was too long. She thought I'd used the week to make up a good story when in fact it took me that long to gather up the nerve to approach the subject. I thought Lana knew me better, but I guess she didn't. Thanks to Sherry, I lost one of the best friends I'd had in a long time, and I was so depressed that even the radio lost its appeal.

It rains a lot in Vancouver and sometimes the gray clouds wrap themselves around the whole city for days and I hated it. My life felt as gray as the sky and as bitter as the rain. I was so lonely and disheartened after what happened between Lana and me, that life seemed pointless.

All the questions, like why she didn't believe me instead of Sherry, or why Sherry had to be so mean continually filled my mind. I'd analyze how I could have done things differently, but in the end I couldn't change a thing. I'd lost a friend.

What was the point of living if all it meant was heartache? So often, I'd hoped things would change, but hope was a word meant for someone else. I didn't have any. I knew that my friendship with Lana was over, and I'd spend the rest of my life alone. I was at one of the lowest points of my life, and I emotionally began to shut down.

Because the gang never saw Sherry for who she was, they believed every lie she told about me. They believed I was the person she made me out to be and no one ever gave me the chance to defend myself. To be honest, I'm not even sure what she told them. Whatever it was, they treated me like a second-class citizen. I was so gullible I was sure that they would come to their senses and I'd become part of the group soon. I just needed to be patient and eventually they'd see the truth.

One night I was sitting on the couch when Sherry came in and sat down beside me. We had barely looked at one another let alone talked since the incident with Lana.

I will never understand why I always believed in the goodness of people. When they did awful things, I'd think it was all my fault, or they'd made a mistake. Mostly I was quick to forgive, and allowed people the chance to change because that's how I wanted others to treat me. I think I was like my Grandmother, because she always saw the best in everyone. So when Sherry started to talk to me I instantly forgave her.

"Hey Laura," Sherry said, smiling as she spoke. "A few of us are going to a Nazareth concert in Nanaimo. Do you want to go? I have an extra ticket and everything will be free." She flashed the two tickets in front of my face.

"Holy smokes, you're asking me?" I couldn't believe she was asking me to go with her to a concert when she could have chosen someone else.

"That sounds awesome," I said, not quite convinced.

I thought this was her way of saying she was sorry. Totally unaware of the real reason they were inviting me.

I found out later that, the three men that had invited her, wanted her to bring along another girl, and it wasn't just to keep her company. She couldn't risk asking one of her good friends to go, so she picked me. She knew that the men wanted sex, and there would be lots of drugs and partying. I was the one person she knew who would do anything to be accepted and would go along with whatever they planned. I'll say one thing for her, she knew how to read people.

To Sherry, sex, drugs and rock and roll were like four dishes at a dinner party. It was all about the here and now, and the more fun you could have the better. I am not sure she ever thought about tomorrow or if that word was even in her vocabulary. She did whatever she wanted no matter how much it might hurt someone else, and I was in such a dark place all I wanted was to be accepted.

I was so tired of being alone that the thought of going anywhere seemed like a great idea. I liked the band and Sherry seemed to have changed towards me, so I felt like I had nothing to lose and everything to gain.

"Are you sure," I asked. "I mean I'd love to go, but, wow. Are you sure you want to take me?"

"Yup I'm sure. It'll be a blast. Are you in?"

She gave me a sweet innocent smile.

I'd never been to a concert before and the guys graciously paid my way so there was no reason not to go. It was the first time in a long time I'd been invited anywhere and it was something to look forward to.

"Yup I'm in," I squealed as I wrapped my arms around her and gave her a big hug.

She smiled, and I couldn't wait for the big day to arrive.

Sam, one of the guys going to the concert owned a blue van with a bed in the back. He and his two friends picked Sherry and me up, and we headed for the ferry. While we were waiting in line we started drinking, and the party was on. I thought they were so sweet because they said they had made me a *special* drink: rum and Coke.

I thought it was strange that I was the only one with the *special* drink, but I thought they were being extra nice, and I seemed to be the center of attention. It felt good.

Everyone else was drinking beer, my favourite, but hey, if they wanted to treat me special, that was okay with me.

I never saw them mix the drink, which turned out to be a big mistake. They put a drug called Spanish Fly into it that dissolves easily into any liquid and has no taste. It's used to enhance a woman's sex drive, which was what they were after. I should've known something was wrong when they kept telling me to down my drink so I could have another one. I was happy to oblige because I loved booze and it'd been a long time since I'd been to a party. I drank a few of my *special* drinks before we got to the front of the ferry line-up.

We started to move and the man pointed to our parking spot on the ferry. The drug was beginning to work and all I could think about was having sex with one of the men. It was like a demon inside me driving my thoughts and body in one direction, and the desire was so strong I felt like I'd go crazy if I didn't fulfill it.

Sam noticed I'd become very flirtatious and said, "Hey, why don't you guys go get some fresh air. Looks like Laura's ready for a little fun." He smirked and the others laughed as they left the van.

The moment they were gone, he was all over me. I don't remember much as I went from black out to black out with only a few minutes in between. The only thing I really remember is how tired I felt.

When the Ferry reached Nanaimo, the others were back in the van and I was still in the bed, completely out of it. Time seemed to be racing, and before I knew it, we were at the concert.

"Where are we?" I asked, rubbing my eyes.

I was having trouble figuring out what time it was, where I was or what I was doing. I felt so confused. My legs felt like rubber and my body didn't feel like it belonged to me. I couldn't keep my eyes open, and when I did, everything was blurry.

I felt numb and all I really wanted to do was sleep. I was surprised at how wasted I was because usually a few drinks didn't affect me that way.

"Come on, Laura, get dressed," Sam insisted. "I paid for these tickets and you're coming with us."

"I can't," I whined. "I'm too tired, leave me alone and I'll be here when you get back."

"Get dressed," he yelled as he threw my clothes at me.

I had a lot of trouble getting dressed, and when we went into the concert, the music was so loud I could hardly stand it. I felt like my whole body was going to explode with the pounding of the drums.

I couldn't keep my head up so Sherry let me rest my head on her shoulder. How kind! I missed the whole concert, and after the band stopped playing, we went back to the van to find a hotel room for the night.

We found a hotel with a hide-a-bed and a bedroom. Sherry and her man took the bedroom and I ended up in the hide-a-bed. Sam eventually spent the night in the van, but not until he used me first. It was all part of their great plan.

Most of the night was a blur, however I did have enough brainpower to know that I'd started out in bed with Sam, and Vance was the one lying beside me in the morning.

I was disgusted with myself, and couldn't believe the alcohol had such an adverse effect on me. I'd never had a hangover like this one before. Shame and guilt pilled up on me until I thought I'd suffocate under their weight.

"Anyone hungry," Vance asked.

"I'm starving," I said.

"I bet you are after last night," Sam laughed.

All I wanted was to get home, but I was so hungover I thought some food might help me to feel better.

When we left for the restaurant, Vance kept trying to hold my hand, but I wanted no part of him or his handholding.

"Stop it." I said grouchily.

I ordered my breakfast and listened to them talk about what a great time they'd had at the concert, and how much fun I'd been afterwards. I felt like a hooker. I had a hard time looking anyone in the eye, and wished that everyone would shut up so we could finish our breakfast, and go home.

Once we got into the van, I never said a word. I should have known better than to go anywhere with Sherry. Why I thought she'd changed I'll never know, and once again she made me look like a fool.

When the guys dropped us off at our house Sherry couldn't wait to tell Karin what happened. As she told the story, I could see the disappointment in Karin's face. I just stood there like a whipped puppy, with my head hung down as the tears flowed down my face and hit the floor.

I went to my room while Sherry yakked and laughed about how I'd do anything to have a friend and it's a good thing I didn't have a gun because I might have shot her.

When I got to my room, I closed the door, flung myself on the bed, and covered my ears so I couldn't hear her laughing.

Kimberly, one of Sam's friends moved in with us a few weeks after the disastrous weekend in Nanaimo. We spent most of our days together, and I started asking her a few question about Sam and Vance. I told her I'd gone to the concert with them and she suddenly became very quiet; I knew I had her attention. I went on to say how awful I felt after drinking the Rum, and then somehow ended up in bed with Sam and Vance.

I could tell by the look on her face she was horrified. At first, I thought it was because she thought I was a real loser, but that wasn't it at all.

"They drugged you Laura," she said with great compassion. "They had the whole thing planned before they left." She looked me straight in the eye and said, "I'm so sorry it was you. You can't blame yourself for this one. You had no control over what they did." Then she said thoughtfully, "I never dreamt they'd actually go through with their plan. I'm so sorry."

I'd been feeling so guilty and ashamed that I tried to avoid Karin because she didn't treat me with any respect. I knew the only way to restore our friendship was if she knew the truth, so I asked Kimberly to tell Karin what she knew, and she was more than happy to set the record straight.

When Karin heard the truth, she was furious. The moment Sherry came home from work Karin threw her bag of things at her and yelled, "Get the hell out of here and never come back you lying bitch!"

"What's the matter?" Sherry asked dumbfounded.

"You know exactly what's wrong, now get out!" Karin hollered.

I found great pleasure seeing Sherry squirm because I think it was one of the few times she wasn't able to lie herself out of a sticky situation. The minute she saw the look on Kimberly's face she knew the secret was out so she picked up her stuff and left. That was one of the most satisfying moments of my life.

Good-bye to a bag full of garbage was my only thought, and the smile on my face was the biggest it had been in a very long time!

Karin and I moved to Burnaby and got another apartment because I wanted to go back to high school. My good intention only lasted about a month because as hard as I tried, I just couldn't understand what was going on. They didn't give me a teacher's aide to help me, and I felt like I was drowning. Then to complicate things Karin told me she was pregnant.

She never stopped sleeping with both Mark and Danny so she had no idea who the father was, and to say she felt a little panicky is a huge understatement.

She knew she had to make up her mind as to whom she might spend the rest of her life with once the baby was born, so she picked Danny.

I was in the living room when he came over for a visit and heard Karin say, "Danny, how do you feel about becoming a daddy?"

"What are you talking about?" he asked, "Are you pregnant?" There was shock written all over his face.

Karin hung her head and started to cry, "Yes, and the baby is yours."

"I'm not ready to be a father. I love ya' babe but I'm not ready to have a kid."

I could tell by Karin's face she was disappointed by his reaction.

"What do you want me to do?" she asked.

It was quiet for a few moments and then he said, "Well, have the baby and give it up for adoption. I do love you-ya know that-and I want to spend the rest of my life with you, but it's too early for us to have a kid."

He moved over to Karin and wrapped his arms around her. "It's okay, I'll help out as much as I can, we'll get through this."

"Okay," Karin said between the tears.

Poor Mark was so hurt when he found out the news. Really, between the two of them, he was the better pick because he was way more stable and likely would have made a great husband and father.

I wasn't sure how much money Danny was going to give her, and suddenly I felt responsible to make sure we had enough food. I didn't know a lot about being pregnant, but I did know that Karin needed to eat if she was to have a healthy baby.

She had always been the one with the job supporting us, and now it was my turn. Sadly, I didn't have a very good track record when it came to keeping a job, and felt sick inside at the idea of having to find one.

When I quit school, Karin and I spent most of our days playing crib and eating Lipton chicken noodle soup with an egg in it for protein. It was our favourite dish, but I knew it wasn't enough, and decided it was time to look for work.

I went to work as a carhop at A&W, and lasted a whole three days. Unfortunately, I couldn't make change or legibly write down what the people wanted, so the manager told me he didn't think the job was for me. It's hard to say if anyone got what he or she actually ordered! Although I was very disappointed, the up side was I did get us some burgers and fries for those three days, and it was a nice change from the egg and soup mixture.

Then I applied at Captain Scott's Fish and Chips, not far from where we lived, and was so excited when they hired me. I washed floors and cut potatoes into French fries. This job lasted only two weeks because they were not happy with my work. They said I was too quiet and not suited for the job. I'm not sure what being quiet had to do with floor washing or cutting potatoes.

I felt so stupid and worthless every time someone fired me. I could never figure out what it was that they wanted and was too shy to ask. I couldn't even peel potatoes right for goodness sake. I could understand not being able to write or make change, but cleaning floors and peeling potatoes anyone could do that, unless you were me apparently.

I got twenty dollars for the two weeks, which helped with groceries, and for that, I was thankful.

I couldn't seem to make any money legitimately so I decided to rob the corner store. Stealing wasn't new to me, however I'd never actually held anyone at gunpoint to do it. I'd watched enough TV to know that I needed a gun, a black mask and an escape route, and I knew if I could pull it off we'd be in great shape financially.

The first problem was I didn't have a gun, and I knew you couldn't hold up a store without one, so I decided to use a roll of deodorant. You know the kind that has a ball on the top and it looks like a gun when you put it in your pocket. I stood in front of the mirror and practiced just to make sure the deodorant looked like a gun, and it really did. Well, that was the first step figured out.

Then I had to dress in black, and wear a ski mask. I certainly didn't want anyone to recognize me after I took all the cash or have my picture on a WANTED poster. Thankfully, it was cold outside so wearing a mask didn't seem out of place.

The store I was going to hold up was close to home so I could get away quickly and be home before the police arrived. Now the only thing left was to go and do it.

Karin didn't have any idea what I was up to, and I wasn't about to tell her for fear she'd talk me out of it.

"Where are you going at this hour?" she asked.

"We need some money Karin so I was thinking I might go and see if I could find some somewhere." I answered, trying not to sound suspicious.

"Good luck with that," she said with a big smile on her face when I went out the door. I often wonder where she thought I was going to get the money from. A tree maybe?

Thankfully, she never asked any more questions. Otherwise I would've had to lie to her, and she could always tell when I wasn't telling the truth.

I left the apartment and walked to the store. Something I never thought about was how much guts and courage it took to rob a store, and those two words didn't describe my personality. Somehow, though, I was able to talk myself into being brave because I thought this was the fastest and easiest way to get some cash, and we needed the money.

When I went into the store, the reality of what I was about to do hit me like a punch in the gut, but I was determined to try.

The store wasn't very big and I walked casually around the aisles and looked like I was going to buy something. I was so nervous my stomach was tied into a million knots, and I was sweating like crazy under the ski mask.

I finally went outside to cool off because the store got busy, and for two hours I waited for my chance, but the store never emptied out.

The real problem was I couldn't talk myself into trying to stick up the clerk using some deodorant, and thank God, I had enough sense to take my deodorant and go home.

When I arrived home, Karin looked up, "You were gone a long time, did you find any money?"

"Nope, no luck tonight."

"Don't worry about it, Laura. We'll be okay," she said encouragingly.

She always seemed to keep positive, and usually things did work out for her, but I was worried about her, and once again I'd failed.

Karin gave the baby up for adoption as planned and it was very difficult for her. Once she'd held her little boy I could see the turmoil in her eyes as she gazed at her son. Her eyes were so tender, and when she let him place his little fingers around hers, the tears started to fall. As much as she loved her child, she knew she couldn't look after him, so she did the unselfish thing and gave the baby away.

Karin and Danny moved in together shortly after she came home from the hospital, and I stayed with them for a couple of weeks until I met Tim.

Tim was a friend of Danny's. He was about 5'9", tattooed, and wore muscle shirts that showed off his muscular arms; I thought he was cute. We dated for about a week and then we moved in together. I needed a place to live, so if I lived with Tim I'd have free room and board.

Tim worked at Donald's Delivery as a truck driver and was a reliable kind of guy. He had a regular pay cheque, and it was nice not to worry about where the next meal was coming from.

Grocery shopping was kind of fun when you didn't have to shop from the bargain bin.

We lived like husband and wife, however there was no love between us. We partied every night with his friends, smoked tons of pot and drank lots of booze. Before I knew it, the days were all running together, and I was drunk or stoned most of the time.

Eventually our little gang started to use LSD. Two friends of Tim's who lived close by, Janice and Jillian loved using acid and made sure we had a healthy supply at our parties.

LSD, or acid, as some called it, was a drug that was either awesome or awful, depending on the person. For me a good trip meant everything was wonderful and stimulating and I felt like I had an understanding far beyond anything I'd ever known. It made colours, smells and sounds so intense it was hard to explain. Sometimes it felt like you could actually feel the colours and see the sounds.

Karin and I called it the laughing drug because it made us laugh uncontrollably at anything until the drug wore off.

The bad trips made me feel anxious and out of control because of the hallucinations. Everything seemed so real that at times I felt like I was going insane.

Once we started taking the drug, it didn't take long before we needed to up the dose in order to get the same kind of high.

To make things sweeter, Danny and Karin became drug dealers so our acid was free. That allowed us to buy the booze and other party supplies we needed because we had extra money.

Karin and I, once in awhile, took a few hits of acid and wandered the streets; we laughed and saw the hidden colours and sounds of the world.

Our trips on acid were usually a riot and this one started out great, until we stopped into McDonald's for fries and a burger. We had just sat down to eat when the fries started to dance and the burgers started to talk.

"Please, please don't eat me! I have a family!" the burger said to me.

It freaked me right out. There was no way I was going to eat a talking burger with a family!

"Don't touch that food!" I yelled.

"Why not, I'm hungry," Karin said.

"Because they're alive you moron!"

"What's alive?"

"The burger and fries, can't you hear them!"

"Shit, I'm not eating live food," Karin said.

We ran out of McDonald's like it was on fire. It was so real I had us both convinced the burger was chasing us, and it wasn't until we came down from our high that we could laugh about the talking burger and dancing fries.

What a life. I was seventeen years old, sleeping and living with a man I hardly knew, and drunk or stoned most of the time. My life was one big party, but the more I partied the more depressed I became. I hated to think that this was all there was to life, yet everyone I knew lived their lives this way, and I knew no different.

I found out that Tim was not only sleeping with me, but Janice, one of the girls who supplied the acid. Living with him was a necessity more than a desire, yet it still hurt to think I was never enough. At least for three months I had a roof over my head, good food, and company, but now it was time for me to move on.

The next morning I phoned Social Services to see if I could go back and live with the Rodgers. They were always kind enough to give me a place to stay when I needed one, and I was glad to be going somewhere familiar. Not mention it was time for one of her famous apple turnovers.

They gave me a bedroom in the basement, and although it had old dark paneling on the walls and a very small window, it felt safe. Making my own decisions hadn't worked out very well, and I was tired inside. I just wanted to be taken care of for a while because I wasn't very good at looking after myself.

Mr. Rodgers' mother visited every so often and she was a sweet, beautiful little old lady who reminded me of Mother Theresa. She lived with her daughter, who for some reason didn't treat her very well, and I felt sorry for her.

When I'd visit her at her house, I'd make her cream of wheat or bake her some cookies.

"Oh sweetie, you have made my day," she said every time. We always had a great time together, and I never grew tired of her stories, even though they were the same ones over and over again. She reminded me of my own Grandma, which brought back wonderful childhood memories, the only good ones I had.

Karin had a strange hold on me for some reason. Her happiness was more important to me than my own. I always wanted to buy her presents, or do something for her, because I never wanted to lose her friendship.

I never had any money, so I started to steal money out of Gramma Rogers' purse every time I visited her. I rationalized it by telling myself she was close to dying anyway, and didn't need all her money. I had myself so convinced it was for a good cause, it never bothered me. I didn't have a conscience anymore.

At one time, I would have felt guilty and beat myself up for weeks on end, but I was void of any emotion. I felt like a hollow shell that moved from place to place, and the only person who really mattered was Karin.

From time to time, while I lived with the Rodgers I'd check on my mother to see how she was doing, only to find her the same or worse. When I saw her I had so many mixed emotions, I felt schizophrenic. I loved her and hated her; she was pretty, she was ugly; she gave me life and killed me everyday with her mean spirit. She was a drunk and thanks to her, so was I. I never once thought I'd be any different than she was, because we were more alike than I wanted to admit.

The only thing I could thank my mother for was *her* mother.

Gramma was a wonderful woman. Too bad Mom didn't use her for a role model and save me from this hellhole called life.

I never stayed long with Mom because it was too discouraging, and I was discouraged enough already, but somehow I just couldn't stay away. I felt responsible for her, as crazy as that sounds.

I called Gramma about once a month, and the sound of her voice warmed my heart like a hot summer's day. She told me that Grandpa was suffering from Alzheimer's and they placed him in a home. Lucky him. He could forget all the awful things he did to me, while I would relive those awful memories for the rest of my life.

Gramma moved in with Aunty Kim, and although I hadn't seen much of her since I quit living with her, I knew I'd see even less of her now.

I hoped she knew how much I loved her and what a difference she'd made in my life. Those times we spent together when I was a little girl were the only good memories I had, and sometimes I wished I could go back in time and play the "Stinky Feet Game." When I was with my Gramma, I always felt like God was always a part of the time we spent together.

I didn't stay with the Rodgers for very long because their son was a pervert and I didn't want anything to do with him. I called Social Services and told them it wasn't working out at the Rodgers' house, packed up my stuff and moved.

When I left the Rogers' I moved back to Vancouver. I was still on the Independent living program so it was up to me to find a suitable place to live.

I found a place that provided room and board, and I loved the idea I'd get three meals a day.

Henry and Susan were a cool young couple, but they had some marriage problems, and before I knew it I was looking for another place to live, because she left her husband for a younger man.

I moved in with Karin for two weeks until I got a job as a nanny.

Karin's life had become a little complicated because she and Danny were selling drugs full time. Although I was excited for her because she didn't have to worry about money, I was afraid they'd get caught and she'd go to jail. She always reassured me they were too smart to get caught and I believed her.

Karin and Danny's closest friends, Zak and Donna Johnson, were drug dealers as well. They had a little girl named Tess who was three, and I loved watching her play with her dolls and pretending to be a princess. Even though I was seventeen at the time, I always made sure to spend some one-on-one time with her.

The first thing Tess asked for when they came to visit was me.

"Here I am Tess, how about a big hug!" I said as I picked her up. I loved her, and I think the feeling was mutual. Then we'd play while the others visited. After the Johnsons left, Karin said she had something she needed to ask me.

"Laura, the Johnsons are planning a trip to Hawaii because they are thinking they might find some new drug connections. Their only problem is they needed someone to look after Tess. How would you like to go to Hawaii and look after Tess while Zak and Donna do a little business?"

I should have been over the moon with excitement, yet I felt uneasy. I tried talking myself into thinking I was afraid of the plane, or it was too far away, but I knew it was something else, something I couldn't put my finger on. Thinking back, I think it was God trying to warn me but I couldn't say no to Karin.

"Sure, sounds like fun," I lied.

"Great, I'll let the Johnsons know. They're going to be so relieved!" Then she raced over to the phone to pass on the good news.

The plans were made, and we left by car for Los Angeles. I thought there was only going to be the four of us going and was very surprised when we picked up Ray, Zak's brother. He apparently wanted to be a musician and needed a ride to LA. He had written a song and wanted to see if he could make a record deal. Good luck with that.

We had a great time on the road drinking eighty percent rum, and the drunker I got the more hyper I became. Chatty Laura came out and was the life of the party. We all told stories and laughed until our sides hurt. How we stayed on the road is a miracle, and poor Tess had to sit in the backseat with us drunks. At the time, I never thought anything was wrong with what we were doing, because a drunk raised me and I survived.

After I'd consumed enough booze, the knot in my stomach was gone and I couldn't wait to get on the plane and hit the beach; I was ready to see for myself those beautiful Hawaiian sunsets they put on the post cards.

It took us almost twenty-four hours to get to Los Angeles and although we were tired, the minute we saw the Hollywood sign we caught our second wind.

Karin was right. It was a good idea for me to come. After all, when would I ever see any other part of the world? The sun was shining, the streets were busy and I was in the USA.

Los Angeles was hot! Even with all the windows down in the car it felt like we were inside a hair blower. You could see the heat rising off the pavement, and everyone was in either bathing suits or tank tops and shorts.

I had never seen a palm tree before, and couldn't believe how tall they were. The orange trees were beautiful too, and you could smell their sweet fragrance in the air.

We drove around until we found a hotel room close to the airport. The room was clean and had one bedroom with a fold out couch. I knew right away that Ray and I were going to have to share the couch and I wasn't thrilled with that idea. To take my mind off the sleeping arrangements, I looked out the window only to see the hookers standing on the street corner.

Their clothes were clean, and all of them wore super short skirts and low cut blouses. I noticed the amount of make-up they were wearing—likely to make themselves look older—and it made me wonder how old they really were. For some reason, I remember their pretty long hair and their sexy, spiked, high-heeled shoes.

I never judged them for how they made their living, because I often thought if I'd taken Clive's money that day to have sex with him, I could have been on one of those street corners, too. Like anything in our lives, once we cross that invisible line, it's easier to cross a second time.

Looking at them also reminded me of Allison, and I wondered how she was doing.

I no sooner closed the curtain than I started to feel queasy. I got sick to my stomach and started to ache all over. Of all times to get the flu, it had to be now.

"Anyone hungry," Zak asked.

"I am," Tess said rubbing her tummy.

"No, thanks. I think I have the flu," I said.

"Oh no," Donna replied. "Is there anything we can get for you?"

"No, thanks. I think I'll just go to bed. Have a nice dinner."

When everyone left, I pulled out the hide-a-bed and went to bed, hoping I'd feel better in the morning.

When they came back from dinner, it was late and everyone got ready for bed. Ray crawled into bed beside me, and you'd think because I was so sick he wouldn't be interested in me, but he was. He kept moving closer to me and I kept moving away from him until I had nowhere to go.

"Aw, come on Laura. What's the matter?" he asked.

I couldn't believe anyone could be as self-centered as he was. He told me he really wanted to make love to me the normal way, but was afraid he'd catch what I had and wouldn't be able to sing for his audition.

"Go to hell, Ray, and get back on your own side of the bed!" I said thoroughly disgusted with him. The last thing I wanted was to become his sex slave, and I guess I turned him off because he moved over to his own side of the bed and went to sleep.

I told the Johnsons what he was trying to do and they didn't seem to think it was anything to be concerned about.

"Oh just ignore him and he'll eventually get the picture," they said.

Easy for them to say when they weren't the ones he was trying to molest. I had to put up with his fondling and begging for seven days and was ready to shoot him by the time he left.

Finally, the day arrived, and we were on our way to the airport headed for Waikiki. I was so thankful that Ray was out of the picture, and there'd only be the four of us.

I'd never been on a plane before, and felt giddy inside as I walked to my seat. When I was younger, I wondered what it might feel like to fly in an airplane, never dreaming I might be in one someday.

I loved the way I felt when we lifted off the ground. It was like a big gust of wind was holding my head to the back of the seat, and my ears started to pop.

The snacks were good, and I enjoyed the hum of the plane as it glided through the air.

The stewardess' were so professional looking in their uniforms, and they were all so friendly. It was fun being the one waited on, rather than the one doing the serving.

We watched the movie "Heaven Can Wait" with Warren Beatty, and I loved the little bottles of booze they served, it was one of the best five hours of my life.

Before we landed in Waikiki, you could smell the flowers.

They smelled like the perfume you could buy at the Hudson Bay, sweet and pretty.

When we finally got off the plane, the beauty was breathtaking. There were trees full of flowers that made your nose tickle with their smells. The soft gentle wind blew the palm trees, keeping the scents of the island alive, even in the airport.

The airport was super busy and everyone seemed to be in a hurry to get their bags so they could start their holiday, and we were no different.

Tess was so sweet, and her enthusiasm was contagious. "Can we go to the beach, daddy?" she screeched.

"Not today, honey bunch, but I promise: first thing tomorrow," her dad replied.

I could tell she was disappointed but she was also tired so she just nodded her head in agreement.

We picked up our bags and headed into the city. As we followed the shoreline, the beauty of the city and the sounds of the ocean seemed to be welcoming us to the island.

We found a nice condominium that had two bedrooms, a bathroom, a common living room and kitchen. We unpacked our things and enjoyed the newness that was all around us. Between the sun, the breeze, and the smell, I was sure this had to be like heaven on earth.

We could smell the ocean through our window, and hear the waves as they crashed onto the beach. It was like the ocean had its own rhythm and its beat was strong and steady.

I found the ocean interesting, because sometimes the waves were so high it was hard to distinguish the difference between the ocean and the sky, and other times the waves were small, rolling gently onto the beach.

We went to bed that night all dreaming of hitting the beach the next day. I couldn't wait to get my feet in the water and spend some time with Tess.

After breakfast, we cleaned up the dishes, and Zak said, "Hey, girls, it's time to put on your bathing suits and hit the beach."

I didn't know what to say because I didn't own a bathing suit and was thinking I'd just use a tank top and a pair of shorts.

"I don't actually own a bathing suit, Zak," I said as I headed for my bedroom.

"Well, we'll have to fix that!" Donna chirped. "You need to get a tan before you go home, and you'd look great in a bikini."

On the way to the beach, we stopped and they bought me the cutest little white bikini I'd ever seen. It was adorable, and brand new.

When we got to the beach, the sand was warm, and I loved the way it slipped through my toes.

I was so fair that I had to find a shady spot to sit otherwise I'd have looked like one of the red flowers blooming near by. It was a wonderful day, and every so often, I felt like pinching myself just to make sure I wasn't dreaming.

There were lots of open markets in Waikiki and hundreds of vendors set up little booths all over the place. They sold necklaces and rings made out of shells, and you could buy just about anything you wanted to at the market. I loved scouting out all the shops. Everything was so new and different from anything I'd ever seen. I loved the hustle and bustle of the vendors as they bartered with the tourists, and the place was full of smiling people.

The markets were not only busy, but beautiful. One market was under a huge tree shaped like a gigantic umbrella, and it provided shade for all the shoppers. We spent a lot of time strolling around the markets, and every day I noticed something new. It was fantastic!

After a few days of wandering the market, Zak informed me that he wanted to mentor me in the art of stealing. I must admit I smiled inside, because Karin and I had learned the fine art of stealing a long time ago. There were many times we'd go shopping in our old clothes, and walk out with new ones. There were no cameras or tag sensors in those days, so stealing was easy. You just needed some patience and courage. Stealing was second nature to me and, sadly, I was good at it.

"Alright Laura, there are a few things you need to keep in mind when you go into a place to steal something," he said seriously. "The first thing is you need to be calm and make eye contact with the person at the till. Buy something little so they won't suspect you have something under your blouse or purse, and look at things on your way out of the shop. Do you think you can do that?" he asked.

It was funny listening to him as he told me how to act when I stole something. Those were all basic stealing skills put into words. The fact that I stole never bothered me; however, the idea of going to jail in Hawaii was something altogether different. It should have scared some sense into me, but it was more important I please Zak than worry about jail.

After a few trips to the market and successfully stealing whatever I wanted, it became a game. Zak's birthday was coming up and he showed me the slippers he wanted for his birthday present. That wasn't a problem for me; I just went out the next day and stole him a pair.

"Yes!" he said the moment he unwrapped the slippers I'd stolen for him. "These are perfect, how much did they cost?" he asked teasingly.

"Well, I don't remember paying anything for them, Zak. I think they were free."

"Good job, Laura. I'm really proud of you. Now, I think it's time for a drink!" I liked the fact I'd made him happy, and it wasn't often someone was actually proud of me.

We celebrated his birthday by drinking too many Blue Hawaiians. They tasted so good and were so smooth I'm not sure how many I drank. When we first started to party it was a blast, we danced and sang "We Are Family" around the condominium.

I actually felt like part of a family, because I had someone who appreciated me and my very own little sister.

Thankfully, Tess had gone to bed. We had a great time until the room began to spin, and I could feel the burning in my throat from the vomit that was trying to escape. I ran to the bathroom, and puked my guts out. I lost my two retainers to the toilet that night. My teeth, in order to stay straight, needed those retainers, and now they were gone. I should have reached into the toilet and tried to find them, but at the time, that was the last thing on my mind.

After I quit puking, I put my head down on the toilet bowl and let the coolness soothe my aching head. Those Blue Hawaiians may have been as smooth as a slushy the first time around, but the second time around they were downright gross!

I'm not sure how the Johnsons met the Chinese limo driver, Chang, but all of a sudden he became a regular at our parties. Maybe they thought he'd be a good person to get to know because he was driving around rich people all day, or someone had given them his name. Either way they looked at him as someone important.

He often took us in his Limousine for a ride around the city, and I have to admit it was lots of fun. He seemed like a nice enough man, but so did all the men I met at first.

Everything seemed to be going okay with the Johnsons for the first couple of weeks. I enjoyed looking after Tess while they did whatever it was they were doing, and it was fun spending our days at the beach. Between the sun, building sand castles, and playing in the water, we were tired by the end of the day. Life seemed simpler on the beach.

One night after we had our dinner, everyone was tired so we all headed for bed. I could hear Tess's breathing as she fell into a deep sleep. I could feel myself starting to fall asleep too when all of a sudden the door to our room began to open. I took a quick look and saw Zak coming into the room. I closed my eyes thinking he was coming to tuck Tess in when I felt his hand traveling over my body.

I was horrified, his little girl was in the bed beside me, and his wife was in the other room, what was he thinking? If the scream I felt inside my head could have reached my mouth, it would have ripped the roof off, but I just kept my eyes closed and pretended I was asleep.

I hated what he was doing to me, but I didn't dare tell him to stop. They were my only ticket home.

In the morning, Zak acted as if nothing had happened, and it made me feel furious and dirty inside. Nothing looked the same that day. The waves acted angry, and when they hit the rocks, they sounded more like a jackhammer than a lullaby. The sand seemed to be dirtier on the beach, and the sky, although it was blue, was too bright to enjoy.

Why didn't I stand up for myself? I asked myself that question almost everyday of my life. I could have slapped his hand, and quietly told him to leave without waking Tess. Maybe I liked it and didn't want to admit it. All I know is the knot was back in my stomach, and I didn't know what to do.

The next night when I went to bed, I knew that even if I closed my eyes I couldn't sleep because I was afraid Zak would come back, and I was right.

Once again, the door opened, and Zak quietly came over to my bed and started to touch me with his wet, sweaty hands.

In my head I kept saying, *Open your eyes Laura, open your eyes. He'll go away if you open your eyes.*

I finally talked myself into opening my eyes, and the moment our eyes met, he smiled.

Was this some sick joke? Then I noticed standing beside him was his wife! When I saw her, my heart began to race so fast I thought I was going to have a heart attack. The tears started to sting my face, and in no time at all, my entire pillow was soaked. She was no better than my mother was.

Suddenly, my mind was full of questions. How could she watch her husband molest a young girl and not stop him? Her daughter was in the next bed. Didn't she care if she woke up? What if they were molesting Tess? The thought of that made me want to kill them both. She was so sweet and innocent. Was there anybody willing to save her from her parents? Did all men treat young girls this way?

I closed my eyes thinking they'd leave, but I guess he wasn't finished. When he finished fondling me, he grabbed his wife's hand, and they left. Another sleepless night, wondering what the next day would bring, and what I should do about Zak.

The next morning I was afraid to leave my room. I didn't want to face him or her, and wasn't sure how I was going to muster up the courage to put a smile on my face and enter another day. Hunger always took first place in my life so I made myself go to the kitchen to get something to eat.

When I entered the kitchen, everyone was sitting at the table having a nice visit.

"Good morning, Laura, did you have a good sleep?" Donna asked as she took another sip of her coffee.

"It was okay," I said as I watched Tess laugh and giggle with her dad. Then I prayed to God that he never touched her in the wrong way. As long as he left her alone I'd gladly take the abuse. I tried to pretend nothing had happened, but the lump in my stomach was back, and all I could think of was I needed to go home.

Chang invited us over to his apartment for a party, and I could tell he was interested in me. He lived in a rich part of the city in a high-rise apartment that had security guards. The lobby was so beautiful. Everything was made out of glass or brass, and the marble floors looked like ice they were so shiny.

He lived on the sixteenth floor so the view was spectacular. You could see the ocean, and I used to look for the pigeons because they always made me feel calmer. As the evening progressed, we started to drink, dance and party together, and I was glad to be getting my fill of alcohol because it made me feel better. Even the fondling that had gone on the night before didn't seem like such a big deal when I was drunk. It wasn't the first time someone molested me, and the more I drank the less significant the abuse became. Maybe that was his way of showing he liked me. Wasn't that how all men showed women they liked them?

"Hey, Chang, why don't you take our little Laura on a date? She can't spend all her time working," Zak said with a twinkle in his eye.

"Now that's the best offer I've had in awhile," Chang said, grinning at me like he'd just won a prize.

"What do you think, Laura? Do you want to go out with Chang?" Zak asked.

I was drunk at the time so I said, "That sounds like a wonderful idea. When are we goin'?" I walked over to Chang and sat on his knee.

"How about day after tomorrow, and I'll take you to the best restaurant on the island. To make it extra special, why don't I buy you a new outfit before we go out." He stared into my eyes as he spoke.

It was all just part of the fun, and as long as I was drunk I could do, or be, anything I wanted without a worry in the world. I thought it would be great fun to go on a date, especially if he was going to buy me a new outfit. It all sounded like a wonderful fairy tale, but the next morning when I sobered up, it looked very different.

The next morning besides being hungover, I was worried about the date I was going on in a few days. It was too late to change the plans, and the Johnsons told me I was to be very nice to Chang, and I knew what that meant! I felt like I had nowhere to go, no one to turn to, and was being forced into something I didn't want to do.

That night, I tossed and turned, wondering how I was going to get myself out of this mess. I hardly knew this guy, and I no longer trusted the Johnsons. I decided the only way to get home was to do as I was told, and once I had enough to drink everything would be fine. I just needed to remember that. A few beers would help me get through the evening.

Chang picked me up from the condominium and drove me to the most expensive store in the city.

I have to admit it was kind of fun trying on all those new clothes, and I knew he was enjoying the modelling session too.

"What about this one, Chang?" I teased, twirling around in front of the mirror. "Do you like it?"

"Oh, yeah. That's the one." He was almost drooling, and the fact he thought I was pretty made me feel good.

Going shopping was a real treat for me, and once we'd decided on an outfit we went to the cashier to pay for it. I couldn't believe how much money he had in his jacket. There must have been hundreds of dollars, all rolled up in a big wad.

I grabbed my new outfit and headed to the limousine thinking, *Karin will never believe this story.* It was just like a romance movie. Now all I needed was a drink.

On the way back to his apartment, the reality of what was going to happen next suddenly hit me. I reminded myself that all I needed was a drink to calm my nerves and then the party girl would show up and I'd be all right. Chang was talking, but to be honest I never heard a word, I was too nervous. By the time we arrived at his house my nerves were shot.

"Why don't you go into the bathroom and get ready," Chang said as he threw his coat jacket onto the chair.

"Okay," I said, anxious to get all dolled up. I went into the bathroom, did my hair, put on my make-up and new clothes, and when I looked in the mirror I liked what I saw. I looked good for a seventeen year old, which was more of a curse than a blessing in this situation. I'd been around enough men to know that no man gives you something without wanting something in return, and the thought of that made me uneasy.

When I got out of the bathroom, I could feel his eyes lingering on my body. Mom's friends looked at her that way, and she always took it as a compliment, and for a brief moment, I did too.

"Wow, you look great! How about you fix us a drink while I have a quick shower?" he said.

"Sure, that sounds like a great idea!" I couldn't wait to get a few stiff drinks into me so I'd calm down and relax.

As I was mixing us a drink, I started to think about the evening, and I was so afraid I started sweating and my heart began to race. I needed to get out of there.

Suddenly, I remembered the wad of money he'd rolled up and stuck into his jacket pocket after paying for my outfit. I could hear the shower running, so I knew this would be a great time for me to steal his money, and get out of the apartment. The adrenaline was pumping so fast through my body I felt like I could do anything. I dug through his coat pocket, grabbed the money and ran to the door, but for some reason I couldn't get the door open, and then I heard the shower stop running.

I ran back to his jacket, and put all the money back except for sixty bucks, hoping he didn't notice it was missing. Then I headed to the kitchen to finish making the drinks.

I tried to look as natural as possible when he came into the room, but my face must have given me away.

"What's the matter Laura, are you okay?" He asked suspiciously.

"Ya, ya I'm fine," I said, taking a quick glimpse towards his jacket.

He caught my glimpse and immediately went over to his jacket and counted his money. I could see him, and when he realized he was short sixty dollars his eyes started to bulge out of his head.

"Where's my sixty bucks," he growled.

"I have no idea," I said trying to sound convincing.

"You little bitch, you took my money and I want it back right now!"

"Okay, okay, here's your money!" I said as I tried to hand him the sixty bucks. "Now let's just forget about the whole thing and I'll go home." He grabbed my arm.

I was hysterical by this time, praying he'd let me go, but all he did was raise his eyebrow and give me a little smirk.

"Oh, I don't think that's going to happen. Do you want me to call the police and the Johnsons and tell them you're a thief? I think if you were to earn that sixty bucks you wouldn't be a thief, and I wouldn't have to say anything to anyone."

All of a sudden, the money took on a completely new meaning. As much as I detested the idea, I knew it was going to be the only way I'd get home. I suppose I could have started to scream, but I was too afraid that he would call the police and I would end up in jail for stealing his money. I never once thought that what he was making me do wasn't right because I always assumed I was the one in the wrong.

"Please, please don't call the cops or the Johnsons. I'll do whatever you want, I promise."

"Well," he said, "the sixty bucks is yours then."

"I'm not on any birth control. Just let me go home and I won't say a word, I promise," I pleaded.

"I don't care if you're on birth control or not," he laughed. "I think it's time we made our way to the bedroom, don't you? Ladies first." He waved his arm towards the door.

I went into the bedroom and he closed the door behind him.

"Take those nice clothes off and get into bed," he ordered.

I felt numb as I took my clothes off, and if I could have willed myself to die I would have, but I didn't have any control over that either.

It wasn't long before he was lying beside me, and I felt like a robot doing as I was told. I felt filthy inside and out, and after it was all over, he fell asleep. I quietly went to the bathroom, cleaned myself up, and got dressed.

For some reason I didn't have any trouble opening the door so I slipped out of the apartment, took the elevator down to the main floor, and started to walk back to the condo.

I felt so worthless inside. I had crossed that invisible line, and I hated that man for making me. I hated the Johnsons for their part in all this, and I hated the fact I was at their mercy. I hated the clothes he'd given me, and if I could have, I'd have ripped them into a million pieces and walked home naked!

My mind was racing with each step I took. Why didn't I fight him off? Why did I just lay there and let him have his way with me? Why didn't I get drunk BEFORE he picked me up so I could've handled everything better? The more I thought about the evening the faster I walked. I wanted to walk the memory away.

My emotions went from fear to anger, then guilt, until I was crying so hard that the black mascara I'd put on earlier ran down my face as a reminder of how dirty I was.

I had done what I vowed I'd never do: I had traded my self-worth for a measly sixty bucks. I was just like the hookers in L.A. on Hollywood Boulevard that stood outside of our hotel, and I wondered if they felt as dirty as I did the first time they turned their first trick.

As I walked home, I tried to occupy my mind with something positive, but I couldn't. The smells of the island weren't as sweet, the breeze felt cold and it was dark.

I needed something bigger than myself to lean on, and those Sunday School classes I'd taken as a little girl reminded me once again of a God who forgave, and loved me for who I was. I wasn't sure why he would love or forgive me, yet something inside me knew it was true. Maybe someday I could actually forgive myself. I hung onto that thought as tightly as I could as I made my way home.

I'm not sure how I got home, but I did. The managers of the

condominium were outside enjoying the warm breeze when I arrived, and when they saw me, they immediately came running to see if I was okay. I looked awful because of the streaked mascara and the fact I was crying was a good clue too.

"Are you alright?" The manager asked. "You look awful! Did something happen to you on your way home?"

"Oh, I'll be alright. I just need to get home," I said choking back the tears.

"You don't look alright. I'm calling the police," his wife said, picking up the phone that was lying beside her.

"No, please. I was at a party and someone tried to rape me. I'm okay, really. He didn't hurt me. Please just keep this between us. I don't want the Johnsons to worry or the police involved."

She put the phone down and gave me a hug. Then they walked me to my condo.

"Thank you," I said as I opened the door.

"You're welcome. Let us know if there's anything we can do." Then they left.

I appreciated their love and concern, but was glad when they were gone. The moment I got into my bedroom the phone rang and I knew right away it was the managers filling the Johnsons in on what they'd seen.

I should have known that a rape was too juicy a story to keep a secret. When the Johnsons confronted me, and wanted to know what happened I told them the truth.

I could tell by the looks on their faces they were angry, and instead of showing me a little sympathy, they just shook their heads in disgust and it got very quiet. You could have cut the air with a knife from the tension in the room, and I knew I was in trouble.

"I want to go home. Please, just let me go home." I was shaking and crying uncontrollably, and I needed them to understand how desperate I felt.

When I went to bed that night, I was afraid to go to sleep because I was unsure of what the Johnsons might do to me. I kept going over all that had gone on since I started on this trip, and other than Tess, and the fun we had at the beach, the whole trip had been one disaster after another. Why hadn't I listened to that little voice warning me not to go?

"Laura, we want the money and the outfit Chang gave you," Zak ordered the moment I got up in the morning.

"No problem," I said quietly. I didn't want the money or the outfit because it was a reminder of what I'd done.

I assumed they were going to return the outfit for a refund, and use the sixty bucks I had earned to purchase me a ticket home, but that was a silly thought.

They went to Chang and told him they needed to get rid of me and could he please buy me a ticket home. They must have convinced him because he bought me a ticket, and the moment I heard I was going home, I felt like I'd finished my life sentence in jail.

The next day we went in Chang's limo to the airport, and it was a very quiet ride.

"Laura, before you go, don't you think you should give Chang a big hug and thank him for the ticket home?" Zak said with a smile.

How humiliating. However, I didn't care because I was on my way home. "Thanks, Chang," I said, giving him a quick hug before I boarded the plane.

I was apprehensive and relieved about going home; apprehensive, because I had left my purse in L.A. and had no identification to get back into Canada, but relieved to be on my way home away from the Johnsons and Chang.

I boarded the plane and immediately began to calm down. I was a little concerned about how Karin was going to take my quitting the job she found for me, but for the most part I felt relieved. The return trip home was just as exciting, and those little bottles of booze went down really smooth.

When I arrived in Canada, I couldn't get back into the country without my identification. I called Karin and asked her to get in touch with my social worker and have her come to the airport to prove I was a Canadian citizen. After a few hours, my social worker arrived, and they let me back into the country. I could have danced the whole way home I was so happy.

Eventually, we arrived back at Karin's apartment and she wanted all the details.

"So, how was it?" she asked curiously.

I couldn't bring myself to tell her any more than how beautiful Hawaii was, and how much I enjoyed being the nanny. She seemed okay with that, even when I told her to be careful around the Johnsons because they were not who they seemed to be. She never asked me any more questions, making me wonder if she knew more than she was letting on, or didn't really care.

I stayed with her for a few weeks and asked the social worker to place me into another foster home. I recognized I needed some stability in my life and wasn't ready to be living on my own.

While the social worker was trying to find me a place to live, I ran into Jillian.

"Hey, Laura, I haven't seen you since you broke up with Tim. What you been up to?" she asked.

"Oh, not much. I'm just waiting to be placed into another foster home," I said. "What have you been up to?"

"Same old, same old," she said. "Why don't you stay with me instead of going to a foster home? I'm sure Mom and Dad will let you come if you want to."

That was the best offer I'd had for a while, so I told her to ask her parents and get back to me. The only thing I was a bit worried about was her sister Janet. She was the one who was sleeping with Tim when he and I lived together, and I wasn't sure how excited she'd be if I moved into her house.

Normally their parents didn't take in foster kids, but Jillian persuaded them to give me a chance. The moment she introduced me to her parents, they told me the house rules.

"You are welcome to stay as long as you agree to obey the house rules. There will be no partying, no alcohol or drugs in the house, you need to keep your room clean, and you'll have a curfew time. Do you think you can keep those rules?" they asked.

"Yes, I can, and thank you so much." I smiled at Jillian and she grabbed my hand and showed me my new home. Their house was beautiful. It was big and clean and had an in-ground pool in the backyard.

I didn't know until I moved in that Jillian had two brothers that lived in the house too, but I hardly ever saw them. As for Janet, I tried to stay away from her because I knew she wasn't thrilled with her new roommate.

I was hoping in this stable environment I could find a job and put the past behind me.

I did find myself a job wrapping panelling at a wood working plant. It was manual labour so I didn't need to worry about reading, writing, or making change. It was a good outlet for me. I came home tired after a hard day's work, and liked the fact I had a job I could handle. I guess in a way, this job was one of the most encouraging things that had happened to me in a long time. It showed me that I could be successful at something, and I hadn't felt that way since I'd left Royal Oak.

Jillian was looking for work too, and I was able to get her a job at the plant. She was strong and a good worker, and it was nice having her around.

People come and go in our lives, but there are always those that remain special. Lana was one of them. I thought of her often and wondered how she was doing. I was convinced if Sherry had not lied about me our friendship could have lasted forever. I missed her and often wondered what she was doing with her life. While Jillian and I were working at the plant, Karin called one day and told us that Lana was killed in a terrible car accident .

"What happened?" I asked Karin, feeling a sense of sadness I'd never felt before.

"I guess Lana, her brother, and one of his friends were out driving around and her brother lost control of the car and hit a pole," Karin said, sobbing. "Lana's brother and his friend were hurt, but she hit her head on the rear view mirror, and got severe brain damage. They put her on a respirator but eventually her mother had it disconnected and she died. Can you believe that?"

I was speechless.

"And the other bad thing," Karin said, "is Lana's brother is feeling so guilty he's like a walking dead man. I feel sorry for his mother. She's lost her whole family."

"Yes, she has," I sobbed, and I hung up the phone.

I loved Lana, and when I told Jillian what happened she got very quiet. The word sad didn't come close to how I really felt. She was so young and beautiful and even though our friendship had ended, I knew I'd always hold a soft spot in my heart for her.

I wanted to say good-bye to Lana, but Karin said her mother was going to have a wake for her, and only those invited could go. I knew after Sherry had filled Lana's head full of lies about me, I wouldn't be getting an invitation.

I had never forgotten Lana and all the crazy times we had together. I especially loved the memory of when we stole her mother's car and thought it was so funny. My only regret was I lost her as a friend because I was too afraid to stand up for myself.

I met with Karin after the wake, and she filled me in on all the details. Everyone was wasted from all the booze that was consumed, and the Beatles song "Here Comes the Sun" played over and over because it was Lana's favourite song.

Sherry finally let her true colours show for everyone to see, and in her drunken state, decided she'd help the men through their grief by letting them sleep with her. Karin said there was a line up of men outside one of the bedrooms waiting to take their turn.

What was wrong with her and all those men who took advantage of Lana's death to do such a disgusting thing? I couldn't even imagine what they must have been thinking. All I know is it made me hate Sherry more than I thought possible. She was the sickest person I'd ever known.

Janet became very mean spirited towards me and started telling her mother lies. We all had to keep our rooms clean, and I was always careful to leave mine nice when I went to work, but one day I came home to a very upset mother wanting to know why I hadn't cleaned my room.

I gave her a blank look and couldn't understand what she was talking about, until I went into my room and saw my clothes spread all over the floor. Honestly, I never would have thought to purposely go into someone else's room and throw their clothes around, just to make them look bad.

Janet obviously wanted me out of her house, and because she appeared to be the parent's favourite child, I stayed quiet. I knew there was no way that I could make the mother understand what happened, because it was my word against her daughter's.

"I'm really sorry, and I promise you I won't leave a mess again," I said as I shot a nasty look towards Janet. It was hard for me to get those words out, but I didn't want to have to leave, so I did what I thought I needed to do.

Jillian's mother seemed okay with my apology, but I knew Janet was fuming mad, so she had to up her game.

It was on the weekend, and Jillian and I were just kicking back enjoying our day off when Janet walked in. Their parents were out shopping when she appeared with this sad look on her face.

"Hey, Laura, I really shouldn't have lied about you to Mom, so how about a truce and we smoke a joint together?" she said sincerely.

Janet knew the rules about no drugs in the house, but miraculously she had some weed on her and wanted to share it. That old feeling of wanting to be accepted reared its ugly head, and I believed every word she said. I looked at Jillian to see if I was actually hearing correctly, and she shrugged her shoulders, so I took that as a yes.

We rolled a joint, and the moment it came for me to inhale, the parents walked into the room. If there was such a thing as luck, mine was bad. Even if I could have swallowed that joint, the smell all by itself gave us away. Labelled a bad influence, they asked me to leave.

Janet was ecstatic. She had accomplished what she had set out to do. I was so disappointed in myself for screwing up a good thing, it made me think of my mother. She was good at screwing up a good thing, too. Maybe we were both stupid.

Jillian decided that we should live together, so we ended up in a motel on Kingsway. I had to let the social worker know what had happened, and tell them where I was moving, which was starting to get depressing all by itself.

Jillian and I were never good for one another. The moment we moved in together, history started to repeat itself. We drank, partied, and started hanging out with some of the old gang again.

In my happy place, drunk or high, Jillian and I swapped stories. We both loved to laugh so the stories we told were the funny ones.

Eventually I couldn't keep up at work because I was too hungover every morning, so they fired me. I was devastated, and yet I knew I couldn't stop the drinking.

Jillian liked to drink as much as I did and her job lasted a little longer than mine, but eventually they fired her, too. With just our welfare money coming in we had to move and stay at Karin's for a few weeks while we looked for another place to live.

My social worker found us a newly renovated basement suite that was much nicer than our last place. The landlord was a nice man, and seemed easy to deal with. He had a wife and a little boy who ran all day long. Sometimes it felt like the roof was going to cave in, but we didn't mind the noise because we both liked kids.

Our new basement suite needed furniture so we had some donated to us from our social workers, and used our welfare cheques to buy pots, pans and groceries, forgetting we needed to pay rent.

Being desperate, I went over to Karin's place and asked, "Do you think you could lend me enough money for our rent? It's our first month and we're a bit short."

"I can do better than that," she said as she handed me a bag of weed. "Sell this and you'll have more than enough. "

"Thanks, Karin! You've always been my best friend!" I said giving her a big hug.

"Keep what you need for the rent and give me the rest of the money once you've sold it."

"No problem," I said, and rushed out the door.

We'd been planning our house warming party, and decided we'd use a quarter of the dope to celebrate and we'd hide the rest in the living room vent to sell later.

We invited everyone we knew to our party, and before long, the suite was hazy from all the pot smokers. We had lots to drink too, which made me happy, and everything was going along fine until the people upstairs started yelling at us through the vent.

"Hey, quiet down, down there! You're going to wake up the baby!"

Even though we could hear them yelling, we were so drunk we thought they were funny.

"Hey, quiet down up there! We're tryin' to have a party," one of the guys mocked. We all thought he was super funny, but the yelling from upstairs didn't stop.

Jillian finally had enough of the landlord, and was determined to go and tell him what she thought. I decided at that point the party was over and got everyone out of our basement suite as fast as I could.

Even after everyone was gone, I could still hear Jillian arguing so I went upstairs to try to calm things down. She was like another person. I had never seen her so angry.

"Come on, Jillian, let's go home," I pleaded, grabbing her arm.

"Bugger off, who do these people think they are, yelling at us and bustin up our party?"

"Jillian, it's their house and we've only been here a few days. Come on, let's go," I said, but as hard as I tried, there was no way she was coming with me.

We hadn't realized the landlords had already called the police, and it wasn't long before we could hear the sirens, and see the flashing red lights.

"Jillian, we need to go!"

"I am not going anywhere!" she screamed.

When the police officers arrived, the landlords let them in, and one cop grabbed me and threw me up against the wall.

"Alright, everyone," I shouted, "this has gotten way out of hand. We're on our way home," I said as I pushed the cop away from me and started towards the door.

All of a sudden one of the Police Officers stepped in my way, and when I tried to get around him, he pinned me to the wall.

"You're not going anywhere, miss, until we get this figured out," he said sternly.

"Get your hands off of me," I yelled. He scared me when he tightened his grip, and started to pull me towards the car.

I was spitting mad! I had tried to get Jillian calmed down and come home, and somehow we reversed roles once the police arrived. I was the ballistic one and she calmed right down.

She was so calm, in fact, that they told her she didn't have to come to the police station at all—they were only going to take me! I refused to go by myself, so Jillian offered to come with me. How kind!

All the way to the police station I was swearing, arguing, and kicking the back of the front seat.

"Who the hell do you think you are? I wasn't doin' nothing wrong. I was tryin' to get my friend to come home." I tried to defend myself, but I didn't stop there. Oh no. I was on a roll.

"Why don't you try to catch some real criminals, like those ones that kill people, hey? No wonder people call you Pigs—"

"If I were you I'd shut my mouth. Otherwise we'll take you to the psyche ward. Would you sooner go there?" one of the cops threatened.

I was ready to say a lot more, but when they threatened to take me to the psychiatric ward, I shut up. The last place I wanted to go was there, and I was sure jail was the better choice between the two.

When we arrived at the police station, they wanted to know our names.

"My name is Laura Gilbert," I spit out angrily.

"And you, miss?" he said to Jillian.

"My name is Jane Smith," she said sweetly.

I burst out laughing because I thought she was just joking around, so I never corrected her—which caused us some huge problems the next day.

They put each of us in a different cell. Because I was so angry, they thought I might hurt Jillian. Who knows? Maybe I would have.

Being in separate cells really didn't stop us from being obnoxious. Once we became friends again, we came up with the idea that we should sue the whole police department for the way they treated us, and we both thought our landlords had been very unreasonable.

Thanks to me, we were both in jail. Even though Jillian may have started the whole mess, I made sure to finish it on a high note! Luckily, it was just the two of us in jail that night. Otherwise, it may have been a disaster. I was in a fighting mood, and anyone was fair game.

Eventually, I used up all my energy and passed out. By the next morning, we were both sober, and they let us go.

When the cops threw us into their cars the night before, we didn't have any coats or boots on. With all the commotion, I don't think they had time to worry about our clothing. It was winter, the wind and rain felt cold against our skins, and we were freezing to death when we got outside.

The only way we had to get home was to hitchhike, so we put out our thumbs and prayed someone might have pity on us.

We must have been quite a sight. Two teenagers standing in the pouring rain in bare feet.

Thank heavens it wasn't long before a guy picked us up, and gave us a ride.

Once we arrived home we tried to use our key to get in, and quickly realized that the landlords had changed the locks while we were gone. We knew we needed to get back into the suite to get Karin and Danny's weed and our personal things, so we broke one of the windows and crawled inside.

Although it was early morning, someone saw us, and called the police. Now it was a nightmare. We couldn't find the drugs and the police showed up with their dogs, megaphone, and paddy wagon. It was one of the most terrifying times of my life. I couldn't figure out why so many cops had arrived, and my first thought was the landlords had found the weed in the vents, and had blown the whistle on us. It didn't cross my mind that breaking into our own apartment might cause such a fuss.

"Come out with your hands in the air," they yelled through their megaphone. The only problem was we couldn't get out; when the landlords changed the locks, they used a lock that needed a key to open both sides of the door. They'd already gone to work, leaving us locked inside the house.

I am sure the police officers were very surprised to see two young girls, climbing out a broken window with their hands in the air shouting frantically, "Don't shoot, don't shoot!"

Fear was dripping out our pores. We kept screaming at them, "We're not criminals, we live here! We just needed to pick up some of our things and we forgot our keys."

The whole time we were yelling, we were crawling out the window trying to explain to them that we'd spent the night in jail and the landlords had changed the locks. The more we talked, the more confusing everything got. It was like a zoo. The cops had us surrounded with their guns, the dogs were barking, and there was a lot of yelling.

When we finally made it out of the suite, I'm sure those cops were inwardly killing themselves laughing. Here were two hungover teenagers, with no coats or boots on, hands in the air, talking at the same time. What a sight! The more scared we felt the faster we talked.

"Okay, stop!" one of the cops ordered. "You," he pointed at me. "Tell me the story."

I calmed myself down, and told our story. One of the cops returned to his car to check it out and when he returned, everything started to settle down.

I was glad I'd told the truth when we went to jail the night before, because my story checked out, and I was no longer the person they were interested in.

Jillian, on the other hand, had lied about her name, and they had no record of her. She tried to explain why she lied, but no one was listening. We were loaded into a police car, and taken back to jail until our social worker bailed us out.

Once again we were homeless, so Jillian went back to her parents, and I convinced the social worker to let me live with my mother.

Mom had just arrived home from staying a few weeks in the psychiatric ward when I arrived. I guess one night she passed out in her chair with a lit cigarette, and if it hadn't been for the neighbour, she would have burnt to death. She was so sick she really shouldn't have been living on her own, so when I moved in at least there'd be someone there to look after her.

"Hi Mom," I said when I entered her hotel room.

"What are you doing here?" she asked, half asleep.

"I'm going to live with you for a little while, until you get feeling better." I said.

"Whatever," she said. Then she passed out.

All I ever really wanted was for her to love me. I wanted us to have the kind of relationship Lana and her mother did, but I could tell by looking at her that that was never going to happen. She was so far gone mentally and physically from all the booze and drugs she'd used, I'm not sure she knew who she was, let alone who anyone else was. She was desperately thin and dirty because she refused to eat or take a shower, and all she wanted to do was drink and pop pills.

I thought if I could get her to move to a nicer place on the west end, she could see how much better her life could be, but she didn't want to move from the slum. It was her home.

There's and old saying: "The eyes are the window of the soul." Mom's eyes were hollow and dark, and there was no life left in them. Maybe it was my fault for all her failures. That thought haunted me when I was with her. Her life and mine might have been different if she had given me away, because I think we both felt like our lives were a prison sentence.

Living with her again took me back to when I was young and had to look after myself. To her, I was just something to use, and she ignored me unless she wanted money.

From time to time, I had to check-in with social services, and I think they could sense my emotional state was dwindling daily. They finally told me I needed to move somewhere else, and I ended up in another group home.

Mom eventually moved to Look Out, one of the Salvation Army's homes for the destitute. The saddest part was I didn't find out she'd moved until after she died.

It's funny sometimes how our perspective of things can change. Instead of seeing the group home as a kind of punishment, I now viewed it as a place for me to dry out, and get my head on straight.

I loved the look of my new home. It looked like it should be in a movie. It was beautiful. It had a big wrap around porch and pointed roof. It had eight bedrooms and a huge kitchen and I instantly felt like I'd come home.

There were five other kids staying there, including me, so we each had our own room, which was a real treat.

Sylvia, the housemother, was a wonderful person. She had an English accent, was tall and thin, with loads of beautiful gray hair, and a smile that never quit.

I loved listening to her stories, especially the ones about England. She had great family stories too and it didn't take long to see how deeply she loved them all. Her husband had died some years earlier, and she had two daughters she absolutely adored. I often wondered if they knew how lucky they were to have such a wonderful mother.

Sylvia was strict, but loving and fair, so we didn't mind her house rules and chores. She even taught us how to cook.

Every weekend she'd take a break, and a relief worker came for the weekend. They were good to us too, but we all looked forward to Sunday night when Sylvia came home. I stayed in the group home for eight months, and then I started to feel restless. Maybe I was part gypsy like my mother was. I was eighteen.

Jillian and I had kept in touch, and when I said I needed a roommate, she was more than willing.

What a mistake that was. We found a basement suite to rent, and it didn't take long before the cycle of partying started all over again. The more I drank, the more I believed the lie that booze gave me the peace and happiness I so desired. It had to be the truth, because when I wasn't drunk I was miserable; so I stayed drunk to get through life.

Blaine lived next door to us and it wasn't long before we started to date. He liked to party as much as I did, so we weren't good for one another. I thought everything was going along just fine until a rumour started that Jillian and I were lesbians. How ridiculous was that? I had a boyfriend and I loved men.

I'm not sure if Blaine was just tired of dating me, or really believed I was a lesbian. Either way, the outcome was the same.

We were all partying at his house one night when he dropped the bomb.

"Laura, we need to talk," he said.

"Sure," I'd had enough to drink by this time that I didn't catch the seriousness in his voice.

"Laura, this is hard for me to say, but here goes. I'm straight so I don't want to be dating someone who isn't. If you and Jillian are happy together, more power to ya', but we're done."

"What are you talking about? I'm not a lesbian! you should know that!" I said angrily.

"Well, that's not what's going around so—"

"Screw you!" I yelled.

The good time I was having left immediately and I was

furious. I couldn't believe my ears. He knew I wasn't a lesbian. I was so angry and upset that if looks could've killed he'd have been dead, but they don't, so I left slamming the door behind me instead.

When I got home, I started pouring as much booze into me as I could. I gulped each mouthful so fast I started to choke. I cried, and banged my fists on the table. I was so frustrated with everything I didn't know which way to turn.

I could see Blaine's house from the kitchen window and the more I drank the more pissed off I got. Everyone was having such a great old time, laughing, drinking, and dancing and I wasn't a part of it.

The more I watched the quicker the booze flowed through my veins until I was so worked up I punched the kitchen window so hard I broke it into a million pieces.

I was too drunk to feel the glass as it cut into my hand because at that moment I was more concerned with being dumped than anything else.

All of a sudden, I noticed the blood gushing out of my hand and dripping down my arm. I turned the water on in the sink to see how much damage I'd done and my thumb had a huge gash in it. As drunk as I was I knew I needed some help and the only one I could think of was Sylvia.

I didn't own a car so I had to hitchhike. I ran out to the side of the road, put my bloody hand behind me, and prayed for someone to stop and give me a ride. I was having a hard time standing up because I was so drunk, so I leaned on the lamppost for balance as I stuck my thumb out. The first car that stopped, I hopped in.

Once I was inside the car, I heard the doors lock, and I knew right then I should have waited for the next ride. My drunken state had blurred my judgement, and I was about to suffer the consequences.

"Where you going?" he asked.

"13562 Willow Avenue," I told the guy bluntly.

When he started driving in the wrong direction, I knew for sure I was in trouble. By now, my hand was hurting, the blood was soaking into my clothes and I wasn't sure what I should do.

He stopped the car on an unlit street with lots of trees around and started to grab me. As hard as I could I started to pound on him with my good hand while trying to get the door unlocked with the other.

He never said a word, other than the odd groan now and then, so when I finally managed to get out of the car and my feet hit the ground, I ran for the bush.

He was determined to get what he wanted, and jumped me from behind pinning me down on the ground.

"Settle down, you're going to like this," he said.

I started to flail my arms and legs around, and screamed for help. My thumb was bleeding like crazy, so both of us had blood all over us, and I think that's what scared him.

The moment he saw the blood, he ran back to the car cursing and swearing as he tried to wipe the blood off his shirt. Then he drove off in a rage and I ran through the bush to the freeway. I walked to Sylvia's house and when I got there, I started pounding on her door.

"Sylvia, are you there?" I sobbed. "Open the door! I'm hurt! Open the door!"

I was frantic, drunk, bloody and disgusted with myself for not staying away from the booze. It was always the booze that got me into trouble, and yet I was in love with it.

When Sylvia saw all the blood, she went pale, and quickly got me into the kitchen to see how badly the wound was.

"Oh dear God, Laura. What happened?"

I could tell by the expression on her face, I'd done a real number on myself this time. She grabbed a clean towel, put it around my hand, and called a cab to take me to emergency.

When I reached the hospital, they put me into a room until the doctor arrived. Because I was so drunk, they weren't able to do the surgery I needed, and I had to spend the night sobering up. Some people may have been embarrassed, but to tell you the truth, I didn't care, because I was warm and dry, and the bed felt good.

They wrapped my hand with a clean dressing and mumbled something about my cutting a tendon in my thumb.

I wanted some painkillers, but I had too much alcohol in my system and hospitals don't mix drugs and alcohol. I spent two days in the hospital after my surgery, and was thankful for the rest.

I had just closed my eyes when I heard, "Hi, Laura. How are you doing, love?"

It was Sylvia. "Do ya know yet when ya might be able to go home?" she said in her cute little accent.

"I think I can go home tomorrow," I replied.

"Well then, love, I'm thinkin' it might be a good idea if you move back in with me for a spell. What do you think?"

Her eyes were so full of love and concern.

"That would be so good. Thank you, Sylvia," I said, and then I started to cry.

She came over, gave me a kiss on the forehead, and said, "We'll see ya tomorrow. Your bed's all ready."

Poor Jillian. I really was an unreliable roommate. She ended up moving back home again, which was probably a good thing for her, too.

Part Three
On My Own

Once I turned nineteen, I was no longer a ward of the court, and was completely let go to fend for myself. I stayed at Sylvia's for as long as I could and then, before my nineteenth birthday, I found myself a small basement suite to rent. Sylvia was excited for me and encouraged me not to get a roommate, which was really good advice.

The suite was completely furnished and had a bar in the living room. The kitchen looked like a bowling alley with a big laundry tub at one end, and I needed to share the bathroom upstairs with the mother and daughter.

My rent was only one hundred and fifty dollars a month, which included everything. The only problem was I was lonely, so I got myself a cat and named him Smokey.

Mrs. Reimer was in and out of my life, and when I was doing well we spoke often. However it had been a while since I'd talked to her because of all the trouble I'd been in. I had disappointed too many people in my lifetime, and I never wanted her to be one of them.

When I moved into my own place, I called her and told her all about my new home. She was happy for me and I could feel the love drifting through the phone line. She always believed in me more than I believed in myself.

Judy, her niece, had a little business making sandwiches, soup, stews and Dad's cookies for an engineering firm in downtown Vancouver. Mrs. Reimer knew I was looking for a job, so she got in touch with Judy, and before long I was working full time. I was so wound up I could hardly contain myself. I just knew this job was going to be the one that could help me get back on the right track.

I loved working for Judy, and we had lots of fun making the food together. It wasn't long before we knew all the engineers by his or her name and had a good idea what they wanted to order.

Fridays, after we served lunch, we went shopping for the next week's supplies. When we had time, we stopped for a Strawberry Daiquiri before we went back to work, and if I'd had my way we'd have stayed at the bar all afternoon.

Fridays were special in many ways because we ordered in donuts to sell, and the engineers invited us to have happy hour with them at the end of the day. It was fabulous! The booze was free, and I thought that maybe professional people drank differently from others. I was wrong.

I quickly realized that anyone that got too drunk acted just as stupid as anyone else did. It didn't take me long to figure out who the drinkers were in the crowd, because they were always the last ones to leave.

My work with Judy was going really well, and I looked forward to going to work everyday. After a couple of months however, I missed having someone to talk to in the evenings. The nights dragged on and it was no fun drinking by myself.

One Saturday I was doing some shopping when I bumped into Darla. I met her at a party awhile back, and as we talked, she told me she was looking for a place to live.

"Why don't you move in with me?" I said. We seemed to get along okay. If she moved in with me, it would help pay the rent and I'd have more money to buy beer.

"Sure, that sounds great!" she said without hesitation. The fact

I barely knew her never entered my mind. It seemed like a win-win situation for me, so within the week I had a new roommate. I was always so impulsive!

Her boyfriend was a drug dealer named JJ who'd just gotten out of jail for trafficking. Apparently, his stay in jail hadn't changed him because he was back selling drugs the moment they let him go. Because the police knew him, he asked Darla and me to be his partners in crime.

The plan was that JJ would pick the drugs up from the supplier and bring the drugs to us. Then he'd give his clients our address so they could pick up their order. For us it seemed like a great opportunity, because we could make some extra money and get free drugs.

Honestly, it was thrilling at first. The phone was always ringing, and Darla and I were two of the most popular people around. For once in my life, I had something someone else wanted that had nothing to do with my body.

We really thought we were living the high life. We had loads of "friends" and between the drugs and the booze, life was awesome.

I was still working for Judy, too, so I felt rich. It was the first time in my life that I'd made so much money, and it felt great.

With a little extra money, I went with our little group to the clubs downtown more often. We liked going to Cabo Blanca, a bar that had a mechanical bull, because they had good music, and the bull riders could be very entertaining.

One night when we got to the bar, we got drunker and drunker until everything was hilarious. We drank, danced, and laughed, until all of a sudden we realized we'd spent all of our money.

We were getting ready to leave when the manager came over.

"Where are you going?" he said.

"We're out of money," one of the guys replied.

"That's no reason to leave. I'll make you a deal. The mechanical bull's been kind of quiet so if one of you can stay on the bull I'll pay for your drinks for the rest of the night."

I was tickled at the thought of one of us riding that bull, especially if it meant we could stay longer.

To this day, I am not sure why I was the one picked, but I was. I staggered over to the bull and hoisted myself onto the saddle, letting the booze do all the talking and laughing.

Now everyone in the bar had gathered around the fence and was yelling, "Go, Laura, Go!" The more they encouraged me, the braver I got. I felt invincible.

The man running the bull told me to hang onto the saddle horn, and then counted down: three, two, one. The bull started to rock back and forth, and the crowd cheered as I somehow managed to stay on that dizzy bull.

"Yahoo! Bring on the beer!" I yelled.

If I'd had an ounce of good sense, I'd have gotten off that bull. But, oh no, I was unstoppable now, especially with all the encouragement I was getting.

"Okay, cowboy, one more ride," I said to the guy operating the bull. I was sure that bull could never buck me off.

This time the bull was bucking a lot harder and faster than the first time around, and when it reared backwards the back of my head hit the back of the bull, and when the bull reared forward I'd hit my forehead on the saddle horn.

I never fell off, but by the time the guy operating the bull stopped the ride, I had a nosebleed, a big bump on the back of my head and a ringing in my ears from the crowd. I was too drunk to feel any pain, and couldn't stop laughing even though I had blood all over me.

I jumped off the bull, smiling as if I'd won a huge contest when out of nowhere a man jumped over the fence, scooped me up like a knight in shining armour, and took me to his table. He gave me a cool cloth to put on my bloody nose—and he was cute!

Holy smokes, this had turned out to be an awesome night. I'd ridden my first mechanical bull, been saved by a handsome man, and had free drinks until the bar closed. In my world, it didn't get any better than that.

I spent the whole evening with the guy who saved me, and I'm not even sure I found out what his name was, but when the bar closed, I invited my new best friend home so I could thank him properly.

Everything was perfect, until the cab we caught ran out of gas on the way home, and we had to push it to the nearest gas station. At first, we were a little ticked, but eventually we got the giggles, and ended up saving money.

When we got to my house, it didn't take us long to get to the couch and start making out. It was late, and although we both intended on doing a lot more, we passed out. So much for a romantic evening. He left before I woke up the next morning, and I never saw him again.

Up until this point, I had been good at partying and keeping up with my job. The odd time I was late for work, and knew that Judy was starting to wonder how reliable I was going to be. She knew I was visiting Mrs. Reimer drunk, something I had never done in the past, and that concerned her. The old song, "Here We Go Round the Mulberry Bush," could have been my theme song.

The morning after the bull ride, I missed work and didn't call Judy to tell her I wasn't coming in because I had a splitting headache, black eyes from hitting my head on the bullhorn, and bruised thighs. I was in no condition to work. She never fired me. However, I did get a warning, which I am sure was because Mrs. Reimer begged her to give me another chance.

Darla and I were evicted a few weeks after we'd been in the basement suite together because the landlord told us we were too noisy. Looking back, I think the real reason we were kicked out was because they knew we were selling drugs out of their home and didn't want us around.

I moved back to the Rodgers' for a few months and Darla moved in with her boyfriend. In the end, it probably was a good thing because we were headed for disaster.

During the time I lived with the Rodgers I started going to a club called The Traffic Jam. It was close by, and always had good music. I was still working for Judy, and drinking everyday, but I quit selling the drugs.

I started to get a potbelly from all the drinking, so to help stay slim I became anorexic. As much as I loved food, it was secondary to the beer, so the food had to go. Sometimes when I got really hungry, I'd eat and make myself sick, because I didn't want to gain weight. Besides, when I was skinnier the fun part of Laura popped out quicker, because it took less booze to get her drunk.

Part Four

Babies and Marriage

The Traffic Jam was like most bars. It had lots of tables and chairs to sit on, but I preferred sitting at the bar. It was where all the real action took place.

I was sitting and enjoying the music and my drink when one of the nicest looking men sat down beside me.

He was about five foot ten inches tall, with a thin build, shoulder length dark hair, and a black moustache.

"Hi, my name is Wayne. What's yours?" he said as he sat beside me.

I was interested in this man. Maybe it was his big smile, his sexy Scottish accent, or the fact I'd already had a few beer that made him look so good.

"How do you do, Wayne. My name is Laura. It's nice to meet you," I said as I leaned in closer to him.

It wasn't long before we were dancing around the dance floor, and in between dances, we drank and talked.

My only means of transportation during those days was the bus, and before I danced onto my horse drawn carriage, Wayne asked for my phone number. I literally felt like Cinderella going home from the ball that night. I had just danced with Prince Charming, and now I was going to have to wait to see if the glass slipper showed up at my door. I smiled all the way home, and wondered what tomorrow might bring.

The next day I was on edge. Every time the phone rang, my heart raced as I ran to see who was on the other end. Mrs. Rodgers was just as excited as I was, and we were like two giddy teenagers. I had almost given up when the phone rang again.

"Hello?" I said trying to sound calm.

"Hi, is this Laura?" a male voice asked.

"Yes it is. Is this Wayne?" I replied.

"Good guess," he laughed. "I was wondering if I could come over for a visit and maybe later we could go for a drive."

"That would be great. Come on over, lover," I said, full of anticipation. "See you in a few minutes."

After I hung up the phone, I went to my room to pretty myself up. When the doorbell rang, I'd have ploughed over anyone to get to the door first. I wanted to be the first person Wayne saw when the door opened.

"Hi," I said, out of breath, "come on in."

The whole family sat in the living room and visited with him and I felt so special. He sat close to me, and we made lots of eye contact. He smiled lots, and joked around, and I knew that everyone really liked him. We were both nineteen at the time, and I sensed he came from a good family by the way he spoke.

He was so polite and easy to talk to, and he had a confidence about him that wasn't cocky, but refreshing. I liked everything about him, and I was sure he felt the same about me.

After he'd visited for a little while, he said, "Laura, would you like to go for a drive?"

"Sure, just let me get my sweater."

I couldn't wait to be alone with him, so we said goodbye to the Rodgers, and went outside to his car.

I always liked cars, and Wayne drove an older VW van that

was a rusty colour. Life was more fun when you could get around, and we spent as much time as we could together. Time for me meant nothing. A week with the same boyfriend was reason enough to move in together, and that's exactly what we did.

We moved into a basement suite, which we furnished with some of Wayne's furniture, and my favourite piece was the waterbed. I loved the warmth it gave me when I laid down at night, and the shushing of the water was peaceful.

Wayne's mother was a sweet lady. She was beautiful inside and out, and always made me feel like I was part of the family.

His dad, on the other hand, was a mean drunk. It wasn't unusual for him to thump on his wife and boys, and when Wayne fought back, his father saw him as a rebel.

"Wayne was a real handful growing up, Laura," Wayne's mother said sadly. "He and his dad never did see things the same. The other boys never fought back, but Wayne did, and it was never good. I hope you'll be happy together; he needs to settle down."

"I'll do my best," I said. I was really looking forward to getting to know her better.

Wayne worked as a longshoreman part time, and we never knew from week to week what his paycheque was going to be, so thankfully I was still working for Judy.

Every so often, the engineering firm posted a job opening, and I happened to snag a job working in the mailroom. Although I was sad to be no longer working for Judy, the money was better, and it felt like a promotion.

The job was great for me, because all I needed to do was deliver the mail to the engineers, and I could read well enough to do that. I was delighted to be doing something different, and it made me feel good to know I could get a better job.

While Wayne and I were living together, he played on one of the local soccer teams. He was so talented that The White Caps' farm team invited him to try out for their team. In the end, they had to take back their offer because he didn't have his

Canadian Citizenship. Instead of going and getting it, he just became depressed and moped around the house for days.

"Why don't you go and apply for your citizenship papers so you can play?" I asked.

"By the time I get them it will be too late," he said. "Besides it's just the farm team so it's no big deal."

I knew he was lying about his feelings and couldn't understand why he didn't apply for his citizenship. By being stubborn he was giving up his dream.

Wayne skipped work if it fell on one of my days off, and I was so in love I took his laziness as a compliment. It took me a little time to realize he wasn't staying home to be with me, he just didn't want to go to work.

When he did decide to work, I'd clean the house, and make sure there was always a good meal waiting for him. I was obsessed with making him happy, and thought he'd be the one I'd spend the rest of my life with.

Our first month together seemed to fly by as quickly as a jet races through the sky. Wayne was working more, and I was busy trying to be the best "almost wife" possible. We laughed lots, and drove around in his VW, and I thought life was good, but perspective is a strange thing. If anyone asked me how I thought we were getting along, I'd have said great. But Wayne's perspective was quite different.

It was the oddest thing. One day Wayne was sweet as could be, and the next day he was acting as if he didn't care whether I was around or not. Instead of coming home for dinner with a smile and a big hug, he often came home late to a cold meal. There was little conversation between us, and I was confused because I couldn't figure out what I'd done wrong.

He became more and more verbally abusive, and I was an emotional wreck.

"Wayne, what's wrong?" I asked, positive whatever it was that was bothering him was my fault. "Just tell me and I'll try and fix it," I pleaded.

I barely had the words out of my mouth before he'd storm out of the house without saying a word. I thought that maybe he was upset because his dream of becoming a soccer player had died, and then I heard from a mutual friend that he was seeing his old girlfriend.

That could explain the change, but I refused to believe her and give up on our relationship. I just thought I needed to try harder. I thought if he saw how much I loved him, he'd go back to the Wayne I first met, and things would be good again.

I tried as hard as I could to be the best woman in and out of the bedroom because I thought that was the only way to win him back. I was so stressed out I'd forget to take my birth control pills, and it wasn't long before I was pregnant.

Once I found out, I was sure a baby would be just the thing Wayne and I needed to get our relationship back on track. I couldn't wait for Wayne to come home.

I made a special dinner and it seemed to take longer than normal for him to arrive home. The moment he stepped through the door I blurted out "Wayne, I have the best news, you're going to be a daddy!"

"What!" he said in surprise. "Who's the father? Because I sure in hell can't be."

"Of course you're the father," I said, broken hearted. "Why would you think anything different?"

"There's no way I'm the father of that baby, so if you think I'm gonna look after you and some kid, you're nuts!"

I was shaking by the time he got through with me. I felt like a mirror that had a rock thrown at it, shattering into a million pieces.

"Please, Wayne, a baby will make us closer," I cried. "Can't you see how wonderful our lives will be? We'll be a family. I love you, Wayne, please." He refused to listen, and time became our enemy.

He was no longer nice when he was sober, and was meaner when he was drunk. Even though he knew I was pregnant, he pushed me around when he got angry, and one time he threw a glass of beer in my face.

I started to feel my faithful friend depression starting to visit, and knew it was time I spoke to Wayne's mother. I knew that she'd understand, and I needed some advice.

When I told her I was pregnant, and Wayne was mad, she grabbed me. I was sure she was going to hit me, but instead, she gave me a hug. She was excited to think she was going to be a Grandmother, and her response to the news was like giving food to a starving girl.

"Don't you worry honey, I'll talk to Wayne," she said as we hugged and cried.

I'm not sure what his Mom told him, but things got better... for about a week, then the abuse started all over again.

I desperately wanted our baby to have a family. I wanted our child to grow up in a good home where there was love and laughter, and I was prepared to do everything in my power to make that happen. I just needed to figure out what I was doing wrong, so things could get better.

I was still working, but the stress at home was starting to affect my work. Our home had gone from a peaceful place to a war zone, and I was starting to shut down. Wayne's dad stepped in and told Wayne to smarten up, but Wayne just ignored him.

Jillian had moved into a basement suite down the street from us, and when I got tired of being told how fat and ugly I was, I'd stay there.

Usually, Wayne ended up on her doorstep in a day or two saying how sorry he was, promising to be a better man, and begging me to come home. I was desperate to believe him, so I'd go home to try again.

We were like a boomerang that went back and forth. I'd move back home, Wayne within a week started being mean again, I went to Jillian's, Wayne said he was sorry, I'd move back—it was crazy.

Eventually, I had to quit my job because I got sick with

pneumonia and was in bed for days. I didn't have the energy to pack up every time Wayne threw a fit and left so sometimes, I tried to manipulate him into coming home. I'd phone him and tell him how sick I was, and if he ignored me, I'd call the ambulance and they'd take me to the hospital.

Even when I ended up at the hospital Wayne never came to visit or give me a ride home. His mother was usually the one I'd call for help. I could tell by the disappointment in her eyes, that she wished Wayne were different and the ride home was always quiet.

Once I was back inside the apartment, I'd go to bed and cry myself to sleep feeling lost, because I had no idea how to fix our problem.

Karin happened to get pregnant a month before I did, and she was full of anticipation because she could keep this baby. We spent every waking moment we could together.

I had the craziest cravings while I was pregnant. I was hooked on Pickled Herring and Shreddies. Food was always important to me, and eating for two made me hungrier. Karin laughed and shook her head every time I'd devoured one of those slippery fish, and I was happy I never had to share.

We always had a good time together discussing our changing bodies. When we first felt our babies kick, you'd have thought we were the first women in the world to be pregnant. It's so funny how you know there is a child growing inside of you, yet it doesn't seem real until you feel it move.

We both wanted to be good mothers, and our love for our babies grew with our tummies. We made sure to put cream on ourselves to prevent any stretch marks, and compared the sizes of our tummies monthly. She made being pregnant an adventure, and helped me to enjoy mine.

Wayne was getting more and more abusive, to the point where I tried staying out of his way, unless he was in a good mood.

One night when I was seven months pregnant, we were driving around having fun when all of sudden he wanted to fight. He started to drive like a maniac, and without any warning, he quickly turned into a gas station.

"Wayne, what are you doing?" I yelled the same time as my car door flew open. I fell out of the car onto the pavement and to tell you the truth, I was surprised he even stopped to see if I was okay.

Luckily I landed on my side, and other than the road rash and hurt feelings, I was fine. I wasn't sure if I should scream or cry. I wanted to hate him, yet there was something in me that couldn't hate the father of my child.

We co-habitated—I don't say lived—in the same house with few words spoken between us, and my dreams of being this happy little family were shattered. Wayne was drinking so much that he missed a lot of work, and his laziness seemed to be growing like a nasty weed. Most nights he drank so much he'd pass out on the couch until morning. I guess that was his way of coping.

Thank God for the time I'd worked, because that allowed me to collect Unemployment Insurance. Otherwise, I don't know what we would have done for money.

Finally, the nine months was over, and I knew the baby could come at anytime. I was still battling with pneumonia and the moment I thought I was getting better the coughing and chest pain started again. Through the night I slept in a chair because it was more comfortable, and I coughed less. I was tired of being pregnant, and couldn't wait for the baby to arrive.

Other than not feeling great, it had been a relatively uneventful day.

"Wayne it could be anytime now," I said, hoping to start a conversation.

He just grunted and didn't even look up from his dinner plate.

"I haven't been feeling very good today, so maybe it will be today. Are you ready to be a father?"

"Bugger off, Laura, and leave me alone. I just want to eat my dinner okay?"

Then he moved to the couch and fell asleep. I'm not sure what I expected him to say, but a little enthusiasm would have gone a long way.

I left him on the couch, and got busy cleaning up the dishes and putting the food away, when suddenly I started to get some pain in my stomach, and felt a little nauseous. As I grabbed my stomach, it felt like it was getting harder, and I was scared.

I knew something was up, so after a few hours I called the hospital, and the nurse told me to go and see my Doctor the next morning. I couldn't believe my ears... the next morning! I wasn't sure I could make it through the next hour.

All night I felt so uncomfortable, and morning couldn't come fast enough. As soon as the clock struck nine, I tried to wake Wayne.

"Wake up, Wayne, I need to go to the hospital and I need a ride to the Doctor," I said as I shook him. "Can you hear me?" I asked.

"Fuck off, I'm tired," he grumbled as he put his pillow over his head.

As soon as I got myself ready, I caught the bus, and went to see the doctor. The pains were getting stronger, and I was hoping the baby wouldn't be born on the bus.

When the Dr. checked me, she sent me right to the hospital because my labour had started. I caught the next bus to the hospital, and struggled to keep my composure between the labour pains. I wasn't completely over my pneumonia, and I wasn't sure what hurt more, the coughing in my chest or the pain in my stomach. The saddest thing was, part of me was looking forward to being a mother, and another part of me was too tired to care.

Once I got to the hospital, they admitted me and took me to the maternity ward. I was thankful to be there, because like many mothers having their first baby, I was afraid and unsure of what to expect. I knew the nurses knew what they were doing, and that brought a sense of peace to my tortured soul.

I called Wayne and told him where I was, and that our baby was on its way. He went and got his Mom and Dad, and they all arrived with big smiles. It occurred to me when they arrived this was what a family does when a baby is about to be born. They all gather around, anticipating that first cry.

I was so thrilled to see Wayne. I was sure that once the baby started to come his feelings would change, but I was wrong. He was not going to spend his precious time waiting around the hospital, he dropped his Mom and dad off and left. I was so angry I wanted to beat him over the head with something—however, I was a little busy.

After thirty-six hours of labour, the doctor decided to call in a specialist. They knew the baby was big, and were contemplating whether I needed a caesarean. Apparently, they thought I was going to be okay to deliver naturally because they broke my water about the same time as Wayne arrived at the hospital. Even though I was in a lot of pain, I was glad he came back. I thought maybe if he saw his child being born he'd soften up.

I immediately started to push, and the baby was so big the doctors had to use forceps. Wayne was there for the whole delivery, but left the moment after we named him Joseph. His Mom and Dad were excited to be grandparents but I knew they were disappointed in their son. His Mom was furious with him, and I could tell by the look on her face she was beyond disappointed this time.

The nurses thought Joseph sounded too old for a baby so they called him Joey. He was huge! He weighed eleven pounds, and the poor little fella was born with a broken arm and a punctured lung that made him squeak when he breathed. I knew the baby had been hurt during the delivery by the way the doctor was talking, and then they quickly took him away so they could clear his lungs and put a little cast on his arm. I didn't even get to hold him.

As soon as everyone left, I went right to sleep. I was exhausted.

I never saw Wayne for two days after the baby was born, and when I did, all he could talk about was the hitchhiker he had picked up and screwed in our bed. It was the first time I acknowledged how mean-spirited he really was, and the joy he got out of hurting me was just a game.

During the delivery, the doctor cut a tendon in my leg so I couldn't walk, and bruised my bladder so I needed to use a catheter for two months. To make matters worse, I couldn't go with Joey to Vancouver General Hospital when they transferred him because I still had pneumonia and had broken out with cold sores. They put me in isolation, and by that point, I was sure nothing else could go wrong.

When my cold sores and pneumonia were gone, they transferred me to where Joey was and I was ecstatic. I missed him, and my arms ached to hold him, but for some reason I never saw him even though we were in the same hospital.

After two weeks, I'd had enough of the hospital and discharged myself, but Joey ended up having to stay so his lungs and arm could heal.

I moved in with Wayne's parents, and they were so thoughtful, they'd gone to my apartment and gathered up my belongings so I'd have something to wear when I got home. Their kindness touched my heart.

I was afraid of the future for the first time in my life. I knew my dreams of having a happy little family with Wayne were over and once again, I felt like a failure. Nothing in my life ever seemed to turn out the way I thought it should, and I could never figure out why.

One night during dinner, I knew there was something not right. Everyone was quiet and other than the odd yes or no to a question, there was an uncomfortable feeling around the table.

Little Joey was still in the hospital and we were all getting ready for him to come home.

Eventually Wayne's mother said, "Laura, there's something we'd like to discuss with you."

I was sure that they were going to kick me out, and I had such a sinking feeling inside my gut I thought I was going to get sick. Her gentle eyes and smile made me think that what she was about to say couldn't be bad, or could it?

"Laura," she said kindly, "we're wondering how you plan on looking after Joey? You don't have a job, and a baby is a big responsibility. We know you love him, but sometimes that's not enough, so we'd like to look after him for you, and you can visit anytime you like."

I didn't know what to say at first, but eventually my voice arrived and my eyes met with hers.

"I know I don't have a very good track record," I said, "but I want to raise my own baby. I promise you I'll be a good mother to Joey, and you can have him anytime you like. You just need to give me a chance to show you I can be a good mother. I promise you I'll take good care of my son," I said with as much conviction as I could.

"Alright," she said hesitantly, "but we want to be a part of his life regardless of what happens between you and Wayne. He's our grandson and we'd like to help you raise him."

I was thrilled. I knew how important my Grandmother had been in my life, and wanted the same for my son.

"That would be fantabulous," I said grinning from ear to ear. "I know you only want what's best for us, so you can have him anytime you like, I promise."

"Good," was all that she said, and everyone went back to eating their dinner.

I knew part of what she was saying was true, but there was no way on I was going to abandon my baby. I knew they loved their grandson, but he was my son, and I was not going to give him to anyone. I wasn't so naïve as to think that if they wanted to push the issue they could involve Social Services, and they'd find enough ammunition against me to take Joey away; but unlike my mother, I wanted to raise my baby, and give him all the love, food and guidance a mother is supposed to give her child. I wanted to love my child like my Grandmother loved me.

Finally, we got the phone call tellin us it was time for Joey to come home. I never went to get him from the hospital—his grandparents did, which is strange when I look back now. But I remember trying my hardest to keep busy, so the time would go by quicker.

When I heard the car drive into the driveway, I ran out to meet my little boy. Although his lungs and arm were healed, you could still see the little dents on his forehead from the forceps.

I took him out of his car seat and I couldn't believe how healthy he looked, and how big he was! He looked so cute and chubby, and the moment I held him, the word "mother" took on a completely new meaning.

"Welcome home Joey," I whispered tenderly in his ear. "You're home now and mommy's going to take good care of you."

I was determined to be the best mother in the world. Gramma and Grandpa both had tears in their eyes; I knew they loved Joey too, and I was thankful for their support. Their love and kindness towards us far exceeded my expectations. They told me not to worry about the hospital bill; they'd paid it before they left. It had been a long time since I had felt loved unconditionally.

We all went into the house and Gramma helped me feed

our new little treasure. I don't know what I would have done without her because I had no idea how to look after a baby. She was patient with me and taught me how to care for Joey, which was such a blessing.

I let my mother know she was a Grandmother after Joey came home from the hospital, but I could tell the news didn't thrill her the way it did Wayne's parents. I knew babies were not her thing, so I should have known better than to think she'd be excited. I guess I just wanted her to know that I could do something good, and be proud of both Joey and me.

Babies are such miracles. My entire world revolved around Joey. I loved my little son more and more every day. When he'd smile at me, my heart melted, and when his little fingers wrapped themselves around mine I used to wonder what he would be when he grew up.

I wanted to be a good mother so I made sure that I kept him well fed and clean, but most of all he had lots of love. I loved to play with him, and looked forward to each new day.

Wayne's grandparents from Scotland came to visit, and his Mom told me after they left they thought I was a wonderful mother. My only regret is they never told me how they felt—I could have used some encouragement because I was forever second-guessing myself.

The only way I could be independent was to be on Welfare, making me eligible for BC housing. Their apartments weren't fancy, but they were clean and safe, and within two months of applying, Joey and I moved into our first new home.

It had two bedrooms, and Joey's grandparents bought us everything we needed to furnish the apartment.

I received four hundred and twenty-five dollars a month and my rent was one hundred and twelve, which didn't leave a lot for baby food and other necessities. We never went without anything because Joey's grandparents made sure we had whatever we needed without my asking. There were times I wasn't sure how to act towards them and felt a little guilty because I had no way to pay them back.

Wayne started to come and visit, and at first seemed genuinely thrilled to be a father. He told me he was sorry for all the hurt he'd caused me and wanted to start again. I wasn't sure what to do until he bought me an engagement ring.

"Oh, Wayne, are you sure?" I said as he slipped the ring on my finger.

"I want to try and make this work," he said.

I wanted Joey to have a family so badly it clouded any good judgement I may have possessed, and so I agreed to try again.

Wayne moved in with us, and it was easy to see he loved his son, but he didn't love me. He did try to take a few more shifts at work, but it wasn't long before the ugly side of him was back.

Our lives were not great, and Wayne and I fought a lot, however I never lost hope that someday we'd be a happy family. I kept myself busy with the baby, and the days were full of firsts.

It seemed like every day Joey did something new. I'll never forget his first smile that eventually turned into a giggle, or his first little *goo* that formed a word. It was no time at all before he was crawling, and then walking. He was so busy exploring everything around the house that it took me all day just to keep everything cleaned up behind him. I was so tired by the end of each day that sleep was never a problem.

Wayne was around physically, but emotionally he'd checked out. He liked being a father when it was convenient; however, there is more to being a father than just playing with your child. He was so irresponsible. He rarely went to work, and never helped around the house. He was drunk a lot, and I was starting to detest him. Instead of him bringing out the best in me, he brought out the worst, a side I didn't like.

I was sick and tired of hoping that someday our house would

contain a family; it was just a stupid, unrealistic dream, and the more things deteriorated the more discouraged I got.

The saddest part was I wasn't sure what I should do about the whole situation, so I just buried my head in the sand, and kept going.

Joey had his first birthday, and then his second. Since he had arrived, it seemed like time had flown by twice as fast as it did before. Each birthday was a victory for two reasons. Our son was growing into a beautiful young boy, and Wayne and I were hanging in there. As long as I never spoke to Wayne, and did whatever he wanted, we fought less. I was tired of fighting.

When Wayne's lazy streak took a break and he went to work, it was like letting a bird out of its cage. With Wayne out of the house, I'd have coffee with a woman named Ida who lived down the hall from us. She was from Czechoslovakia, and I loved the way she viewed life. She was so positive. She had a rough side to her, yet inside she was as soft as a marshmallow. She was a great friend, and since her little boy was two months older than Joey, the four of us spent hours together when we could.

One morning we were having coffee and she asked me if everything was okay between Wayne and me. The truth was, everyday was a little more abusive than the one before, and when she asked, my feelings poured out like a spilled cup of coffee. Ida encouraged me to leave, but I didn't know where to go, or what to do, and it wasn't just about me anymore. I had a baby.

One day Wayne decided to skip work because he was too hungover, and when Ida showed up for coffee he was asleep on the couch.

"Wayne, you might want to move into the bedroom because it will be quieter," I said, trying to be nice.

That bit of kindness backfired on me, because he jumped off the couch and with a closed fist came after me. He grabbed me by the front of my shirt pushed me up against the wall yelling, "Why the hell did you wake me up? Couldn't you see I was sleeping? Maybe a good smack will smarten you up!"

"Wayne, what are you doing? Stop it you're scaring the babies!" I screamed, but it was as if I was yelling under water and he couldn't hear or understand me. The only thing that got his attention was Ida—she wasn't afraid of anyone.

She grabbed Wayne by the back of the shirt and yelled, "Back off, Wayne, I mean it!"

The babies were crying and the whole scene was horrible. I am not sure to this day why he listened to Ida. Perhaps he heard Joey crying or was afraid of her. What really mattered was he stomped out of the kitchen, and went into the bedroom.

Once I quit shaking Ida said, "Laura, no woman deserves to be treated like that. You deserve way better. What kind of a man treats a woman that way? Not a good one, that's for sure!"

Maybe I did deserve something better. It was the first time I'd ever entertained such a thought. I started to cry, because I didn't want this kind of life for Joey or me. If Ida hadn't been around that day, I don't know what would have happened, and that scared me.

Once she had everyone settled down, she went home, and I knew right then that I was not going to bring Joey up in a family that fought all the time. I wanted him to think of his home as a peaceful place, a place to go for hugs and love. A place he'd always feel safe and secure. I was not going to give up that idea, so the next day, I called Wayne's mother and together we asked Wayne to move.

Joey was two and half years old when his father moved back in with his parents, and it was the best thing for everyone. Wayne could see Joey whenever his parents had him, and our house was no longer a war zone.

In an ideal world, a child gets two parents that love one another and are good role models. Sadly for Joey and I, we had neither.

I knew in order to make ends meet I was going to have to look for work on the weekends. Joey stayed at his grandparent's house every weekend, and that was a treat for both of them. He loved his grandparents, and I am sure that he did pretty much whatever he wanted. They were good, loving people, and did anything for their grandson.

While Joey was at his grandparent's house, I went job hunting. The only job I could find was selling flowers and Teddy Bears in the bars and clubs. Because I wasn't the only one out there doing the same thing, I made sure I dressed up really nice so I'd be noticed.

One good thing about drunks is they can be very generous, and I made eighty dollars my first night in tips. It felt like a lot of money to me, and I hadn't stolen it.

"Those look like nice flowers," one of the men at the bar said to me one weekend. "I'll buy some, how much are they?" He reached for his wallet.

"They're five dollars," I answered. Then he did something very strange.

"Here," he said, "why don't you keep these they'll look nice in your house."

His kindness blew me away, and I was in shock. In the past, I'd have sat down and struck up a conversation with him, but I wasn't in any rush to get involved with anyone so I simply thanked him and went on my way.

I'd finally reached a place in my life where I was making better choices and an honest living. I lugged around so much guilt from the past that any good honest accomplishment, no matter how small, was something to celebrate. The guilt might get me eventually, but for now, I felt good about my life.

With Gramma babysitting Joey on the weekends, it allowed me to get out and be around other adults again. I loved Joey, yet there was a yearning inside of me that was trying to claw its way out. My life seemed like it was missing something.

My first few shifts at work I never accepted any drinks from anyone, but after I got to know the bartenders, and the regular customers, I found myself stopping for what I told myself would be one drink. *HELLO?!*

I loved alcohol and it loved me. I loved the taste of it, the feeling it gave me, and the person I became. I started drinking every weekend, and the party girl came alive.

I was back on the roller coaster, ups and downs. Ups meant the weekend, and downs meant the weekdays. I made sure Joey had everything he needed during the week; however, Fridays never came quick enough. I looked forward to all the parties, and the way everyone in the bars and clubs seemed to love having me around. I started to take drugs again, and I knew my life was spinning out of control, but had no idea how to stop.

Usually I never drank through the week, but because I had made some extra money at work, I bought myself some liqueurs and made an alcoholic milkshake to drink after Joey went to bed one night. Booze always helped me sleep, so I drank half the milkshake, and put the rest into the fridge for the next night.

The next morning, Joey, that little stinker, crawled out of his crib, got into the fridge, and drank the rest of my milkshake. By the time I got out of bed, I noticed the blender was on the floor, and he was staggering around the house acting goofier than normal. I couldn't believe my eyes. He was stumbling around, and he thought everything was funny, and so did I. I knew he shouldn't have drunk it, but honestly, at that time, I never thought it would hurt him. It made him sick to his stomach, and he was cranky for the rest of the week, which made me think that maybe I needed to get out of bed before he did in the mornings. Other than that, I never thought anything of it.

When Fridays came along, I couldn't wait for the break. I'd get dressed up for work, drop Joey off at his grandparents for the weekend, and hit the bars.

After the bars closed, I'd go to a party where there was lots of booze, weed and acid and go on a trip. It was hard being a mother and I was thankful for my little getaways.

Usually acid had a good affect on me, but this particular night it made me feel sick, and I was so ill I had to leave the party early and go home.

The next day I felt worse, and the day after was no better, so I went to the Doctor. I thought the acid must have come from a bad batch, and was shocked when the Doctor told me I was pregnant. She explained that the child could likely have some kind of birth defect because of the drugs and alcohol I'd consumed, and suggested I have an abortion.

I knew the baby was Wayne's, because he was the only man I'd slept with, but there was no way he was about to care for another child, especially if it was sick.

I was in the same place my mother was so many years ago, and was beginning to identify with her more and more as time went on. I walked and walked and walked, hoping that my mind would clear enough to make sense of what I'd just heard, but I felt like I was in a fog and I couldn't decide what I should do.

I knew Wayne's parents would never want me to have an abortion; but I also knew I was the one that had to make the decision. There was no way I could care for a sick child, or pay for all the medical bills, and I felt like I was drowning. As hard as it was for me to make the decision to terminate the baby's life, I felt like it was the only fair and rational thing to do.

I told Wayne's parents that I had a tubular pregnancy and had to go to the hospital. The last thing I wanted them to know was that I was drinking and doing drugs while they looked after my son, because I knew they'd take him away from me. Not to mention the fact that I was about to abort one of their grandchildren, proving to them I really wasn't a good mother.

I thought I was ready for the abortion, and went at the appointed time for the procedure, but couldn't go through with it. I felt tormented inside. I knew I was killing a life regardless of whether the baby was okay or not, and seriously, I had no one to give me any guidance.

After a few days of crying my guts out, I made another appointment at the abortion clinic not really knowing whether my decision was right or wrong. All I knew was I couldn't look after a sick child, so I kept my appointment.

The procedure went fine, but I felt empty as I waited outside the hospital for Karin to pick me up. I never thought I'd ever have an abortion, and I was starting to hate the person I was becoming.

"Are you okay?" Karen asked.

"I guess so," I said, smiling weakly.

"It'll be okay," she said, and as much as I wanted to believe her, I didn't.

For about a month, I tried to keep myself sober on the weekends, but I began drinking again, all I could think about was that next drink. I was thin and dishevelled looking on Sundays when I went to pick Joey up, and his grandparents knew what was going on.

My old companions of guilt and depression set in through the week, and as hard as I promised myself that I wouldn't drink on the weekends, I couldn't keep my promise.

I was hurting so bad inside from all the garbage life had thrown at me, that I couldn't take it sober. The only good thing that had happened in my life was Joey, and I was starting to screw that up, too. My mother's voice continually called me stupid, dumb, worthless, and baby killer, and the only way the voice went away was when I was drunk.

I was having so much trouble by this time that there were

many times I couldn't finish my flower route. There were no consequences in my thinking when I drank. I just knew I needed the booze because it was the one and only thing that made me come alive. In my drunkenness, I thought I was the best woman, mother, worker, friend—you name it. I felt invincible, and deception was my best friend.

After Wayne moved out, Ida and I continued to have coffee through the week. She was a good mother and helped me out a lot. We took our boys on long walks to the park and I thought she seemed a lot more stable than I was. She was married to a nice guy, and their family was the kind I'd dreamed of having.

I remember one time after a routine doctor's visit for Joey he was low on iron, Ida encouraged me to keep trying to introduce fruits and vegetables to him along with the cereal and formula I gave him every morning. I knew he needed to be eating more fruits and vegetables, but I was a lousy cook, and didn't have a lot of money for food because I was drinking again. Thankfully, he ate really well on the weekends, and Gramma made sure he got all the healthy food he needed.

Most Sundays, Gramma invited us to stay for dinner and the smell of her steak pies made my taste buds come alive the moment I entered the house. I think she tried to get as much nutrition into both of us as she could, and I knew they hated to see Joey leave with me. I bet they wrestled every weekend with whether they should let him go or fight to have him stay. Maybe Joey would have been better off with them. God knows I would have been better off living with my Grandmother, but he always came home with me, just like I always went home to my mother.

My drinking was out of control by now, and as much as a part of me wanted to change, another part of me fought tooth and nail for the booze. My weekend binging was all I lived for, and the alcohol made me feel vivacious. I liked the drunken Laura better than the sober one; she was more fun and didn't have a worry in the world.

I often sang that little song "The Wheels on the Bus" to Joey, and the sad part was it described my life. As the wheels on the bus rolled round and round, so did my abuse of alcohol and drugs. The bus never stopped, and neither did I. The cycle of drinking and partying had started again, only this time it was worse because I had a child.

One weekend Jillian and I stayed at the pub until it closed, and then went over to a house with some men for a few drinks. Around three o'clock in the morning we were ready to go home and needed a ride, but our new friends were in no condition to drive.

Across the street, we saw a station wagon running with no one in it. With big smiles on our faces, we made eye contact, ran to the car, got in, and drove away. We were killing ourselves laughing and feeling super smart, until we realized it had a standard transmission.

"Oh shit, Jillian, do you know how to drive a standard?" I asked.

"Nope, but you seem to be doin' alright, other than all that noise," she said laughing.

"I wonder what gear this one is?" I giggled as the car lunged forward.

"It's not backwards," Jillian replied, "because we're goin forward."

And then we both roared with laughter. There was lots of lunging and grinding of the gears going on, and I wonder to this day how long the transmission lasted after our little joy ride.

Before we got home, I realized I had left my purse behind. I knew I needed it so I tried to turn the car around, but my perception was a little off and I side swiped two cars.

"Holy smokes," I said, "where did those cars come from?"

"I have no idea," Jillian said, looking a little pale.

God only knows how we got back to the house, but we did—only to find a bunch of cops looking for a stolen car.

"Now what are we going to do?" Jillian slurred. "I don't want to end up in jail again, do you?"

"We gotta get out of here," I said and then I pushed down on the gas pedal and we screeched out of there.

Obviously, I'd watched too many cops and robbers shows on TV. The cop cars started chasing us through the alleys and streets until I slowed down enough for us to get out of the car, jump over a few fences, and hide in some person's back yard.

We heard the cops stop at the car and after they took a quick look around, they drove the stolen car home.

After they had driven away and everything was quiet, we slowly made our way back to the house and got my purse.

I was scared for weeks, thinking that they might find out who stole the car, and I'd end up in jail. Then for sure I'd lose Joey to his grandparents. I felt so guilty, and yet I didn't have what it took to change.

After that night, something snapped inside me. That restless side I blamed on my mother I started to own as my own, and I followed it into a deep dark hole.

I had gone from taking acid, to having an abortion, to stealing a car. Then to top it off, one weekend Jillian and I broke into some kind of a Temple just for the fun of it. We were racing around in cars, and doing donuts in parking lots thinking sirens were just something to laugh at and run from. It was like I went crazy and was willing to do anything for the fun of it.

I even entered some wet tee-shirt contests so I could make some money to buy more booze. Some of the men liked to spray us girls with ammonia so we'd take our shirts off, but as bad as that stuff stunk, I never took mine off. They'd have to be a lot nicer to me before that would happen.

When I was drunk, I'd do most anything to feed my habit. I was no longer in control of my life, the need for a drink had taken over.

I had convinced myself that Joey's grandparents thought I was doing a fine job of caring for my son, and started to lie to them about why I couldn't pick him up on time.

I was extremely late picking Joey up one night when I spent the night in jail for trying to eat in a restaurant and leave without paying the bill. Jillian was part of the "eat and run" scene and it was a good thing. If she hadn't been in on it, I don't know who I'd have left Joey with when it was time for me to do my community service.

Every weekend I looked worse than I had the week before. Every time I looked in the mirror my eyes had that hollow look to them. I was super skinny and sickly looking. When I went to pick Joey up I always smelled like booze, and the saddest part was, I was too stupid to realize I was only fooling myself.

Being the dutiful daughter that I was, I decided to check in on my mother because I hadn't seen her in awhile. When I got to her hotel room, I was shocked when I saw her. She was using a walker, and looked so old. Her corns had deformed her feet, and she had ingrown toenails. You could tell it hurt her to walk, and for a woman in her forties she looked awful.

My heart ached for her. She had lived such an awful life, and the saddest part was she chose it. The drugs, booze and men had really marked her. She was dirty and unkempt, and had lost the outer beauty she once possessed. The only heads that would turn towards her now, would be ones filled with either pity or contempt. The saddest part about the whole thing was I didn't realize how the life I was living was patterned after her.

"Mom, why are you using a walker?" I asked when I first saw her.

"Hit by a damn car," she mumbled. "Broken pelvic bone."

"Why didn't you call me?" I asked.

"What would I do that for?"

Her answer shouldn't have shocked me. She never once phoned and told me to come over and visit, so why would she let me know she was hurt?

The only good thing that came out of the accident was the twenty thousand dollars insurance paid her. For her it was as good as winning the lottery. I thought once I told her how broke I was she'd offer to give me some of her money, but she just looked at me, and never offered me a dime.

"You need to take me home with you," she said, "I'm sick and it's your responsibility to look after me." For some strange reason I did feel responsible for her so I agreed to take her home with me for a while. Plus I wanted her to meet her grandson because I was convinced that once she saw how cute he was, she'd automatically fall in love with him.

That certainly was a ridiculous thought. Even though Joey was excited to see her, she didn't even acknowledge him. The harder he tried to talk to her, or play with her, the more she shut down. She never did have any patience for children. I couldn't believe anyone could be so cold towards a child. I don't know why I expected her to love her grandson when she didn't even love her own daughter, but one can always dream.

I'd never understand my mother. Life was all about her and no one else. I knew she'd never change, and frankly, I was tired of trying to make her happy. After her response to Joey, it made me feel very blessed that he had other grandparents that loved him.

She lived with us for about a week, and it was a nightmare. I finally had to take her back to her house, because one night after I went to bed, she fell asleep with a lit cigarette, and burned a hole in my couch. I was furious with her. She could have burned the whole place down with us inside. I couldn't watch her every waking hour, so I explained to her that she needed to go home.

"Well," she said, "I certainly didn't do a very good job raising you. You won't even look after your own mother!"

Now that was a strange sentence coming out of her mouth. She left so upset I was sure she was going to have a heart attack. Part of me felt sorry for her, and another part realized she'd told me the truth; she really didn't do a good job of raising me.

The only thing that changed about my mother was her age. She was still self-centered and angry and I doubted if she even liked herself.

Before she left my house, I wrote myself a three thousand dollar cheque on her bank account so I could buy myself a car. I should have felt guilty stealing from my own mother, but I didn't. As far as I was concerned, she'd gotten off cheap!

I was lonely during the week and even though I had Joey and Ida, I was ready to share my life with someone. I wanted to have a man who could help me settle down, and clean up my act. I wanted someone who loved me, and wanted to take care of me by working, and making a good living. I wanted someone to love and accept Joey as his own son. I wanted to grow old with someone I loved. Maybe if someone loved me I could learn to love myself. I thought if I had a man in my life I could quit drinking; Mom did when she was so in love with Jack. I knew if she could stop drinking for love so could I. That's all I ever wanted out of life, was for someone to love me.

We were drinking at the bar one night and one of my girlfriends asked, "So Laura, you ready to start dating again? "

"Yeah, I think I am. Hopefully I have better luck the next time around," I said bitterly. "It couldn't get any worse than the last one." We all laughed and ordered another round of beer.

"Girls, did I ever tell you about the guy who bought flowers from me in the bar awhile ago?" I said.

"No, what happened?"

"Well, I sold him some flowers and he gave them back to me and told me to take them home. I was blown away. I think maybe I should have gotten a little friendlier with him when I had the chance."

"So what'd he look like?"

"Well, from what I can remember, he was tall, around six foot two, and big. He had a moustache and that all by itself made me think he was cute! He was a bit overweight too, but I thought he was gorgeous."

Like any good memory, the more I spoke about it the more it grew into one of those love stories where two people briefly meet, fall in love, and then never see each other again.

About the time I was ready to move onto another subject, I looked up and couldn't believe my eyes! I saw the very man I was talking about walk into the room. I thought for sure the stars had aligned, or something in the universe was right to have him come at the very moment I was talking about him.

"That's him," I whispered to the girls, "that's the flower guy!"

I was exceptionally drunk by this time, which meant I was very brave. I propelled myself off my bar stool, and ran towards him, adjusting my boobs and hair as I went.

"Hi, do you remember me?" I flirted.

He didn't say anything, but gave me a really sweet smile.

"I'm the lady you bought flowers from and gave them back to one night here at the bar. Do you remember?" I cooed. "I never forgot you, in fact I was just telling the girls about you before you came in."

He seemed impressed that I remembered him, and his eyes lit up when I sat down beside him.

"My name is Kurt and yours is..."

"Laura. It's a pleasure to meet you, handsome," I winked.

For me it was love at first sight. We talked and drank for hours and before the evening was over, I told him about Joey. He said he liked kids, making that hurdle easier to jump because not all men are willing to get involved with a woman with a son.

"I had a great time tonight Laura, is it okay if I give you a call and we could go out?" he asked.

"Of course," I said and scribbled my phone number on a serviette that was sitting on the table.

"Thanks," he said, and then he kissed me on the cheek.

I wanted to melt.

When Kurt called the next day for a date, he asked if Joey could come too. It surprised me to think that he wanted to take both of us.

We went to the "Spaghetti Factory" for lunch, and he gave Joey a little "Cabbage Patch" hockey player. I could tell right away that Joey and Kurt were going to get along just fine. Not to mention, there is no better way to get to a mother's heart than through her child.

We saw each other every day, and I loved our times together. As we told each other our life stories I found out he was a longshoreman like Wayne. The big difference was Kurt worked every available shift they gave him, which was encouraging. There was a sense of stability about him that I liked.

I'd never met a man like Kurt before. He was kind and loving and I was so in love with him that he moved into my place a week after we met. The fact we barely knew one another didn't seem to matter. We were in love.

Kurt was in the middle of a divorce when we met. He said his wife was crazy, and very good at making things difficult for everyone. One of the reasons they split up was because she was unfaithful to him. I couldn't imagine anyone being unfaithful to Kurt, because he was so sweet.

He didn't have any feelings for his wife, but he deeply cared about his little three-year-old son. He wasn't even sure this little boy was his, but that didn't matter to him. He was the only daddy this little guy knew, and he loved him. His biggest disappointment was his ex-wife wouldn't let him visit his son anytime he wanted to. She made such a scene when he dropped by unannounced that he thought it was best if he only visited when she said it was okay.

Because of all the trouble she had caused in his family, Kurt was a little afraid to introduce me to his parents. He said his mother was a very out spoken woman, and the fact that we only knew each other a week before we started living together, would make her very sceptical of me.

I loved Kurt and I was determined to show his Mom that I was not like his wife, so I went to visit her without telling Kurt. To say it was awkward would be a huge understatement.

I rang the doorbell, and before she answered the door, I was wishing I could've run and hid in the trees. I suddenly was terrified of what she might say, and felt like I was frozen to the step.

When she opened the door, she had a scowl on her face, and it took all the courage I had to speak.

"Hi," I said, "you don't know me, but I am Kurt's girlfriend, and I thought it might be nice if we met." I smiled, hoping she'd smile in return, but her expression got worse instead of better.

"Come in," she ordered, and if I hadn't noticed the smile on Kurt's Dad's face, I think I might have fainted.

"So," she said, "I'm going to be very blunt with you, and let you know that if you last six months it will be a miracle. You don't even know one another, and you're already living together. Kurt's been hurt once and I don't want to see him hurt again, do you understand?" She banged her fist on the table for more emphasis, and I was glad she hit the table instead of me.

"I understand," I said as I started towards the door, "but, I just want you to know I love your son, and I will make him very happy."

After that most uplifting conversation, I left feeling as if I'd been shot! The only positive thing was Kurt's dad wished us the best of luck. Boy, Kurt was right when he said his mother was outspoken!

That night I scrambled up enough courage to tell Kurt what I'd done.

"I have something I need to tell you," I said sheepishly.

"What is it?" he asked.

"I went to meet your mother today, and it didn't go very well. I know I should have waited for you, but I just wanted her to like me," I said timidly.

I was expecting him to holler and yell at me, but instead he just gave me a hug, and said, "Don't worry about it Laura, she'll come around."

I loved him. He was the first man in my life to take my side, and look out for my best interest. He restored my hope in the dream of having a loving family; a dream I had given up on too many times to count.

We'd been living together for three weeks when Kurt came home one night after work with the biggest twinkle in his eye.

"I have a very important question for you Laura, maybe you better sit down," he said seriously.

Had I misread the twinkle for something else? I knew from past experience I wasn't very good at judging someone's character.

"What's the problem?" I asked cautiously.

"Well," he said, "I was wondering if you had any plans for the rest of your life?" Then he grinned and pulled out a ring. "Will you marry me?"

"Yes, yes, yes." The words popped out of my mouth so fast I'm not sure my brain even had time to process the question. I couldn't believe I was going to be someone's wife. Finally, someone loved me enough to want to spend the rest of their life with me.

We went over to tell his parents we were getting married, and thank the good Lord his mother was civil. His Dad was happy for us, and as we visited more often, his mother warmed up to Joey and me. I knew she didn't approve of me because of my background, but I wanted to show her that people could change. The frustrating part was the harder I tried to gain her approval, the more evident it became I was never going to be good enough for her son.

I made sure to help her whenever she needed me which helped a bit, but she judged me on my past not my present. Kurt continually told me not to worry about her, but I'd been seeking approval from a mother all my life, and I thought maybe being a daughter-in-law would be different.

She was constantly comparing me to her other daughter-in-law who came from a good family, and if I'd had enough courage, I'd have told her if given the choice I would have chosen a good family too. I think she forgot that none of us gets to choose our parents, we all just have to take who we are given.

Kurt worked as much as he could and my world was more stable, and had more meaning than ever before. I loved knowing someone cared enough to take care of Joey and me. We were a family.

I continued to visit with Ida and Karin when Kurt was at work, and from time to time Karin needed a break from her colicky baby, so I babysat for her.

One day when she came over to visit, she looked awful. For the past week, the baby had kept her up all night, and she was exhausted.

"Karin, why don't you let me look after the kids for you tonight so you can get a good night's sleep?"

"I'm not going to turn you down. I haven't slept for weeks and I'm exhausted, so if you can come tonight, that'd be great." She was so tired it seemed to take her forever to get the sentence out.

"Well it's payback time, don't you think?" I said as I gave her a big hug. "I'll drop Joey off at his grandparents' and meet you at your house later, okay?"

"It's more than okay, believe me!"

She went home while I gathered up Joey and took him to his grandparents' before I headed over to Karin's house. She went right to bed the moment I got there and I spent the night babysitting.

What had I gotten myself into? Her little one never quit crying from the moment her mother went to bed until she got up the next morning. My arms and back were aching from trying to keep the baby quiet and I was so tired I could hardly think straight.

When I got home, I was exhausted. I felt sick to my stomach and was thankful that Joey wasn't due home until the following day. I went to bed hoping I'd feel better in the morning after a good night's sleep, but I didn't.

When Joey came home, he was chattering a mile a minute about all the things he'd done at his grandparents' house, and as hard as I tried to look interested, I was too sick to take it all in.

As I began my morning routine, I started getting awful cramps in my stomach, and then I noticed blood running down my leg. I was so scared I called Ida to come over and help me.

"You better get to the hospital," she said, "clean yourself up and I'll call Kurt," she rushed around the house, got Joey ready and we waited for Kurt to arrive. I knew she was worried, which made me more anxious.

Kurt must have broken every speed limit there was because it didn't take him very long to get home. I was so relieved to see him that I burst into tears.

"It's okay, honey," he said, "we'll get this figured out. Just get into the car. Ida, I'll pick Joey up later."

"No problem at all," she said worriedly.

He took my hand and helped me into the car and then we drove to the hospital.

I knew it wasn't a good thing to compare people, but I couldn't get over the difference between the way Wayne treated me when I needed him, and the way Kurt did. They were like night and day, and I was so relieved I'd ended up with the day. It was times like these my mind wandered back to the God I'd heard about in that little church in Penticton. What they said was true. He was watching over me, even if I couldn't see him.

When we arrived at the hospital, they took a bunch of tests and it seemed to take forever before the doctor came with the results.

"You had a miscarriage," the Doctor said.

I couldn't believe my ears; I didn't even know I was pregnant. Kurt and I were both heartsick. I buried my face into Kurt's shoulder and sobbed. Before we left the hospital, the Doctor gave me some painkillers to help with the cramping, and although the pills would be good for one pain, they wouldn't help the unspeakable pain in our hearts.

When I was hurting emotionally, I used alcohol to take me to a better place. So instead of staying home and taking it easy, we decided we'd go out and drown our sorrows. Joey stayed with Ida for the night, which turned out to be a very good thing.

We went to the bar and the moment I finished my first drink, I passed out. Kurt had to pack me home because I was so out of it, and when he couldn't get me to wake up, he took me to the hospital.

When I finally woke up, I was embarrassed. The doctor must have thought I was stupid for mixing painkillers and alcohol, but I'd done it before and it took way more than one drink to get me to black out. I'm not sure why I thought getting drunk was the solution to all my problems, but I did.

As soon as the Doctor told us it was okay for me to go home, we left. I had a terrible headache, and I scared Kurt half to death, which made me feel guilty. I never wanted to worry or disappoint him, and I managed to do both in the same day.

Why does misery always come with a friend? We were still upset about the miscarriage when we heard that Kurt's Grandfather passed away. I felt extremely sorry for Kurt because I knew how important his Grandpa was to him. It was the first time I'd seen him cry, and it broke my heart. I wanted him to be happy, but I knew that only time could heal this kind of hurt. I gave him lots of loving, and I knew he appreciated it, but in the end there was really nothing I could do.

Joey had outgrown most of his baby furniture so I decided to sell it at the flea market on Terminal Avenue and First. It was an exciting place and there were lots of vendors selling everything from food to furniture. I loved the noise and activity, and it was a good place to forget about your troubles.

After I'd sold everything, I went to see what the others had for sale. I found a little red fox head that the taxidermist in one of the booths had stuffed. It looked so real that at first I was a little afraid to get too close. I think it was its eyes; they seemed to follow me wherever I went. Even though it was a little creepy, I knew that Kurt would like it, so I bought it for him.

"I have something for you," I said as I opened the door.

"Really, now what would that be?" he asked, smiling.

I handed him the little fox head, and his face lit up; mission accomplished. His happiness became my purpose in life.

His divorce became final, too, around that time, which also made him happy because he was free from his ex-wife and we could get married.

I continued my regular monthly visits to see Mom, but each one was harder to take. Every time I saw her, she looked older and more depressed. The car accident had really taken what life she had out of her, and she never left her room. She was a walking, cranky zombie, and it was all I could do to make the effort to see her.

She phoned one day and wanted me to bring her some cigarettes, but I couldn't go, and if I had known that I'd never see her again, I would have made more of an effort, I think.

About a month after Kurt's Grandfather passed away, there was a knock at the door, and I nearly fell over when I saw Aunty Kim.

"Your mom is dead," she said without any emotion.

I was speechless. What did she mean my mother was dead? When I finally found my voice I asked, "What happened to her?"

"I'm not sure, but if you want more information she was living at 'Look Out'. They might know something." Then she turned around and walked back to her car.

I guess she'd done her duty and now she could go home and never see me again. Even though there was a sense of relief when I heard Mom was dead, I still loved her. She was my mother, and as dysfunctional as she was, she'd given me life.

I wanted to know what happened to her so I went to 'Look Out'.

"Hi, my name is Laura Gilbert and I'm here to find out how my mother, Johanna Gilbert, died," I said, choking back the tears.

"Why don't you come and sit in here with me," the lady said gently as she led me to a quiet room. We sat down on chairs that faced one another and then she started to tell the story.

"Laura, your mother was very sick and she tried to commit suicide three times last week. We took her to the hospital each time, and they were able to save her, except for the third time. I'm really sorry for your loss, but we did everything we could."

Then she handed me a Kleenex and asked, "Are there any more questions you'd like answered?"

I shook my head.

"Thank you. Thank you for everything." I whispered.

"You're welcome, and if there is any way we can help you, please don't hesitate to call," she said.

Then she walked me to the door, gave me a big hug and I left. Well, Mom had finally accomplished what she'd set out to do, and she wasn't even fifty years old. Such a waste of a life. I headed for home.

Welfare stepped in and arranged for her funeral at St. James' Church in downtown Vancouver. I didn't want to go, but Kurt convinced me I should. We were the only ones there other than her social worker.

As the Priest began to speak, my mind started to wander, and I cried for the years of innocence that she had taken away from me. I cried because I could never please her, and knew I never would, but mostly I cried for what could have been, and not what was.

I hated her and loved her all at the same time, and when she died, relief and despair were the two main emotions left in my heart.

She had spent all her money except for four thousand dollars, and because I was her closest relative, it came to me.

I felt rich. I paid off a credit card Kurt had, bought some furniture, and the rest went towards our wedding day. As hard as it was for me to admit, dying was the best thing my mother ever did for me.

Within three months of living together, Kurt and I had chosen a wedding date, a place for the service and a restaurant and bar for the party afterwards. When Kurt and I celebrated, we celebrated in a big way. We were both giddy with excitement and couldn't wait for our special day to arrive.

I bought myself a white dress for eighty dollars, and Ida a pink dress the same style as mine. I hired a Justice of the Peace to perform the ceremony at Karin's house, and Joey was going to spend the day at his grandparents. Now all we had to do was wait for the big event.

As the day got closer, I became more excited. Every day I dreamt about how wonderful and romantic our wedding day was going to be. It was my turn to be the blushing bride, and I was going to love every minute of it.

When the day arrived, I couldn't wait to see Kurt's face when he saw me in my wedding dress. I was so in love, and knew without a doubt Kurt was the perfect husband for me. Just looking at him made me tingle all over, and I thought I was the luckiest woman in the whole world.

Karin cleaned her house, and we had a special place to stand for the ceremony. The Justice of the Peace was Chinese and had such a thick accent, I'm not sure to this day what we said "I do" to, but in the end he told us we were husband and wife, and that was good enough for me!

When Kurt kissed me for the first time as his wife, I was sure I could hear fireworks near by. I smiled so much that day that my face was sore, a new sensation for sure. If there was a Heaven on earth, this was it! Our wedding day was perfect!

Ida, her husband, Kurt, and I all left Karin's house to celebrate at one of our favourite night clubs downtown. Karin and Danny didn't have a babysitter, so they stayed home. Although we were disappointment they couldn't come with us, it wasn't about to dampen our spirits.

To say we got drunk would be an extreme understatement. Plastered was more like it. The drinks were extra smooth for me that night, and each drink went down a little smoother and sweeter than the one before. Even though we had something to eat throughout the evening, the liquor that was running through my veins quickly cancelled out the food.

I was so drunk by the end of the night, that Kurt had to throw me over his shoulder and take me home. So much for being romantically carried over the threshold. I looked more like a sack of potatoes than a blushing bride. I didn't care, I was married and head over heals in love.

Kurt's mother was furious when she found out we'd gotten married while they were on a holiday. I couldn't really blame her, but on the other hand, she wasn't very supportive from the beginning. She was sure the only reason we got married was I'd gotten myself pregnant; that would be the only reason her son would marry someone like me in such a hurry. She had her own ideas of how life should be for her boys and it was all about education and marrying into good families.

The other boys did what she wanted on both accounts; however, Kurt wanted to work on the docks like his dad instead of going to university, and married me who'd been raised by a drunk.

After a few months of married life, I suddenly developed an insatiable urge to eat burnt pizza. I should have clued in that I might be pregnant, but I didn't put the two together until after I'd seen the doctor.

I couldn't wait to tell Kurt because I knew he'd be just as excited as I was. He worked until five that day, and the clock seemed to take forever to move.

Around four thirty, Joey and I jumped into the car and drove to the docks. When I saw Kurt walking towards the car I was so excited I thought I was going to burst. I'm sure the twinkle in my eyes gave my secret away long before the words did.

"Guess what," I said.

"Hmm, let me think," was his reply, but I knew he had a good idea what I was going to say.

"We're going to have a baby!" I squealed. Once the secret was out, we laughed, hugged, and talked all the way home about our baby. Nothing could have spoiled the moment. Joey must have thought we were crazy!

The first year Kurt and I spent together was like a fairy tale. We were so in love, and life was great. Even though he only made a little over eleven thousand dollars that year, our lives were full of love and laughter; two things money can't buy. Kurt's work continued to be very sporadic, and it was hard to pay the bills and eat, but somehow we seemed to manage.

I was determined to have a healthy baby so I never drank, smoked or did any drugs during my pregnancy. Even though I'd get the urge, I never gave in, because I knew if I had one drink I'd have more, and I didn't want to harm our baby. Only a power greater than I could give me that kind of strength.

While I was pregnant, Joey and I went for long walks during the day. One day we stopped at a pet store to look at the Siamese cats, and the other animals in the store. I always loved Siamese cats, because they reminded me of my Grandmother's cat Ming-a-ling. I wanted to buy one, but they cost one hundred dollars, and I certainly didn't have a hundred dollars to spend on a cat.

As Joey and I stroked the cat, the owner came over to me and said, "I see you like animals. I am looking for someone to feed them and keep their cages clean, would you be interested?"

I'd never in my life had someone just walk up to me and offer me a job. I was shocked and speechless.

"I pay three dollars and hour and I'll throw the cat in as a bonus," she said.

"Well that's an offer I can't refuse," I replied. "The only thing is could you pay me in cash?"

"That's no problem." she said with a smile.

"And can you keep my pay until Christmas time so that way I'll have some money for gifts?"

"That's not a problem either, what's your name?"

"Laura. When can I start?" I asked.

"How about tomorrow? And you can take the cat home with you."

She gave the cat to Joey and he beamed from ear to ear!

"I'll see you tomorrow," I said, still trying to comprehend what had just happened.

I was over the moon because I didn't have to read or make change to do what she wanted, and I got to bring the cat home.

When Joey and I got home, I couldn't wait to tell Kurt the good news. I could tell he was proud of me because we definitely needed the money. He even liked the cat, which made the day extra special.

Because Kurt could choose his hours of work, we never needed to hire a babysitter, and that saved us lots of money.

As time went on, I started to broaden my job description and help sell some of the animals when the owner was busy. It turned out I had a real gift for sales, and made the store a lot of money that year.

The owner was good to me, she showed me how to operate the cash register which made me feel important. It told me how much money to give back in change so I didn't make any mistakes, which took a lot of stress out of the job.

I remember one day on my way to work, I found a cat in the alley and brought it into the store. It was just a Heinz fifty-seven brand, but I convinced some naive soul that the cat was part Bobcat. They paid eighty dollars for that cat. Either I was a very good sales person or this person was very naive—either way we got eighty dollars for an alley cat!

I loved my job, but as the months passed, I was getting more and more pregnant, and the fun was starting to wear off. Pregnant women are emotional, and I was no exception.

I was doing okay until I took a brownie to work to eat during my break time, and one of the cats from the store ate it!

"I can't believe your stupid cat ate my brownie," I yelled. I was so upset I started to cry. "I quit!"

I guess that brownie was important. I don't think the owner could believe what was happening.

"Laura, wait!" she pleaded as I stomped out of the shop, crying over a half-eaten brownie, and vowing never to return.

The walk home helped me cool off, and when I finally came to my senses, I went back, apologized for being so silly, and asked her for the pay she owed me. The timing to quit was perfect because the baby was close to being born and I was tired.

The money I saved allowed us to buy Christmas gifts for everyone, and in our little world that was all we needed to be happy and content.

Sometimes I think Kurt was more anxious about the whole pregnancy than I was.

"Do you think the baby might come today?" he asked me at least ten times a week. I felt like we were on a long car ride with a kid in the back seat asking the question, "Are we there yet?"

"I don't know, lover, if it will be today. You'll just have to be patient," I said, trying to answer kindly.

Finally, the day arrived, and I went into labour. Kurt took me to the hospital and I was only in labour for four hours when Shannon arrived. She was a bouncing seven pounds three ounces, with big beautiful blue eyes, and peach fuzz on the top of her head.

Kurt and I were so overwhelmed with her beauty and the fact we'd made something so wonderful; we couldn't quit staring at her. We were only in the hospital for a few days before they let us go home, and Kurt's parents paid for the hospital bill, an unexpected blessing.

As outspoken and cranky as his mother could be, she could also be sweet and thoughtful. She threw a baby shower for Shannon, and I couldn't believe the beautiful things everyone gave us. In some ways, it was overwhelming.

Kurt and I loved being parents. Every smile, goo or movement Shannon made was not only the cutest thing we'd ever seen, but also the cleverest.

We took turns doing the night feedings, and when it was Kurt's turn, he always fell asleep with Shannon in one arm, and the baby bottle in the other. When I went to check on them, I could see Shannon gazing longingly at her bottle while Kurt snored in the chair. She never seemed to mind, it was as if she knew that Mom would come and finish the job. She was a content little one.

The next few years of our marriage were busy. After Shannon was two months old, we decided to start trying to have another baby. We didn't have to try very hard, because it took no time at all before I knew I was pregnant again.

We were outgrowing our apartment so we moved into a little house with an in-law suite. Kurt was still only getting the odd job down at the docks, so the rent from the in-law suite was a great help. Eventually, he snagged a job at BC Place setting up and taking down for big events, and we were thankful for the extra money.

As time passed, I started having trouble with my pregnancy. Somehow, I had gotten a separated pelvic bone, and the only way I could sleep was sitting up. I was so tired. Joey was three years old, Shannon was six months old, and they were busy. I never was one to sit around and do nothing. It was important to me to look after the kids, and keep the house clean no matter how tired I felt.

Babies come when they are ready, and our third baby was no different. One night when I was trying to sleep in my chair the contractions started. In one way I was relieved, because I knew if the baby was born I could go back to sleeping in my own bed, but on the other hand, I wasn't looking forward to the labour and delivery.

I waited for a little while before I went into the bedroom and whispered in Kurt's ear, "Do you think you could give me a ride to the hospital? I think the baby is coming."

He jumped out of bed so fast I was sure he was going to hurt something.

While he got dressed, I called his mother and Karin because they wanted to be with me when the baby was born, and asked the renter if she could look after the kids while we were gone.

Kurt's mother and Karin met us at the hospital, and we were all full of anticipation. It didn't take long before I was on my way to the delivery room.

Finally it was all over, and we were introduced to our second daughter. She too was beautiful, and we named her Christina.

When I decided to get pregnant the third time, it never occurred to me that I would be going home to another baby in diapers. The girls were only eleven months apart, and Joey was into everything. If I thought I was busy with two kids, it never occurred to me that looking after three was going to be a lot more work!

Christina had colic, and cried day and night.

"Kurt, I feel like I'm going crazy. I can't seem to settle Christina down and I'm so tired. Maybe I should be admitted into the psych ward for a rest," I said half-seriously.

"Oh, I don't think you need to go there. Just give it a few more months and things will get better," he said, and kissed my cheek.

Easy for him to say when he wasn't the one trying to manage a house and three kids without any sleep! He was right, though. After seven months Christina was no longer colicky, and things started to settle down.

Poor Joey spent a lot of time playing on his own. I was always there to make sure he was clean and fed, but our playtimes together went out the window the moment Christina came home.

He continued to visit his grandparents every weekend, and loved the time they spent together, which made me feel less guilty. As crazy as our lives were, Kurt and I grew more in love with each passing day. We argued like any other couple, but we were always able to settle our problems without using our fists.

Money, or lack of it, can be such a huge stress in one's life. Kurt still wasn't working full time so I decided to make some cat toys to sell at the swap meet. Jillian said she'd help me, so every Saturday we'd take off hoping to sell everything I'd made.

I loved the swap meet. It gave me a chance to get out of the house, and I loved the challenge of trying to make a sale.

I was so restless during this time of my life. I wasn't getting enough sleep, and although I loved being a wife and mother, I was starting to feel like there had to be more to life than diapers and dishes.

Kurt and I always said if we were to stray from one another we'd be honest about it, and I'd never entertained the idea of another man in my life, until one weekend the guy beside me at the swap meet was so cute I couldn't keep my eyes off him.

We flirted the whole time, and then he offered Jillian and I a drink. Once I took that first drink, I was gone. Before I knew it, I was heading off to a pub with Jillian, a guy I just met, and one of his friends.

It had been a long time since I'd been in a pub, and when I walked into the smoky, dark atmosphere, it felt like I'd come home. There were peanuts at each table with shells piled up on the floor, and the air was full of cigarette smoke.

We were all having a wonderful time, and my newfound friend was so complimentary.

"So how long have you been a business woman?" he asked.

"I'm not sure I'd call myself a business woman," I laughed.

"Well then, maybe the reason you sell all your stuff is because you're too pretty to resist," he said teasingly.

"Do you really think I'm pretty?" I asked.

"Yup, I sure do." Then he smiled and my brain quit working.

After a few drinks, and all the attention, we ended up at Jillian's house. Suddenly, I realized what I was doing and decided it was time to go home. As I was saying good-by, my new buddy grabbed me, and kissed me. There was such passion in his kiss I was sure my knees were going to buckle. He asked me if I wanted to go home with him, and as hard as I struggled inside to say no, I knew in my heart that it was the right answer.

As Jillian and I made our way home, I started to feel extremely guilty. I knew I never should have taken that first drink and yet I did it anyway. I wasn't looking forward to seeing Kurt because the last thing I wanted to do was hurt him and I was afraid it was too late.

When I got home, Kurt was sleeping on the couch. When he heard me, he popped his head up, smiled at me, and asked, "How'd everything go at the swap meet? Did you sell everything?"

"Yes it was a good day, and I sold everything," I said. Kurt knew there was something wrong because I couldn't look him in the eye, and I smelled of booze and cigarettes.

"Kurt, the reason I was late was because Jillian and I went out to a bar with a few guys from the swap meet."

He just looked at me.

"I know I shouldn't have gone, and I'm sorry, it was a stupid thing to do and I'll never do it again I promise. I'm really sorry, lover."

I sat down beside him and gave him a big hug. I'd had enough to drink to think my lame confession was enough because I felt less guilty after I'd said I was sorry. Kurt just looked at me, nodded his head and went to bed. He never said a word, and we never spoke about it again.

I started babysitting to help make a little extra money and with our three kids, plus two others, our little house was full.

Kurt was working more, and financially we were doing a bit better, but we were still struggling. His parents surprised us one day and gave us a down payment for a house. We were amazed by their kindness and generosity and for me it was hard to comprehend that parents did these kinds of things for their kids.

We started to dream. We knew we wanted a house with a big yard for the kids, somewhere near a school and in a good neighbourhood. After much searching, we found the cutest house on a quarter acre. It was only eight hundred square feet and, like the other house, had a suite. Jillian rented the suite, and in some ways, it was nice having her around.

One thing our house could have had was another bedroom because it only had two. We had one room, and the kids had the other.

We had barely moved into our new home when I found out I was pregnant again. I was excited on one hand, and concerned on the other. That meant four children all under the age of seven, and there was a part of me hoping I could manage the stress four kids could bring.

Kurt's mother, when she was in the mood to be helpful, taught me a great deal. She taught me how to clean, and organize my day. I was glad she took the time to teach me, because my own mother never taught me anything useful, and I needed to be organized. Otherwise we'd have lived in total chaos.

Most every week we had dinner with Kurt's family. His dad was Yugoslavian, and he taught me how to make sauerkraut from scratch. It was one of my favourite meals, and his dad made it often when he knew we'd be coming for dinner, which always made me feel special.

Kurt's dad always loved having his family around; his mother, on the other hand, while she loved her family, never seemed to be as happy to see us as his dad did. I know she loved us, but I think all the noise got to her, and small doses of us went a long way for her.

I loved being a mother. I was pregnant with our fourth child, and knew this was going to be our last. I never realized how hard it was to be a good mother.

There were always a million things to do in a day and thankfully, by nature, I was hyperactive. Otherwise I most likely would have gone crazy!

I never saw my children as being in the way or too much work. I smothered them with as much love as humanly possible. I wanted them to know how special they were, and that they were wanted.

We always celebrated birthdays. I only had one birthday party that I could remember, and I'll never forget how important that little party was. It was a day to celebrate me, and I wanted to celebrate each one of our babies too.

Joey, Shannon and Christina's birthdays were all close together and because I was nine months pregnant, I decided to have one combined party that year. The yard was awesome because we had between fifteen and twenty kids come and there was lots of room for them to play.

To make it extra special, I dressed up like a clown. I didn't need any stuffing because I was the perfect size. The kids loved it, and so did I. It was so much fun watching the kids play and laugh together with all their friends.

We had a sack Race, played "What Time is it Mr. Wolf," and had a wheelbarrow race, plus a few other games. Then we had some homemade birthday cake, opened lots of presents and had a party to remember.

After all the kids went home, I started to get a few twinges, and knew I was in labour. I called Jillian to come and watch the kids and I guess after all the excitement, really, what was a little more?

Kurt was in the kitchen when I came in holding my belly and trying to get my silly clown outfit off.

"Kurt, it's time to go to the hospital. We're going to have another baby," I said, and I ran as quickly as I could into our bedroom to put on some clothes.

"Okay, but I need to stop at McDonald's and get something to eat first, I'm starving," he said as if nothing urgent was going on.

"What do you mean you're starving? Didn't you eat some of the cake from the party?" I asked a little perturbed.

"Yeah, but that's not supper," was his answer. What is it with men sometimes? Here I am having contractions every few minutes, and he announces, he's starving and we need to stop for something to eat!

I was too preoccupied with what my body was doing to argue, and found myself in the McDonald's drive thru wanting to push!

"Kurt, we need to get to the hospital, I feel like I need to push!" I said in between contractions. I was feeling panicky by the time his order arrived. When he looked at me, he looked a little pale. With his hamburger in one hand, and the steering wheel in the other, we raced to the hospital.

As soon as I arrived, the pains were so bad I could hardly walk. They took me into a room and laid me on the bed. My water broke right away, and when they checked, I was ready, so it was off to the delivery room. I never seemed to be able to do things the same as everyone else.

I was too far along to get any drugs for the pain so the nurse said, "Find a dot on the ceiling and focus on that, it will help you with the pain."

All of a sudden, everyone in the room started moving at a

rapid pace. I tried to keep focused on the dot, but it was hard to do with all the activity going on around me.

I wanted to push so badly, but they kept telling me to stop. The ultra-sound technician arrived, and started to take pictures of my stomach. As much as I wanted to ask what was going on, all I could think about was the pain and the dot. They wheeled me into the operating room, and I had an emergency caesarean.

When they took me to my room,, Kurt was sitting beside my bed. He looked like someone had run over him with a truck. He grabbed my hand, and said, "We have another little girl."

"Fantabulous!, isn't it?" I said and gave him a big kiss. "Why did I have to have a caesarean?" I asked.

"I guess when they did your exam they could only see a shoulder and no head so they wanted to see what was going on. I think I must have looked a little panicked because they said they knew the baby had a head, but you wouldn't be able to deliver the baby the way it was right now."

I smiled at him and squeezed his hand. "I knew everyone was in a panic, but the pain was so bad all I could think about was that damned dot on the ceiling!"

"You want to know the funniest part of the story Laura?"

"Of coarse I do," I giggled.

"When they noticed I was standing there they asked me who I was and I told them I was the father of the headless baby!"

He always had a sense of humour when we needed it the most. He could make me laugh no matter what was going on around me. We were so happy—another beautiful little girl.

She was perfect, other than the fact that she had one displaced hip, and I had to double her diaper for a while. We named her Amanda, and like the other two girls, she was beautiful. Kurt's Mom came to help after we brought her home, and I was very thankful for the help.

Wow! I never dreamed that one day I'd have four children. My life was so different from my mother's. I had a great husband, four beautiful children, a home to live in, and lots to eat, how could it get any better? Maybe there really was a God that was good like they talked about in Sunday school.

After Amanda was born, Kurt said he thought we had enough children, and I needed to go get spayed. I laughed until I cried. When he looked at me confused, I explained, "Kurt cats get spayed; women get their tubes tied."

"Oh, well whatever! I think we have enough kids, don't you?" I could tell he was a little embarrassed so I thought I'd enter into the fun.

"Yup, we have enough kids and I'll call the doctor and see when I can get spayed," and then we both started to laugh. I made an appointment, and was spayed within a few weeks.

After I had Amanda, I took on four more kids to babysit, and ended up with nine kids running around the house. I charged twenty-five dollars per family and that included a snack. The house was bursting at the seams with all the people during the day, and the bedroom the kids slept in was really full after we added Amanda.

Every night before the kids went to sleep, I sang them the three songs I knew. I'm not sure where I learned them, but somehow the tunes and words had stayed in my head. They were "Kumbaya, My Lord," "Fox Went Out on a Chilly Night," and "Twas in the Moon of Winter Time." I loved our little bedtime ritual, and as I sang, they tried to sing along.

I loved looking at their clean little faces, and chubby little hands. I gave them a kiss goodnight, told them I loved them and to have a great sleep. Then I'd turn off the light. As I looked back into their bedroom, it looked like a boat full of bunk beds, filled with precious cargo.

Karin and Danny's lifestyle finally caught up with them, and they were having marital problems. I tried to help by taking their kids for a few days now and then, and the kids loved coming to Aunty Laura's house. They were sweet little kids, and I was hoping I could help make their lives a little happier.

Eventually, Karin left Danny, and moved in with us for a while. We introduced her to one of Kurt's friends, and after she got her divorce, they got married. I was happy for her and hoped they'd make a good home for themselves and her kids.

For some unknown reason I decided to take a job working in a pub where Jillian worked. It wasn't as if I wasn't busy enough at home, but I think I needed to get out of the house so I'd keep sane. They hired me to be the chef's helper. I liked that better than being a server, but it still meant I was around a lot of alcohol.

After our shifts, the manager always gave Jillian and I free drinks, and it never occurred to either one of us that we could turn them down and go home. We'd sit down and drink after our shift until the wee hours of the morning, and I loved every minute of it.

The only problem was I still had to get up in the morning. My kids had to go to school and I needed to be ready for the kids I babysat. I couldn't handle the late nights and early mornings, so I only worked at the pub for a couple of weeks before I quit.

We lived in our little house for four years when Kurt and his dad decided to build an addition. Even though I knew we needed the extra space, I was not looking forward to the mess and confusion. I wanted to buy instead of renovate, but as usual what I wanted never came before what Kurt's parents wanted.

I was starting to resent the fact that my opinion came second to theirs. To make matters worse, I needed to work alongside Kurt's dad when Kurt wasn't home; as if I didn't have enough to do already. The addition and all the work it took began to make me hate the whole process. I worked hard to please everyone, but to be honest, by this point there were too many people to please.

The day the addition was finished I took one huge sigh of relief; glad to be finished and pleased with all the extra room.

Because we didn't have a church wedding when we got married, Kurt decided on our fifth anniversary we should renew our vows. We used the little church the Reimer's took me to when I was a little girl, making the day extra special.

I had Mr. Reimer walk me down the aisle and everywhere I looked, I felt blessed, because I had so many people around me who loved me. That feeling I had as a little girl that there was a God who loved me was so strong that day, I felt like if I reached high enough I could hold his hand.

Of course, a special event always came with a party. Twelve of us went out for lunch, and I noticed Mrs. Reimer was drinking more than usual. The most I'd ever see her drink was a glass of wine at dinnertime, but that day the wine was going down glass after glass.

We left the restaurant, and went to our house where we met some of our other friends. In the end about fifty people showed up and the more everyone drank the crazier things got. I may have been drunk, but I wasn't so drunk I couldn't see what was happening around me.

I noticed one of my friends was making out with a girl he'd just met, then I heard a crash in the bathroom and found one of our friends had fallen into the bathtub and broken the shower door.

I started to feel panicky inside. This was our home, and I didn't want this to be happening in a place that had been so safe and peaceful, especially with my children around.

I helped the guy out of the bathtub, and was no sooner in the living room when a fight broke out between two of the men. I couldn't find Kurt so I asked Mrs. Reimer if she could help me. She had such a good way with people that it took her no time at all, and the fight ended. By this time, I'd had enough.

"Alright everyone, the party's over! It's time to go home now," I said as kindly as I could.

Everyone slowly made their way out the door, and what should have been a great time, my old friend alcohol had managed to destroy.

I loved every moment I spent with Mrs. Reimer. She had been the only one in my life that had loved me through thick and thin, and I adored her. She was the kind of person that radiated a warmth I know now is the presence of God. She was so warm and kind she was like a magnet that drew people to her.

Since we'd first met, she'd had two sons of her own and of course was a great mother.

There were so many times I wished she could have been my mother.

She was thrilled when we had all the kids baptized, and she never missed one of the ceremonies. Honestly, I don't really know why we had the kids baptized. We never went to church, but I knew deep down it was important –it was just a feeling I had.

I'll never forget one service when the baby's hair caught on fire from one of the candles. I thought Mrs. Reimer was going to have a heart attack.

I was busy dunking my baby's head into the Holy water to get the fire out, the baby was crying and everyone else looked like statues. It smelled like burnt hair for the rest of the service, making it hard for everyone to be serious.

"My goodness, that's one of the most exciting baptisms I've ever been to," Mrs. Reimer said. We all laughed about it when we got home, but at the time, it was frightening until we got the fire out.

Mrs. Reimer passed away with a brain aneurism not long after our last visit, and I was devastated. For most of my life, she'd been the only one, other than my Gramma, who really cared about me. She helped me see I could be a better person, and if it hadn't been for her, I'm sure I'd have ended up on the streets just like my mother. Her faith in God was something I envied. She knew without a doubt God loved her and had forgiven her for all the things she'd done wrong. She was the mother I never had.

Her husband bought her a coffin with angels all over it, and it reminded me of the angel she was in my life. The tears I cried at her funeral were for a very different reason than the ones I cried at my mother's.

I cried because I'd miss her love, I cried because I hadn't spent more time with her, and I cried because I knew I'd never see her again this side of Heaven.

We went back to her house for a light lunch, and as I looked around the crowded room, I felt so broken inside. I hoped she knew how much I loved her, and how her presence made my life have meaning.

Church was a place I was drawn to from the time I was a little girl in Penticton. I'd always felt safe there, and my mind was able to rest from whatever was going on at the time. Although I wanted to take the kids on a regular basis, we only had one car, making it hard to go.

Every Christmas we made a point of going to one of the churches in Langley to see a play. It was a tradition we all loved, because afterwards we'd meet up with Judy, Mrs. Reimer's niece, and her family and go for a treat. Traditions were important to me, because as a little girl growing up we never had any.

Amanda, our youngest, started school, and I didn't know what to do with myself. I had the house clean, laundry finished and dinner prepared before lunchtime. Although a part of me was happy for this new freedom, another part of me was sad because I knew my days of having babies were over.

A few years after the addition was completed we put the house up for sale. Kurt's dad was angry and disappointed because he'd paid for all the materials and worked so hard on the house. I think he thought the house was big enough for our growing family, and we didn't need anything bigger, but we wanted something newer.

My days of not knowing what to do with myself didn't last long, because the house we bought had been a group home and the whole place needed renovating. Thankfully, Kurt's dad and brothers stepped in to help us again.

I loved our new home. It had windows all over the place making it bright and cheery, and the kids had their own rooms. It was in a cul-de-sac with lots of other kids, and the neighbours were easy to get to know, especially when I showed up at their door with a homemade apple pie.

The kids settled into their new school and life was good. We loved one another and laughed lots.

As we got to know our neighbours, our house became party central for the neighbourhood. Most weekends we'd all get together and have a few drinks and the kids played while we partied. Everything seemed to be going along great, until I noticed that Kurt was having more and more trouble with the booze. He no longer could just take a few drinks and stop. He'd become like me; once we started, we couldn't quit until our glasses couldn't reach our mouths.

The more we partied, the deeper in debt we became. We stopped paying some of our bills so we'd have enough money to buy the booze we needed for the weekend, digging ourselves into a deep hole.

Kurt was still working, but it wasn't enough money to make ends meet. It was one thing to have one person in the house that was an alcoholic, but two was a recipe for disaster.

I started to raise Siamese cats to sell because I knew from the pet store I could get a hundred dollars for each kitten. Even that wasn't enough to get us out of the mess we were in, so I took on some house cleaning jobs.

Kurt and I were arguing more and more, and he was home

less and less. I felt like he didn't really care about us anymore, and was only interested in the things he wanted to do.

"Kurt, what's going on?" I asked one night after the kids had gone to bed. "We never see you anymore and it feels like you don't want to be around us." It took all my nerve to ask him that question, because he seemed so angry all the time.

He scratched his head, looked me in the eyes and said, "You know Laura, the other day I was out with the guys, and I saw an old man walking across the road with a cane. I began to think about how fast time goes, and when I saw him, I decided I needed to have a more fulfilling life, otherwise I might end up like that old man who missed out."

I couldn't believe my ears. I was angry, hurt, and confused, because for him, his family wasn't a part of having a full life? For me a fulfilling life meant having a family. He had his priorities all screwed up as far as I was concerned. Not to mention, how did he know the man with the cane wasn't happy?

To make matters worse, he and Joey were starting to fight. Kurt was getting physical with him, and it didn't take a genius to see that he was favouring his own girls. I could see Joey was depressed and feeling like he'd never be able to please his dad. I knew better than anyone how not being accepted by a parent could kill the soul of a child, but I wasn't sure how to help him. I prayed hoping God would hear me, and give me an answer, but the truth was I didn't know what his voice sounded like, so I never heard His answer.

"Mom," Joey said one day as I was cleaning up the kitchen.

"What's up, bud?" I asked as I kept wiping down the counter.

"I want to kill myself," he said emotionless.

I stopped what I was doing, shocked by what I'd just heard, and asked, "Why? Why would you want to do a terrible thing like that?"

"I just think it would make things easier around here if I was out of the picture," he said softly.

"No, no, honey, that's not true. I love you, your sisters love you—"

"But my dad doesn't love me," he interrupted, and started to cry. He was thirteen years old and was so depressed he felt the only way to make things better was to kill himself.

What had happened to the calm that prevailed over our home? I felt sick to my stomach to think that my little boy was hurting so badly that the only answer to his pain was to commit suicide. The more distressed Joey became, the more I tried to fix the problem. I knew deep down I couldn't mend all his hurts, yet I loved him, and was willing to do all I could to help him through this rough patch. I could feel our family starting to unravel and didn't have any idea what to do.

I told Joey's real dad hoping he could help, but he didn't know what to do either. He loved his son and had always been a part of his life, but I could tell he didn't have a solution.

The biggest problem was Kurt raised Joey, so Kurt was his dad too. It was important for his own dad to accept him, which he did, but he also wanted Kurt to accept him and he didn't think he did.

I couldn't cope with the whole mess so I started drinking more. When I was drunk, none of the problems seemed so bad, and I was happier.

For some reason I thought if I helped make some money it would lessen Kurt's stress and he'd be nicer to Joey. His mother gave me the money I needed to enrol in a school for hairdressing, and the renter downstairs took care of the kids after school as partial payment. The only problem was I couldn't read or write very well, and it didn't take long for the instructor to realize I needed some help.

She took me aside one day after school and said, "Laura, I've noticed you're having trouble reading, so if it is okay with you

I'd like to arrange a teacher's aid to help you get through the theory."

"That would be great!" I exclaimed. I always did well at the Royal Oak school because I had help, so I looked at this opportunity for help the same way. The teacher arranged a lady to help me, and everything was going along pretty well until we had a substitute teacher.

She wasn't aware that I needed extra help to take notes and the lady that usually helped me was home sick. When I asked the substitute teacher for some help, instead of helping me, she made an issue out of the whole thing.

"What do you mean you need help reading," she said in front of the whole class. "You can't possibly think you'll get through this course if you can't read," she said sarcastically.

I was so embarrassed I left the class and cried all the way home. I was humiliated, and felt so defeated that the moment I hit the doorway I ran into my bedroom, and cried until there were no tears left.

Then to add insult to injury, Kurt's mom made me feel like I had made her case by being a stupid person that wasn't capable of anything.

Even though the hair instructor called the next day and tried to convince me to come back, I couldn't. It was too late for me, because I no longer believed in myself.

My old companion Depression started to mess with my head once more.

Well, you have really proven how stupid you are this time, it mocked. *Everything you do you fail at. Your marriage is falling apart, not to mention all the other relationships you've had since you were born, and you might think you're a good mother, but really, how could you be? You're nothing but a screw up, and everything you touch, you ruin, just like your mother did.*

As hard as I tried to make the voice in my head quit talking, I couldn't. It slowly shredded me into little bits until I believed everything it said was the truth. I could never hold down a job, or have a lasting relationship. My own mother had hated me, and maybe I didn't really know how to be a good mother—I just thought I did.

The longer I thought about my life the more the darkness grew. I wasn't sure what the truth was anymore, and I hated the fact I might not be a good mother to my kids.

I started to question whether Kurt really loved me or just felt stuck. He had turned into someone he promised me he'd never become; a workaholic like his Dad, and critical like his Mom. All the insecure feelings I felt as a child returned, and I felt stupid and worthless. I lost all confidence in myself, and continually took the blame for everything that went wrong in everyone's life. The voice in my head was starting to win, and the only way to make it stop was to have a good stiff drink.

Karin came to visit one day and it didn't take her long to see I was in a bad way.

"You need to make a doctor's appointment, Laura, and get something to help you cope," she said. She knew what I was capable of when I got deeply depressed and was not going to leave until I made an appointment.

I went to see my doctor and the medication she gave me helped a bit, but the only way I could really cope with all the stress was a beer or two... or three.

Kurt and I hardly spoke anymore, and Joey was getting worse. He was angry and hard to get along with, which didn't improve the relationship he had with his step-dad.

"Kurt, please, you need to spend a little more time with Joey," I begged.

"He needs to grow up!" was his reply, and I knew he had no intention of spending any more time with his son.

Our lives were a mess. We were partying all the time, adding more financial stress, and when I suggested we quit our partying, and Kurt give up some of his sports to save some money, he didn't want to give up either one. To me, that meant the partying and sports were more important than his family, and that infuriated me.

It didn't seem to matter what happened—we fought. If it wasn't about Joey, it was about money. If it wasn't about money, then it was about how Kurt was never home. We couldn't agree on anything, and we were both miserable.

Kurt even made me give away a little puppy Karin gave me because he said we couldn't afford it. It was crazy. The truth was he didn't like dogs, and didn't care if I liked the dog or not.

One night our neighbours invited our family over for a drink, and we never said no. We'd only been there for a short time when Christina asked if she could talk to me.

"Mom, that man tried to make me say I did something when I didn't," she cried.

"What are you talking about?" I asked.

"He took me into one of the other rooms and wanted me to say I did something I didn't."

I kissed her on the top of the head and told her to go and play.

I was furious, especially when he'd taken her aside without us knowing, and then tried to make her confess to something she didn't do.

I took Kurt aside and said, "Kurt, you need to talk to Phillip and tell him if he has any nasty thing to say about our kids, he needs to talk to us first. He had no business talking to her without us being there," I said.

"Oh Laura, forget it, it's no big deal," Kurt said, brushing me aside.

"What do you mean, it's no big deal? He accused her of something she didn't do and she needs to know her father will stick up for her!" I shouted.

"Be quiet, they're going to hear us!" he hissed, and then, smiling, he went back to the party.

I thought for sure Kurt would stand up for his daughter, but he did nothing. I was too drunk to think so I marched into the party and put my face as close to Phillip's as I could.

"Listen Phillip, you better back off and leave my family alone because no one messes with my kids!" I yelled.

At first, he didn't know what to say but when he saw how feisty I was he said, "I think it's time you left!"

I had a lot more to say, but he threw me out of his house, which was fine with me. I never really liked him anyway, and his kids were brats. Kurt came with me, but I knew he wasn't very happy about the way I'd handled the whole situation.

The more we partied the worse things got, until we hit our breaking point.

One night, Kurt's hockey team plus our neighbours came over for a pig roast. We farmed the kids out to their grandparents for the night because we knew this party would likely last until morning.

We ate, and everyone was having a wonderful time until Kurt's drunken cousin Andrew decided he should drive himself home.

"Thanksh, guyzh," he slurred, "I think I'll be going now. Great barty," he said as he staggered across the room.

He could hardly stand up, so I took his car keys away.

"Hey, gimme my keys back!" he shouted.

"I don't think so. You're too drunk to drive," I said as I went to change the CD.

While I was kneeling on the floor, Andrew came up behind me and started to choke me with his arm.

"I said, give me back my damn keys!"

"Laura, give him back his keys!" Kurt yelled. He never told Andrew to stop choking me. All he was interested in was making Andrew happy.

Dennis, a friend who was sitting on the couch, jumped up, and yelled, "Back off, and leave her alone!"

Andrew took his arm away from my neck, and I threw him

his keys. I was so upset I could have killed him and Kurt, given the chance.

One of my girlfriends came over, and tried to cheer me up by asking me to dance. I got up, and we started goofing off while Dennis watched us from the couch. Soon he was butting in, and I was dancing with him instead of her.

I was so drunk that all I could think about was how angry I was at Kurt. Dennis knew how I was feeling, and before I knew it, we were dirty dancing in the living room. I guess he was my rescuer, and I wanted to thank him for his bravery. We were so loaded that the fact we had our hands on one another's butts didn't seem to matter. It was a very inappropriate moment, but at the time, I didn't care.

Kurt came in, saw us dancing and stormed out. Soon everyone left and the party was over, but I knew our marriage was too.

We'd had some good years together, but once booze became the third person in our marriage, our worlds became a train wreck, with one car crashing into the other.

I took the kids and we moved to Kelowna. Joey was thirteen, Shannon was ten, Christina was nine and Amanda was six. I applied for welfare and found a five-bedroom town house for seven hundred and twenty-five dollars a month. The townhouse wasn't in the best part of town; however, it had enough bedrooms and was close to a school.

Wayne, Joey's real dad paid for the move, and helped us settle into our new home before he left. It was nice for me to see how well they got along.

I enrolled all the kids into their new school and the girls settled in quickly, but Joey was rebellious and hard to handle.

When he was at home, he wanted nothing to do with his sisters, or me, and spent most of his time in his bedroom. I knew he was angry, and as hard as I tried, I couldn't get through to him.

He refused to believe that I loved him, and blamed everyone for his unhappiness.

Since we'd moved to Kelowna, Joey took up so much of my physical and emotional energy I had nothing left to give to the girls. Our home was just as stressful in Kelowna as it had been in Vancouver. I was tired and frustrated because I didn't know how to make things better, and my drinking didn't help the situation.

Not long after we'd moved to Kelowna I got a call from the hospital that Joey had tried to commit suicide by jumping off a tall building. They had admitted him into the psychiatric ward, and he had told the nurses he wanted to see me.

I couldn't believe it. I knew he was in bad shape, but I didn't think he'd really try to hurt himself. I felt like once again I had failed, and it was my fault he was so messed up in the head.

I was numb inside as I drove myself to the hospital. History was starting to repeat itself. I knew how depression could lie to a person, making him actually believe death was the best answer for his problems. I knew firsthand how hopeless you needed to feel before you'd jump off a building, but had no idea what to do. I wanted to tell him about the God I heard about when I was little but I didn't know how to explain it. I thought maybe if he knew God would help him he'd get better.

When I walked into his room, I started to cry, "Oh Joey, what have you done?"

Then I wrapped my arms around him and held him as close to me as I could. He hugged me back, but he was so hyper I think he could've climbed the walls. As hard as I tried to get him to calm down I couldn't. He was out of control.

They diagnosed him with ADHD and put him on Ritalin. He was in the hospital for a week and although the Ritalin helped a bit, he was still very depressed and angry.

I felt sorry for Joey because I knew he wanted to come home, but I thought the stay in the hospital might be good for him. He needed some time to think about what kind of life he wanted, and

I needed a break. He had taken up so much of my time I barely saw the girls, and I missed our times together.

When I got home from visiting Joey I sat the girls down at the table.

"Girls, Joey is going to be in the hospital for a few days and I thought it might be fun to walk dogs for the SPCA. What do you think?"

"That sounds like lots of fun. I'm in," said Christina.

"Me too," Amanda and Shannon echoed.

"Great, I'll set it up and we can start tomorrow."

It was the first time in a long time we all had something fun to look forward to. For the three days we volunteered, I walked a little multi-poo named Rudy.

Everyday after we walked the dogs, the girls and I went to visit Joey, and he seemed genuinely happy to see us. It was fun to watch the girls tell him about our dog walking and see him smile. Before we left each day, I tried to reassure him of how much we all loved him, and I think deep down he wanted to believe me, but something was holding him back.

The girls and I loved Rudy so much we wanted to take him home. However, the SPCA was waiting to see if his owner would claim him before putting him up for adoption. We were never good at waiting, so the girls came up with the idea that I should get dressed up and pretend I was Rudy's owner. The more we talked about the plan, the better it sounded. I could be a great actress if I needed to be, so we started scheming.

The next day the girls did my hair, picked out some nice clothes, did my make-up, and gave me a pair of sunglasses. They did a fabulous job on my disguise, and we were all giddy. It certainly was the first time I'd spent so much time trying to look pretty for a dog!

"Good luck Mom," the girls giggled, as I drove out of the driveway.

"Thanks. I might need it," I laughed, and then I drove to the SPCA.

I have to admit I was very nervous. It had been a long time since I had attempted anything like this, but I wanted to make the girls happy, and Rudy was worth it.

I entered the building with as much confidence as I could muster.

"Hello," I said, as I stood tall and tried not to shake. "I was wondering if anyone has brought my little dog Rudy here. He's a cute little multi-poo and he went missing the other day. I thought I'd come down here, and see if anyone turned him in."

The lady at the counter was so excited, "Well, we did find a little Multi-poo, can you tell me where you lost your dog?"

I felt a little panicky when she asked where he was lost because I had no idea, but I said, "Well, we live about five blocks from here, so that's likely where someone found him."

"Awesome," the lady said. "Come with me and see if you can see your dog."

Relief swept over me the moment she said awesome, so now I was on a roll.

"One more thing," I said, as we walked to the back, "Rudy's not neutered, if that helps."

I couldn't believe she didn't know who I was. I didn't think I looked that different!

As I walked into the kennel area, I slipped on the floor right in front of Rudy.

Without blinking an eye I yelled, "Oh Rudy! I cannot believe I found you!"

Of course, the dog got all excited because he knew who I was, and was likely wanting his daily walk. The SPCA worker had tears in her eyes as she took Rudy out of his cage and handed him to me. I stood up and held Rudy in my arms. I cooed and talked to the dog all the way to the car wanting the worker to know for sure she'd done the right thing.

When I got home, the girls and I laughed until our stomachs ached. It was a great break from all the stress. Rudy didn't take long before he was a part of the family, and his presence brought great healing.

Joey came home from the hospital, and he hadn't changed. He was still angry and aggressive and the more stress I felt, the more I drank, never realizing it was beginning to affect the kids.

Karin's sister, Shirley, lived in Kelowna, and we started visiting the pubs regularly. I was back on the hamster's wheel again. The pub was the place I felt most comfortable, and home had too many problems, so I tried to stay away as much as I could.

One night, Shirley and I went out, and we never came home for the whole night. Shannon, who was only ten at the time, had spent most of her night awake waiting for me to come home. The moment I came through the door she ran towards me crying.

"Mom where were you? I thought that maybe something awful had happened to you. Why didn't you come home last night?"

"I'm sorry honey. I just lost track of time. I promise I won't do it again. Now go get ready for school."

When I looked into her worried little eyes, I saw myself looking at my pathetic mother passed out in her bowl of rice, and I swore I'd never do that to my daughter ever again.

It had been five months since we'd left Kurt, and I was starting to question whether I'd done the right thing. Every night when it got quiet, I missed having him around. I missed his laughter, and wanted to go back to the first few years we were married. Maybe I was being selfish, by keeping my kids from their dad?

Kurt visited us every so often in Kelowna, and I'm not sure who looked more forward to his visits, the kids or me. I think the only one not thrilled about him coming was Joey, and I understood because Kurt never did warm up to him. I knew deep down they'd likely never get along because they never seemed to see anything the same way.

Every time Kurt visited, our love for one another seemed to grow. We didn't argue and always had lots of fun with the kids. Neither one of us wanted a divorce so we decided we'd try again. We knew in order to make our marriage work, we were both going to have to quit drinking because we recognized that was the biggest problem in our marriage.

It sounded like it should be simple, but we never realized what a hold the booze had over us. With the best of intentions, the kids and I returned to Vancouver hoping we could put our family back together.

It was hard for Christina to be living beside the neighbour who'd caused all the trouble, so we sold the house and moved into a townhouse. I was only a few minutes from where Karin lived, so when the kids were at school we spent our time together, discussing our lives, and walking our dogs. She seemed so happy, and although a part of me was thankful she had finally found a good husband, another part of me was envious.

Kurt really did try to cut back on his drinking, but I was only able to quit drinking for a month. It was the longest month of my life. I really tried, but the booze had a strange hold over me and I couldn't fight the pull it had. I was extremely restless, and short tempered with everyone; I knew if I had one drink I'd feel a lot better and then everyone would be happier.

Helen, our next-door neighbour invited me over for a drink one afternoon, and I was so desperate nothing could have stopped me from going. The only drawback was I never could stop at one.

The kids knew I was drinking again because I'd leave the house grouchy and come home happy. I think Kurt knew too, but he never said anything because he'd never given up alcohol completely, like I had. I think he liked the happy side of

Laura better anyways, and it gave him a good excuse to keep drinking.

Helen and I decided to start our own house cleaning business so we could make a little extra money. I enjoyed working with her, and although the work was hard, it was fun and rewarding. We'd go into a mess and clean it up; too bad my own problems weren't as easy to fix. Unfortunately, our business didn't last very long because my life was a disaster and I couldn't manage home and work.

I knew deep down I had a problem with alcohol, but denial became my best friend. The moment I'd think I had a problem drinking, denial told me I didn't, and I'd believe the lie because I wanted to. Every day the booze took a little more of me, until I was drinking just as much as I was before I left for Kelowna.

It had been a long time since our family had gone on a vacation so when Kurt's parents wanted to take our family to Disneyland we were thrilled. We were going to take their motor home and see Mickey and Minnie Mouse. Everything was great, until Kurt's mom and dad made it extremely clear that there was NOT enough room for Joey. I felt sick because I knew darn well if Joey had been Kurt's they'd have made it work.

Joey was fifteen and I tried to explain the whole "not enough room" thing, but he wasn't stupid. I could see the disappointment and hurt in his eyes.

"It's okay, Mom, don't worry about it," he said. I knew he'd just shoved his anger down a little deeper, and I hurt for him. He stayed with his dad, and although I knew his dad would take good care of him, I felt like I'd abandoned him.

I should have been excited about the holiday, but the truth was I felt anxious. Kurt's mother was so fussy about everything I thought I might get into trouble if I hung a tea towel in the wrong spot.

When we reached Disneyland, the girls were in awe. There was so much to see and it was fun to watch them be little girls.

On our way home, we went to Sea World in San Diego. Everyone loved the tricks the dolphins did. Then we headed home via Las Vegas, and as much as I thought it was going to be a terrible place to go, we had a good time there too. We went to one of the roller coasters located on top of one of the hotels, and it was amazing how beautiful the city looked. The only thing missing was Joey.

During the evenings, the adults took turns gambling at the casinos. They were amazing, and I loved the sound of all the bells, and the hustle and bustle of the people. Kurt's mother and I went to do a little gambling one night, and I won twenty-five dollars on the nickel machine. When the bell rang, and the money started spilling out into my bucket, I was sure I was a millionaire.

"Holy Smokes, I won! Look at all this money!" I screamed. It was a neat feeling! I hadn't won much money, but the nickels overfilled my bucket, and it looked like a lot.

We stopped in Reno, and then headed for home. The trip seemed to take forever. I was looking forward to seeing Joey, and finding out how his time with his dad had been. The thought *I wish Joey was here*, continually stayed in my head. Maybe I should have fought harder for him to come, but every time I came up with a solution to the "no room" problem, the answer was no.

My poor Joey. I could well imagine how he must have felt the day that we all pulled out of the driveway. I'm sure the disappointment was overwhelming, and only deepened the idea that he was unloved. I made sure to pick up souvenirs from Disneyland, and the other places we visited, so he'd know I thought about him everywhere we went.

We were in such a financial mess none of us should have gone on the trip in the first place. We were overspending again, and hadn't made a mortgage payment in awhile. When we got home, we knew we were going to have to sell the house in order to clear up our bills.

The worst part about all this money stuff was we had to pretend the reason we were selling the house was that it was too small. Neither one of us had the energy to listen to Kurt's parents *what-you-should-have* done speech, so we lied to them. We couldn't let them know that we had screwed up again, and were behind on our mortgage payment.

We sold the house, paid all our bills, and I found another nice home that was for sale. I talked the owners into letting us rent the house for the first five years, and then we'd buy it from them. They agreed, which was a miracle. Now it was up to us to make sure we paid the rent.

Sometimes when I look back it amazes me how often God gave us a second chance to make things better, but we never did. I'm not sure if it was because we didn't know any better or if it was because we were addicts. We would clean up one problem, but we had so many more it was hard to decide which one to work on next. I was trying as hard as I could to keep our family happy and fix every problem that came along, but I wasn't a bit successful. I didn't know anymore what to do. I couldn't fix my own drinking problem so I don't know why I thought I'd be able to fix anything else. The kids and I had only been home for a year, and other than a few good times our family was slowly falling apart.

Kurt and I were both drinking too much again, and we didn't have enough money to pay the rent or buy groceries. The kids were getting older, and that meant we needed more groceries, not fewer. We started to eat as cheaply as we could, and most days we ate macaroni and cheese. The rest of our grocery items consisted of whatever was on sale.

McDonald's always had hamburgers that were super cheap, and often, after a night of drinking, we stopped and bought some for the kids. Sometimes those hamburgers were the best thing we ate all week, as sad as that sounds.

We'd maxed out all our credit cards, and the phone started ringing off the wall with creditors wanting their money. Although we'd promise to pay, we knew deep down we couldn't. I was a nervous wreck. I hated the phone calls, and the fact we were making promises we couldn't keep.

We hadn't paid our rent for a few months so we both knew it wasn't going to be long before we'd be moving again. I felt like I was going crazy.

The kids knew things had changed, and started to act out more. Kurt started spending every waking moment with the baseball team, and we were back where we started. It was a living hell. I knew we'd never get back those first years we were married because we had changed. I recognized the booze was the problem, but I couldn't let it go because I thought it was my only escape.

We were so broke I decided to try foster parenting. I'm not sure why I picked something that could add more stress to my life, but I did. It was okay for a short time, but I had a hard time watching the kids come and go. Every time one of them left, a chunk of my heart went with them, and I used to wonder who they were going home to. I knew how they felt, tossed from one home to another, and it brought back too many awful memories.

Kurt became more aggressive under the financial pressure, and started drinking even more. He'd stopped spending any time with us, and when he was home, he was angry. I tried to stay out of his way and never asked him to help with the kids, but I was tired of raising four kids on my own.

It had been a hard day, and I was at my wits end with one of the girls. I'd been after her all day to clean her room, and by dinnertime, it still wasn't clean. Although I was unsure if I should ask Kurt to step in, I felt like his big booming voice might spur things on.

"Kurt, I have been after her all day to clean up her room and she won't do it. Could you please talk to her so she gets it cleaned, before I go crazy?" I asked.

"Sure," he said. Then all hell broke loose. He started yelling and screaming, and then he grabbed her and started to shake her.

"Stop it, daddy, you're hurting me!" she cried.

I knew he'd never hurt her, but the fear I saw in her eyes made me want to protect her like a momma bear and her cub.

"If you'd listened to your damned mother and cleaned your room you wouldn't be in this mess!" he shouted.

He finally let her go, and she headed for her room in a fit of tears. I was speechless. There was no way I was going to allow anyone to scare my kids that way, and I certainly wasn't about to sit around and do nothing.

"Why did you have to do that?" I yelled. "All you needed to do was tell her to clean her room. You didn't have to rough her up! What's wrong with you?"

"You're the one that asked for the help in the first place," Kurt said defiantly. The look of disgust on his face made me think of my mother. She used to look at me that way too, and it hurt.

"I just thought if you talked to her she'd smarten up, that's all," I cried out of frustration. Kurt stormed out of the house slamming the door behind him.

There was nothing left of me and I was so upset I couldn't think.

The kids gathered around me and all I could do was cry. I'd done my very best and still failed and I was so tired of all the fighting.

"Mom," Shannon said, "we want to leave dad. He scares us when he gets mad, and when you two are together all you do is fight. "

"And we hate it that you and dad are drunk all the time," Amanda sobbed.

"We're worried about you because you seem so sad all the time," Christina piped in.

"You're not good for each other or for us," Shannon added, "so please, we need to move."

Everything they said was true. I was ready to have a nervous breakdown. Between Kurt's aggressiveness, the bill collectors, and my drinking, I knew I needed to do something. None of us were happy.

"Okay," I said taking a big breath, "okay, I'll try and find us a place to live and we'll move. I just need you kids to know that I love you, and no matter what happens, please always remember that." Then I started to cry so hard I began to shake.

Moving did take care of some of our problems, but my depression and drinking gladly followed us to our new home and things got worse.

I applied for welfare and found a nice clean place to live in Port Coquitlam before I told Kurt we were leaving again. I knew he'd be upset with me because deep down he loved us all, but we both knew we were through this time for good. Even though a part of me still loved him, I needed to look after my kids. I wasn't going to allow my children to be neglected like I was. Their opinions mattered to me, and I knew they loved me. I wanted what was best for us all.

Joey was 17 and in his last year of school, Shannon was 15, Christina was 14, and Amanda was 12. I knew that they were looking forward to having a peaceful place to call home, and with Kurt out of the picture at least there'd be less fighting.

Karin helped us move by supplying a truck, and Joey's friends were the muscle. We moved on my thirty-eighth birthday, and we always celebrated our birthdays, with a party.

I bought some booze, and we all got plastered except for Amanda. She didn't like what alcohol did to Kurt and me, so she'd have no part of it.

We laughed, sang, danced, and had a great old time. Although November 28th was a bit early to put up a Christmas tree, we put up ours just to make the evening more special. It was the first time in ages we'd had fun like that, and we enjoyed every minute of it.

Every night the kids brought their friends over, and everyone drank until the booze was gone. I was so naïve I didn't think what I was doing was wrong. After all, at least I knew where my kids were. What's more, I was extremely popular, loved and accepted by my kids and their friends. Three things I'd craved my whole life.

One night Kurt showed up while we were all partying, and I could tell he was upset.

"What the hell are you doing, Laura? You shouldn't be letting our kids get drunk and party like this. Grow up and act like a mother. You're not their friend."

I could tell he was extremely irritated with me, but I didn't care. He was drinking a lot too, and I thought he was just jealous because he wasn't part of our family anymore. At that time in my life, I was sure you could be a mother and a friend to your kids and I wasn't doing anything wrong. I know now that's not the case, but back then, I really thought I was being a good mother to my kids.

I loved having the kids around, but I was lonely for some adult companionship. One night I went to the pub, and found some women who loved to drink as much as I did. We partied the whole night long, and I never realized how much my kids were worrying about me. They were spending their evenings wondering what their drunken mother was up to, instead of doing their homework or getting some sleep. Sometimes they'd call the pub ten times throughout the night to see if I was okay and I still never clued in.

"It's for you Laura," the bartender yelled. He got a little cranky after the fourth call, yet he always handed me the phone.

"Hello?"

"Mom, when are you coming home?" Shannon asked.

"Don't worry about me, I'm just having a few drinks with the girls. Quit worrying about me and go to bed." I'd try to reassure her I'd be home soon, but most nights I never got home until the early morning.

I was drinking so much that I couldn't get myself out of bed to get the kids off to school, and they missed a lot of school that year. I had become completely irresponsible and the kids were now looking after their mother, instead of the other way around.

Sounds familiar, doesn't it? I had completely become the very person I hated.

I met Lynette at the local bar, and we immediately became friends.

"You don't know of anyone renting out their house, do you?" she asked.

I was always very generous when I drank so I said, "Well, you can move in with us, if you want to. It'd be great having another adult in the house."

I took another swig of beer and before the evening was over she and her two kids were moving in with us. Then, to sweeten the pot, she offered me a job helping her with her housekeeping business. I couldn't believe my good fortune; more money meant I could order another round.

Once Lynette and her kids moved in there were eight of us, and at first, we all got along. The house was extremely busy with kids coming and going, and life seemed to be heading in the right direction. My new friend was an alcoholic too, so we were like two peas in a pod when it came to drinking.

Maybe if I hadn't had such a great time when I drank I might have smartened up sooner, but I loved the way the alcohol took me to a happier place. The world was kind when I was drunk. When I wasn't drunk, life was depressing and difficult.

Lynette and I lived our lives going from one party to the next. Although I loved having her around, I missed having a man in my life. I wanted so desperately for a man to love me that sometimes I swear it hurt me physically.

My mother always had men in an out of her life, and I think as a little girl I learned the equation that men plus sex equals love. As sick as that thought might be to a sane person, I grew up with that kind of thinking. Drunk or sober that thought was the truth for me, and for the first time I understood why Mom liked to have men around her. It made her feel loved.

Sometimes when I was at a party, if a man flirted with me, I started to fantasize we were in love. If the kids were around and he was nice to them, it was like a green light at an intersection, and I'd end up in bed with the guy, hoping I'd feel loved in the morning.

I never understood how two people could have sex and not love one another. To me it was like having a peanut butter and jam sandwich without the peanut butter. I really believed at that time that once I slept with someone it meant they loved me, and could never understand the idea of a one-night stand. How does someone love someone else for just a few hours?

I was reliving the past, only now I was my mother and not the little girl. Like her, there was constant fighting around me at the parties I went to, I was drunk all the time, I was buying booze instead of food, and lots of men were in an out of my life. The only difference between my mother and me was I actually loved my kids.

I thought I'd hit the jackpot when I met Rick one night at the Legion. Lynette and I had stopped there after work for a drink and the moment I walked through the door I could sense he was watching me. We sat down at the bar and ordered our first round when he walked over and sat down beside me.

"Hey, beautiful," he said, "I haven't seen you around here before." It didn't take him long to buy us another round of beer and get extremely friendly.

"Well," I said flirting the whole time "you haven't been looking very hard, lover, because I'm here a lot."

"Really?" he said, and he leaned so close to me that I could smell his breath. "Well then I guess we have a lot of catching up to do."

"Oh ya, I'll drink to that!" I squealed.

The whole night I had his full attention, and that deep need of being wanted he fulfilled. It was the first time in a long time a man had paid this much attention to me, and it only took me a few hours to think I was in love.

I thought at the time he was good for my self-esteem, because after all, how many older women can catch a man ten years younger? The drunker I got, the more I was convinced he was the answer to all my needs.

I thought he was such a great guy that after a week of dating I introduced him to the kids. They all liked him, except Amanda. She never gave up on her dad and me getting back together, and she knew that couldn't happen if I had a boyfriend.

My living situation with Lynette had turned sour and the kids were suffering. Lynette and I were fighting about everything so we quit house cleaning together and tried to stay out of each other's way. Suddenly, the house wasn't big enough for both our families so after Rick and I had dated a month I moved in with him and Lynette kept the house.

Joey moved out on his own, which was a good thing, because Rick's apartment was small, and with Christina and Shannon, the place was full. Amanda wasn't a bit fond of him, so she moved in with his sister for a short time before she moved in with her dad. Our family was broken apart, and I was too blind to see what was really going on.

Rick and all his family lived in the same subsidized housing complex so we spent a lot of time together. It felt good being a part of a family again. However, in my rush to get a man, I made one of the biggest mistakes of my life.

During this time, it was all about me, and nobody else. I cared about my kids, but they came second to my own happiness. I suppose in a way I thought if I was happy then we'd all be happy, but that certainly wasn't the case.

The more I drank, the less rational I became, and I had huge expectations of Rick. I wanted him to put my family back together, and keep me happy—not an easy task for sure.

The neighbourhood pub was our favourite drinking hole, and every weekend we hung out with his family and best friends. It never failed: before the evening was over, his dad picked a fight with someone, and soon the whole family, including his mother, were in a barroom brawl. I stayed out of the fights, until one night I thought that maybe another set of fists might help.

"Wait for me," I hollered as I jumped in to save the day. "Here comes super Laura to the rescue!"

I was too drunk to be much good, and was likely more in the way than any help, but it helped me feel like a part of the family, and that was important at the time.

Eventually, they banned us from all our favourite pubs because of all the fights Rick's Dad started. We were ticked off, because as far as we were concerned, it was never our fault. We were just defending ourselves.

Rick and I were a pair of reckless, drunken adults, and as much as I wanted to stop drinking, by this time I couldn't. When I didn't get my fill of booze, I got the shakes, and was super cranky until I had a drink.

One night, some of my girlfriends and I went out for some drinks, and we were having a great time until Rick showed up acting like an idiot. To begin with, all the attention he gave me was nice, but eventually I felt like I was suffocating. He was extremely jealous of me, and always had the crazy idea that I was going to leave him, and go back to Kurt. I don't know why he thought that, but he did.

"What are you doing here? I suppose you're looking for Kurt, you stupid bitch!" he said.

I was embarrassed. I couldn't believe he was talking to me that way. I stood up and looked him right in the eye.

"Don't you talk to me like that," I yelled, and I slapped him across the face hoping he'd shut his mouth.

He grabbed my arm, pushed me against the door of the pub, and said, "No whore hits me! I should have known better than to hook up with someone like you!" he said as he made a fist. I was sure he was going to punch me in the face. I knew I had to get away from him before he hit me so I fought back with everything in me.

"Leave me alone!" I cried, "What's wrong with you? I haven't done anything wrong."

He grabbed my arm and threw me outside into the parking lot.

"Leave me alone!" I cried. "You're hurting me!" I tried to cover my face as he slapped and pushed me around and I was sure he was going to kill me.

"Take your filthy hands off of her" a man said as he walked over to Rick. "If you want to fight, fight a man—or are you too chickenshit?"

The minute Rick saw the guy he quit hitting me and went after the young man.

"Bugger off," he said, as he staggered across the parking lot.

I knew that was my chance to get out of there before he came after me again. The only place close and safe enough for me to go was Joey's place. I was glad Rick never followed me, because I was so drunk I was staggering all over the place, and it wouldn't have taken him very long to catch me.

When I reached Joey's place I banged on the door and hollered, "Joey, Joey, answer the door." Praying he was at home.

Finally Joey answered the door and was shocked at what he saw.

"He tried to kill me; he tried to kill me, Joey." I was hysterical. He grabbed me, pulled me inside and tried to calm me down.

"Mom, calm down, you're safe now." He held me tightly until I quit crying, and was able to tell him what happened. I was so drunk! I was having a hard time forming words and I could tell Joey didn't like to see me this way.

"I'm going to kill that bastard the next time I see him!" he said as he paced around the living room. "You better stay here the night, you can have my bed," he said as he helped me to his room.

"You're shush a good boy, Joey," I slurred. "In fact, you're my favouritest son in the whole wide world, and I'm not even kidding." I gave him a big slobbery kiss and fell onto the bed where I passed out.

When I came to, I kept replaying the night's events over and over in my head. Where had the nice guy I met a few months ago gone, or was he only a figment of my imagination? How was it that every man I loved turned into a nut case? What was I doing wrong? The more I sobered up, the more I hated myself. I wasn't just screwing up my own life, but my kids' lives too. My whole life was messed up.

Mom was right: I was the problem. I curled up on the bed, and let the hours slowly tick by as a shadow of despair covered me.

When I got up in the morning, I went into the kitchen. Joey was standing by the coffee pot and couldn't wait to tell me his news.

"Hey Mom, you're not going to believe this," Joey said. "The guy that helped you out last night is one of my best friends! How cool is that!" He smiled at me as he poured me a cup of coffee.

I was afraid of Rick's family because they were all about revenge, and they either loved you or hated you, and I knew the emotion my name brought to mind.

I sat down at the table and Joey sat beside me.

"Joey, you need to be careful around Rick's family, they're not all there, and they won't think twice about hurting you," I said.

"Don't worry about me, Mom. I can look after myself." He kissed me on the top of my head. "I gotta run. I'll talk to you later."

I finished my coffee and somehow mustered up the courage to go home. When I got there, Rick was sitting at the kitchen table with a black eye and cuts all over his hands.

"You need to leave," I said quietly.

"You're right, we're done," was all he said. Then he packed up some clothes and left. The funny part was I kicked him out of his own apartment. He moved in with his parents a few floors down, and I was relieved I didn't have to move again.

That night I went drinking with some of my friends and was having a great time until Rick and his family arrived. His sister had brought a girl friend with her, and I knew my nice evening was over by the way he looked at me.

Kurt happened to be there that night too, and although we weren't sitting together, I could read Rick's mind. He grabbed his sister's girlfriend, and hauled her onto the dance floor.

I tried to ignore him, but it was hard to do when he was fondling the woman right in front of me, grinning as they slinked across the dance floor. The drunker I got the more I wanted to slug them both. As hard as I tried to ignore them, I was hurt. He'd swapped me for someone else in about ten hours. Reinforcing in my mind how worthless and easy to replace I was.

The drunker Rick and his family got, the more they blew things out of proportion. They were sure the reason I'd left Rick was for Kurt, and the truth to a drunk is the one they make up in their mind. You're sure you know everything, and any common sense you may possess gets drowned out.

I decided I wasn't going to go through another beating, so I said good-bye to my friends and headed home.

Kurt told me after I left the pub, that Rick's family followed him into the bathroom. They cornered him and wanted to fight until Rick's sister appeared and told them to leave him alone. She was the boss, so they listened to her and went back to their table.

I was thankful they didn't hurt Kurt because I still loved him, and only wanted good things for him. Even though we couldn't make things work, he was the father of our girls.

I started cleaning houses again with Helen. She was the lady who lived in the cul-de-sac when Kurt and I were married. I needed to make some money, and keep my mind busy because I was depressed.

I lost my appetite, couldn't sleep, and cried all the time. The more depressed I became the thinner and sicker I looked. I had huge bags under my eyes and was jumpy because I couldn't sleep. I felt nervous all the time, and the girls were worried about me, so they called their dad.

"Dad, you have to come and take Mom to the hospital. She's really sick," Shannon said.

"What's wrong with her?" Kurt asked.

"She's really depressed and her drinking has gotten worse. Please, dad, she needs some help. Will you come?"

There was a short pause and then he said, "Sure. You make a doctor's appointment and I'll make sure she gets there."

Shannon called Kurt and told him when my appointment was and he took me to the doctor. I didn't even put up a fight because there was no fight left in me. The doctor prescribed an anti-anxiety drug for me to try and Kurt and the girls decided that I should put my belongings into storage and house sit for Kurt while he took the girls to Disneyland.

I moved into Kurt's house and felt more alone than ever once the girls weren't around. Joey was busy, so I never saw much of him, and the only thing that kept me going was I knew they'd be back in a few weeks.

I loved my kids more than life itself, and I hated the fact I'd disappointed them. I knew they loved me, and I didn't want them to stop. I knew that I'd loved my mother for a long time too, but when she didn't stop drinking, I started to hate her, and I didn't want that to happen to me. Where was God when I needed Him the most? I know now he was longing for me to turn my life around but at the time, I couldn't find this God who supposedly wanted what was best for me.

The first week they were gone they sent me some post cards that said they loved and missed me, and every time one came in the mail, it made me cry. The only way to make the pain go away was to go to the pub and drown my sorrows, so that's how I spent my time. I'd hook up with one of my girlfriends and we'd drink the night away. Then the next morning we'd start all over again. The longer the kids were away, the earlier I went to the pub, until one day I was standing outside the door waiting for it to open.

"Good morning, Laura, you're here early today," the bartender said as he opened the door.

"Nowhere else to go," I said.

As the pub got busier, and the noise got louder, the more alone I felt. Some of my friends had invited me to sit with them, but I sat by myself because the only ones I wanted near me were my kids.

I drank until the pub closed, fourteen hours later, and was so drunk when I left I don't remember how I got home. The only thing I remember about that night is the hopelessness I felt. It coiled itself around me so tightly I lost the will to live. I'd finally hit bottom. I was done.

All the thoughts I'd had about myself since I was a little girl filled my head. Words like ugly, unwanted, hated, stupid, unworthy, freak, drunk, worthless, and the list went on and on. Every word gouged a bigger hole in my heart until I just wanted to die.

I noticed three full bottles of pills on the top of Kurt's fridge promising me if I took them, I'd never hurt ever again. I was so drunk and depressed I took the pills hoping they'd keep their word, swallowing them as fast as I could without choking.

I sat down on the couch, and let the pills and booze do their magic. Suddenly I got the urge to call Helen and Karin. I know for a fact that had to be a God shot and not the shot of rum helping me to remember those phone numbers. Because there was no way I should have been able to dial a phone.

"Hi, Helen," I slurred, "are you there?" I never heard anything so I dialled Karin's number.

"Hello? Hello? Karin, are you there?" I was crying by this time and never did hear Karin answer the phone, but thank God she called 911.

Karin and Helen arrived at Kurt's house the same time the ambulance did only to find me lifeless on the couch.

I was surprised and disappointed when I woke up. Helen was sitting on a chair beside my bed and the moment she saw my eyes open, she started to cry.

"What's the matter?" I asked.

"Oh, Laura, what were you thinking? You almost killed yourself last night. If you hadn't called Karin and me you'd have died," she sobbed. "Karin called the ambulance and they brought you to the hospital and pumped out your stomach. We were so scared."

As she told me the story, all I could think of was my mother; she'd succeeded in killing herself, and once again I'd failed.

"Helen, will you lie down beside me?" I asked as the tears ran like rivers down my cheeks. "I'm afraid."

She looked so tired and worried. She crawled into bed beside me and then we both started to cry.

"Everything is going to be okay, Laura, I promise." She wrapped her arms around me and became the one eyed Panda I used to hug when I was a little girl.

Eventually we both fell asleep and when I woke up the next morning, I was hiding under one of the beds in the emergency ward afraid to move. I'm not sure if I was hallucinating in my sleep or what, but when Karin phoned the hospital the next morning to see how I was doing, they told her they couldn't find me.

She was furious, "What do you mean you can't find her!"

"Please don't worry, we'll find your friend. She is likely just wandering the halls. Would you like us to call you when we find her?" The nurse asked calmly.

"Yes, that would be nice," Karin said sarcastically, "and you better find her quick before she tries to hurt herself again."

Once they found me, they admitted me into the psychiatric ward where they started to detoxify me. They took away all my booze, cigarettes and anti-depressants, and after a few hours, I started to see rats.

There were huge rats all over my body, biting me, and running from the top of my head to the tips of my toes. My whole body hurt from their claws that dug into my skin, and as hard as I tried, I couldn't get them off me.

"Get away from me! Get away from me!" I screamed, trying to swat them off. But they were too strong. Their black beady eyes, long tails, and stinky breath terrified me. The more I screamed the more rats appeared.

"Help me! Get them off! Get them off! Help me!" I screamed. "Somebody, please! I need help! They're going to kill me!"

I was running from wall to wall in my room trying to stay away from the rats, but they were too fast.

A nurse ran into my room and said calmly, "It's okay, Laura. Laura, look at me."

"Get these rats off of me! They're hurting me! Help me, please!" Then I started to sob, and fell to the floor.

The nurse walked over to me and handed me a pill and a glass of water.

"Here, take this and you'll feel better, okay sweetie? There aren't any rats, you are just hallucinating. That happens when your body starts to get rid of all the booze."

I grabbed the pill out of the nurse's hand, and swallowed it as quickly as I could. After a few minutes, the pill started to take effect and I calmed down.

Once the drugs and alcohol started to leave my system, the rats gradually disappeared. I'd never been that frightened in my whole life, and the whole ordeal left me drained. I ached all over, while alcoholism and sobriety were at war with one another.

It took me a week to detoxify my body before they introduced another anti-depressant into my system. I was so thankful when they gave me the anti-depressant, because I knew I needed the help. I was desperately depressed.

I was dying for a cigarette, so the moment my Doctor said it was okay to go outside for a smoke, my two bodyguards and I went outside. The fresh air felt good, and even the fact I had two strange men watching me smoke didn't bother me because I knew they were there to make sure I didn't try to kill myself again. I took my time because the sun was shining, and I noticed a few pigeons on the lawn. My friends were back.

I seldom left my room, because it was the only place I felt safe. The nurses encouraged me daily to walk down the hall or go to the activity room, but I was too afraid.

"Laura, you really need to get out of your room if you are going to get better. The only way to get over your fear is to face it." But my fear was all consuming.

After a few days of telling myself I needed to be brave and face my fear, I gathered up enough courage to walk to the kitchen for a drink. Honestly, every step took all the courage I had, but I was determined to get better and this was a start.

When I got to the kitchen, there was a man standing by one of the chairs talking to himself. In order for me to get to the fridge I had to walk right past him. The moment I went to walk by him, he grabbed my arm and shoved me into a corner. He never said a word, but the look in his eyes terrified me.

"Nurse! Nurse!" I hollered as I tried to free myself from his grasp.

One of the nurses came running into the kitchen and said firmly, "Frank, you need to let Laura go. Remember, we scare people when we grab them. Let her go." The man let me go and sat down on a chair with his head between his hands.

I was shaking so uncontrollably I couldn't move. I could see the man was sick, and he really wasn't going to harm me, but I still felt paralysed.

"It's okay, Laura, he won't hurt you," the nurse said. "Now go ahead and get what you came for, it's okay."

I quickly grabbed my juice box, and went back to my room. I hated the psychiatric ward and couldn't wait to go home.

When Kurt and the girls came home from Disneyland, they were frantic when they couldn't find me. Kurt's first thought was to see if I was at the pub, and that was a good place to start. However, when he got there and I wasn't there, he started to worry.

He spotted one of the gals I drank with, and quickly walked over to her table.

"Hi, I'm Laura's ex-husband and I was wondering if you knew where she was?" he asked.

"Oh, didn't you hear?" the woman said. "She tried killing herself so she's in the psych ward."

"What!" Kurt said. "When did that happen?"

"Maybe a couple of days ago."

He raced out of the bar and headed right up to the hospital. He was furious by the time he reached me. I was glad he'd left the girls at home.

"You are the most selfish, crazy and stupid person I've ever met!" he yelled at me. "You're no better than your mother was! You don't give a damn about anyone but yourself, not even your own kids!"

His cruel words made me completely shut down. I knew he could never understand the hopelessness I felt, and I didn't have the words to explain.

"I want to see my kids." That was all I could manage to say before he stormed out of the room.

All night I tossed and turned trying to figure out what I was going to tell the kids. I was in a psychiatric ward, and knew by now their dad had told them what I'd tried to do. I just wanted them to know it wasn't their fault. They just needed to know none of this was their fault.

The next day when the girls came up to the hospital, they looked so sad and worried that the only way I could communicate was through my hugs. I hung onto them, and didn't want them to leave. They were old enough to know that they'd almost lost their mother, and I could see the fear in their eyes.

I never wanted to hurt my kids. I knew I'd made tons of mistakes over the years, but having my kids was never one of them. Their presence in my life was the only thing that kept me going, and I vowed that day that I was going to do whatever it took to make things right.

Before they discharged me, one of the nurses handed me a phone number.

"Laura, this is the number for Alcoholics Anonymous. Give

them a call when you get home. They can help you," she said compassionately.

"Thank you, I will," I said, as I tucked the piece of paper into my purse. I left praying I'd never see the inside of that place again.

Part Five
Road to Sobriety

I went back to Kurt's apartment and made my first phone call to find out where I could attend an AA meeting. I asked Kurt if he could drive me to the meeting and he did.

"Welcome, go on in and grab yourself a cup of coffee. The meeting should start in about ten minutes," the greeter at the door informed me. I was afraid to go to the meeting at first, but the greeter made me feel so welcome I felt less afraid, and went through the door.

I grabbed a cup of coffee, and almost instantly I had men and women coming up to welcome me to the meeting. As we visited, it wasn't long before I knew these people understood what I was going through. It was so nice to be understood for a change. No one judged me, they just let me talk. I went to a meeting as often as I could, and when I was really struggling, I'd go twice a day.

At every meeting they talked about the importance of having a higher power in your life. I wasn't sure at first what that really meant but I knew in order for me to get well, I needed help. Supernatural help. Suddenly I knew without a doubt that God was the higher power I would need to lean on if I was going to quit drinking. Mrs. Reimer told me often how she leaned on God to help her and now it was my turn. I had no idea how everything was supposed to work, but I was determined to change and knew I couldn't do it on my own.

I knew I needed to get away from Kurt, because he was still drinking, and his temper was too unpredictable. I felt like I was five again, waiting for my mother to blow up, and I was so on edge I couldn't sleep.

"Kurt, I think you need to take me back to the hospital," I wept. "I haven't been able to sleep for a week and I need some help."

He spoke softly to me and said, "Laura, you'll be alright. Your body just needs to get rested. Believe me, you'll be fine. Go back to bed."

"Okay," I said, and went back to my room.

Over time, the insomnia went away, and I started to feel a lot stronger. My thinking started to clear up and I knew it was time for the kids and me to find our own place to live. All the kids were ready to live with me again, and I was excited because it had been a long time since we'd all lived together.

I'm not sure how this happened, but a woman I had previously cleaned for called me, and told me she was moving and that her place was available to rent. It was perfect for us: it was clean, in a good area, and had a basement suite Joey could use. Maybe my higher power was looking after us after all.

I didn't have a job, so Family Court ordered Kurt to start paying child support or they'd garnish his wages. His cheque every month really helped us keep food on the table and a roof over our heads until I was well enough to go back to work.

Helen, once she heard I was ready to work again, offered me a job cleaning houses, and it felt good to be independent.

I kept going to the AA meetings for the social support, but for some reason I couldn't understand the speakers. It was as if I could hear them talking, but they were speaking a different language. The one thing I did get out of the meetings was that there were lots of people who started out like me and with the help of their higher power had changed and that gave me hope.

My daughter Shannon started coming to the meetings with me for moral support, but I was fidgety, irritable and discontent. I was fighting my addiction as hard as I could, but it was slowly winning.

I missed my old drinking partners and all the fun we had together. I'd promised the kids I wouldn't start drinking again, and I wanted to keep my promise, however the fight going on inside me was making me crazy. The urge to start drinking again was so strong I could almost taste the booze, and the only thing standing in the way of my starting to drink again was my promise. I went back and forth so many times I finally convinced myself I was strong enough to stop at one drink.

Now that was a lie straight from the pit of Hell. I stayed sober for five months, and then I relapsed.

I'd actually convinced myself I could quit after one drink. I went to a meeting knowing full well the moment it ended I was going to go pick up some beer and wine at the liquor store, and go over to Helen's house for one drink. When Helen opened her door and saw me holding a six-pack, a big smile came across her face. Her old drinking pal was back.

"Hey, this is a pleasant surprise, come on in and let's crack open one of those beers," she said as she made her way to the kitchen.

I smiled at her and said, "I'm only coming for one."

"No problem, I'll drink the rest," she laughed.

I followed her into the kitchen and that first beer tasted so good there was no way I was going to quit at one. I was on a roll and completely forgot about the promise I'd made to the kids. I was back on that old hamster's wheel, loving and hating every moment of it.

When I left Helen's house that night I was drunk. I was so ashamed of myself because for the millionth time I'd failed. I'd broken my promise to my kids and I prayed all the way home that they'd be in bed and not see me drunk. The truth was they'd know sooner or later I was drinking again. Why couldn't I stop?

My mother was right. I was stupid and no good. I was a drunk and was starting to believe I'd always be a drunk, just like her. I was so frustrated inside I could have burst but as hard as I tried, I thought I couldn't live without the booze.

One Friday, after Helen and I had cleaned our last house, we went outside and discovered her car had a flat tire. I knew the quicker the tire got fixed the sooner we could get on with our evening routine.

She didn't have a jack so I went to two different gas stations to find one, but came back empty-handed. I'd been drinking for two weeks and my routine of meeting the girls at the old watering hole after work had taken root. The kids were really disappointed with me but I pushed their feelings aside and did what I wanted

"Now what are we going to do?" Helen asked.

I'd remembered hearing at an AA meeting that some of the men who attended the meetings lived in a recovery house five blocks from where we were.

"I know some men who might help. I'll be right back," and I walked as fast as I could to one of the houses and banged on the door.

A man answered the door, stepped out of the house closing the door behind him.

"Hi, can I help you?" he asked.

"As a matter of fact, you can. Our car has a flat tire and we need some help to change it," I said.

He went back inside, and when he returned, he had another man with him.

"I can help you if you like. My car's right over here," he said as I followed him to his car. We jumped into his vehicle and I told him where to go. Little did I know that the next five minutes were going to change my life forever.

While we were driving, he asked, "How did you know about the recovery house?"

"I used to go to AA meetings, and I remembered some of the men mentioning they lived there."

"You used to go to AA?" he asked. "Does that mean you don't go anymore?"

"No, I really don't have time," I answered, suddenly wishing I were somewhere else.

"I remember being in the same place as you. It's tough work staying away from the booze. I know because I am an alcoholic and if it hadn't been for my higher power, I never would have made it."

Then he started to tell me his story and I hung on every word. Everything he said made me realize he knew me, or at least he knew the part of me that I'd been trying to hide. He understood the struggles I was going through, and there was something about him that made me think if he could beat his demon, then so could I. He was a recovering alcoholic, and his addiction had run his life until he found God, attended the AA meetings regularly, and gone through the twelve-step program. He had been sober for ten years, and to give back he went weekly to do in-house meetings.

A warm sensation swept over me, and I knew recovery was the place for me. It was more than just a decision it was a spiritual awakening. Everything he said I had lived through. We were alike in that we'd both tried to kill ourselves more than once, but different because he'd lost his family and I still had mine. It was the first time I realized I needed to quit drinking for myself, because I wanted to live. I wanted to be a good mother to my children, I wanted to see my grandchildren, I wanted my life back, and I didn't want to have the same kind of life as my mother did. Something inside me changed.

When we arrived at Helen's car he quickly pulled over to the side of the road and we both got out.

"Looks like you have a little problem?" he said teasingly.

"Yup, it is definitely cutting into our drinking time." Helen laughed.

I wanted to put some tape over her mouth. It was the first time ever I felt embarrassed I was hurrying off to a bar.

The man just smiled and before long the tire was fixed and we were on our way.

"Thank you so much," I said hoping he'd realize I was thanking him for more than just fixing the tire.

"You're welcome" he said as he left, "and think about what we talked about."

I did, in fact it's all I did.

"What did he mean by that," Helen asked, "did he ask you for a date?"

"Oh no, it was nothing like that," I said quietly.

"You're not talking much, anything wrong?" Helen asked as we drove into the parking lot at the bar.

"No, it's just been a long week."

As we walked into the bar to meet the girls it was the first time I noticed how awful the place smelled and how unkept it was.

The girls sounded like a bunch of clucking hens in a barn, and at one time I would have clucked right along with them, but not that night. As I looked around I saw the same people, in the same spots, and the volume in the place was getting louder and louder. The clinking of the glasses seemed sharper, and although I had two glasses of beer in front of me, I had no desire to drink them. It was as if my eyes were open to a truth I'd never seen before.

I didn't recognize at the time that the voice I heard that night was God's but he said to me, "You don't belong here anymore, Laura. Take my hand and together we'll beat your demons."

There was something so gentle, hopeful and convincing about

that voice that I chose to believe what that little voice said, stood up, and walked towards the door.

"Hey, Laura, where you going? The night's still young," Helen yelled, but I knew I didn't belong in this place anymore.

The moment I closed the bar door that night, I closed a chapter in my life. The man I'd talked to earlier convinced me there was more to living than what I'd experienced, and I wanted to live.

Once I got outside the bar, I knew I needed to go to an AA meeting. I was so excited and full of hope I couldn't get to the meeting fast enough. I felt giddy inside, and was looking forward to seeing my AA friends.

The moment the greeter at the door welcomed me this time around, I knew I was home. I could understand everything being said for once, and every word healed a little of my heart. These people understood the demons I was fighting, and I knew I needed to be honest with myself, accept I was an alcoholic, and move forward.

I quit my job working with Helen because I knew if I didn't it would be too hard to stay away from the bar , and I knew I needed to stay away from anything or anyone that would call me back to the bottle if I was going to succeed.

My only focus was to stay sober, and become healthier physically and emotionally. I also had no idea how often the kids were getting to school, so I did my best to get them back on the right track.

They told me at the meetings that in order for me to get better, I needed to serve God, and help others, so the moment I got feeling better I wanted to help anyone, and everyone. My whole outlook on life was beginning to change, and I hadn't had this much energy for a long time.

My kids had some friends that were having trouble at home, so I told them they could live with us for a while. I was determined to help my kids and their friends so that they wouldn't make the same mistakes I did.

The moment I felt a twinge better, I always bit off more than I could chew, and trying to help all those rebellious teenagers change their lives was one big bite.

To add to the chaos, we also had two dogs, a cat and a frog Amanda brought home one day after school.

The first major disaster was when the cat ate the frog. Amanda was so upset I was sure she'd never get over her loss. Thank heavens time heals all things, because the frog incident was by far the least of our worries.

"Okay kids," I said very seriously, "we can make this work, but we are going to have a few house rules, and if you choose not to obey them, you'll have to leave."

"Sure, no problem. What are they?" they asked flippantly.

"There will be no drinking, drugs or partying in our house. I am serious. If you don't listen to me, I'm going to ask you to leave."

I knew I wasn't strong enough to stay away from the booze, and I was determined to stay sober.

"No problem," was their answer, and then they took off. I knew the kids didn't understand how important the house rules were, because the first time I went to an AA meeting they threw a party. I came home after the meeting to a house full of drunken teenagers, and booze all over the place. If they could've seen the war that went on inside me as I cleaned up their mess, things may have been different, but they didn't have a clue!

For so many years, I'd been more of a friend to them than a mother, and now I was changing the rules. They were used to a fun, drunken mother, who loved to party with them, instead of a sober mother, who knew how alcohol could ruin their lives.

The next morning I rallied the troops.

"I asked you nicely not to have parties in our home, and last night when I got here there was booze and drugs all over the place. This is my home, and if you refuse to keep the rules, you have to leave, I'm not kidding."

"Aw, come on, Mom. Those are stupid rules. We always drank and partied before and you never minded. Lighten up," Christina said.

I knew I needed to make some tough decisions. I knew my kids were going to have the same addiction to alcohol as I did if they kept up their drinking, and I wasn't going to enable them. I'd always wanted to keep them happy, but I understood for the first time, that the kind of drunken happiness I'd allowed them could kill them in the end.

The kids' friends were the first to leave because they refused to abide by the rules. Then I asked Joey to leave, because his anger was unpredictable and I couldn't handle his outbursts.

The girls were resentful and angry because I'd suddenly put some boundaries in place—and kept them. If they'd have known how hard it was for me to make and keep a boundary in the first place, they'd have realized they'd witnessed a miracle.

The more I got to know the people at AA the more I loved going to the meetings. I chose to turn to God and my new friends instead of the booze when I needed help, which at first wasn't easy.

Bob was the man I met at the door when I went to my first meeting, and he became my sponsor, because I couldn't find a woman to sponsor me. He was a lot older than I was, and more of a father figure than anything else. I felt safe with him. He had been sober for thirty years when we met, and was a great encouragement for me.

He knew I was looking for work so he hired the kids and me to help him with his firewood business. Our day started at 6:00am and ended after we'd filled all the orders. It was so quiet in the bush. I loved the mountains, and the presence of God was all around me.

Bob cut the wood, and our job was to load it into his truck and deliver it to his customers. He was the driver, and we were the runners.

"Hey, girls, you ready for a Tim Horton's coffee?" he'd say with a big grin on his face, and then off we'd go for our big treat of the day. The girls loved Bob; he was the Grandfather they never had. He was fun, and he made us all laugh when he told stories about himself. He was a great male role model for my girls and me.

He took me to my first AA Round-up and it was a life changing experience for me. There were so many stories I could relate to, and for the first time I really understood I wasn't a big mistake. I cried through every story, and felt so sorry for the people who were speaking. Their stories moved something inside of me I never knew existed.

God, my higher power, began to show me how precious I was as time went on, and I can't explain the peace and acceptance I felt. I started to like myself, and started to believe I was born for a reason.

I was thankful for the work Bob had for me, but it wasn't enough. I knew I was good at housekeeping so I started my own housekeeping business and called it "An Angel's Touch." My girls and I worked together, and we were able to make a decent living between the two jobs.

One of the first cleaning jobs we did was for a well-known contractor named John. He was the kind of man that always saw the cup half full instead of half empty, and I liked that.

He was also a very giving person. When the girls and I first started our little business there were times we couldn't pay our rent, and he had no problem in helping us out. One time he even bought us some furniture and a bed to make our lives a little easier. The neat thing about him was his heart was a big as he was and he wanted us to succeed.

"Laura, I have found over the years that anything is possible if you work hard enough. Everyone deserves a chance, so you just keep working, and eventually everything will work out," he'd say. "Just keep at it. You can do it. You're honest and hardworking, and you do a good job. Those are the qualities people look for, and it's those qualities that get you jobs."

He blew me away with his kindness and acceptance. I knew he wasn't just trying to make me feel good about myself. He was from the old school where a man's word meant something. When he said something, he meant it, and everyone knew it. In the past, honest and hard working were two words never associated with me, and I liked the fact I'd changed.

John and I became friends and he helped grow our little business by recommending us to everyone he knew. We ended up being so busy we had to hire a few women to work for us so we could keep up. It was awesome to know I wasn't stupid, and could even run my own business. The biggest thing John taught me was that there were men in this world who were good, decent human beings.

One of my biggest hurdles was to learn how to read. I only read at about a grade two level and had little comprehension. By the time I figured out what the word was, I lost the whole meaning of the sentence, and it was frustrating. I was determined to read better so I could read the "Big Book" that AA gave me. Every night, Amanda and I sat down and she taught me how to read. We had lots of fun. I'd often get the word wrong and we'd have a good laugh. The English language is so crazy! Just when you think you can sound a word out, the rules change!

After I'd attended the meetings for a good length of time, I was encouraged to find a woman to sponsor me, so I started to look for one. As much as I appreciated all Bob had done for me, he had become too much like a father, and I didn't feel comfortable sharing some of my past with him.

I thought I had so many things to work through I needed two sponsors instead of one. I think I was afraid I might wear one of them out, but with two, they'd last longer.

The two ladies who agreed to sponsor me were wonderful women, and I felt free to talk to them about anything. They always gave me lots to think about, were very wise, and I trusted them. In so many ways, I hadn't grown past the little girl who hid under the bed while her mother carried on with her male friends. I had no idea what was right or wrong, and they helped me figure out some of my feelings.

One of the hardest things for me was to believe my sponsor when she told me I wasn't to blame for everything that had happened in my life. I knew there were things I did that were wrong as an adult, but when I was a child, I had no control over the things that happened to me, and those unhappy years were not my fault. I can't tell you how many times we discussed my childhood. She would try to make me see I really was a victim during that time and my head knew the truth but my heart still believed the lie.

It was tough. I cried everyday, but these tears were different. I knew from the meetings that the only way to recover fully was to face all my pain, see the truth, forgive others and myself, and move on. So that's what I did, one hurt at a time. I realized from the "Big Book" that it wasn't the things going on around me on the outside that were the problem, it was all the hurts inside that caused me to drink.

For once I allowed myself to feel the pain and deal with it. I gave myself permission to cry for myself, because I never grew up like a normal little girl. I cried because my mother allowed the men in her life to rob me of my innocence. I cried because she always made me feel like a worthless piece of junk and never loved me. It was a slow process, and sometimes I felt like I took one-step forward and two steps back. Thankfully, I had God and the support of the people at the AA meetings. God was my comforter and the people at AA helped me learn from my mistakes, and start over.

Eventually, Shannon started to attend the meetings with me on a regular basis. She'd been drinking and partying right along with me and recognized that the alcohol had a hold on her, too. I was so proud she had the courage to reach out and get the help she needed before she went through what I did.

Harvey was one of the men I met at AA, and there was something different about him. He was quite a bit older than I was and the more I got to know him, the more I wished I could have been his daughter.

His wife was sick with cancer when we met, and yet he seemed at peace. I loved the way he looked after her, and the way he talked about her; you could tell he loved her and was going to keep his vow to care for her in sickness and in health. He said he'd made a vow to God when they got married and he was not going to break it. The love of God oozed out of him.

Shortly after we met, his wife passed away, and I'll never forget her funeral. It was the most touching funeral I'd ever attended. She was a woman that loved children and prayed for them daily, loved her husband and was everything my mother was not. No wonder Harvey's heart broke when she died.

I continued to see him at the AA meetings, and slowly over time, you could see he was beginning to mend. He acted as I believed God would to the girls and me by dropping off groceries unexpectedly, and helping us get back on our feet. He paid me to clean his house after his wife died, giving me the opportunity to earn my own money and restore my dignity.

After awhile, Harvey asked me if I'd like to go to church with him. I'd stopped going to church even at Christmas time once Mrs. Reimer passed away. Church was always something near to her heart, and because of that, I wasn't sure if I could even enter a church again. I knew she'd want me to go, so I told Harvey I'd go with him.

When I walked through the door I immediately thought of Mrs. Reimer, and then I felt such an overwhelming presence of God. I couldn't stop the tears from streaming down my face. I felt like God had his arms wrapped around me, and was rocking me back and forth to show me how much He loved me.

It was also the first time I figured out how that man on the cross-named Jesus fit into the picture. The pastor said Jesus was God in the form of a man and came down to this earth so we could see what God was really like.

I was blown away! For me that meant God was no longer an invisible being, he loved us so much He wanted us to be able to know him by coming in the form of Jesus. It blew my mind!

By the end of the service I didn't want to leave because of the peace and acceptance I felt. Even after I got home, I found myself crying off and on throughout the day, not because I was sad, but because I was loved by the almighty God and forgiven because of his son.

Sometimes, after church, Harvey and some of his other friends invited me to go to lunch with them. I remember thinking how different these people were because they had such full, happy lives with no booze. They seemed to be free in a way I'd never known, and I wanted what they had.

Harvey continued to surprise the girls and me with his generosity. He gave us his old car and I cried when he gave me the keys. I cried because I'd never had anyone treat me with such kindness, and deep down I felt like I really didn't deserve any gift. Every time someone gave me something I could hear my mother's voice saying, *you are nothing but a pain in the ass.* Then that feeling of unworthiness crept into my thinking and I had a hard time making it go away.

My little housekeeping business was getting busier, and my clothes were wearing thin so I used to go to Value Village whenever I needed something new. Although I could have bought something new, I never did, because I didn't think I deserved it.

"Laura, how about I buy you some new clothes?" Harvey said, "yours are looking a little tired."

"Oh, Harvey, you've done enough for me already. what I have is good enough for me." I smiled because he reminded me of a father telling his daughter she needed to dress better.

"Well," he said, "I think it's important you get something new because it will remind you you're worth it, just like the rest of us."

Harvey bought me some new clothes, and I couldn't bring myself to wear them. Somehow, I didn't feel clean enough to put them on, and I knew it was going to take some time before I did. I didn't see the brand new Laura who'd traded her rags for riches, and because of God's forgiveness was as clean as the new fallen snow.

Harvey invited the girls and me to come to his AA home group meeting because they'd asked him to share his story. When he came up to speak, he thanked God and AA for how they had changed his life, then he introduced us to a new woman he'd brought with him. To our surprise, he got down on one knee and proposed to her. I will never forget that meeting! We all loved Harvey, and were thrilled that God had given him such a wonderful gift.

Before Harvey moved, he gave me a tape recorder so I could tell my story, and maybe someday write a book. At the time, I thought it was a sweet thing to do, never dreaming I'd ever write one.

Between working for Bob and housekeeping, my body was constantly in pain. I wasn't able to lift the wood everyday because of my back, and could only manage three housecleaning jobs a week. Because I wasn't making as much money, I knew I was going to have to move to be able to afford the rent.

I applied for BC housing and it only took a month before we moved into our new townhouse. Although it wasn't as nice as the old place, it was something we could afford, and the girls and I were good at making our homes comfortable.

We'd only been in our new home a short time when Christina, who was in grade eleven, met Elizabeth. Her mother had died of cancer and her stepfather wasn't interested in being a father any longer, so she moved in with us. She was such a sweet girl. I loved her like one of my own. The only problem was they were always getting themselves into trouble. What one didn't think of, the other did, and they caused a lot of stress!

Like the time I'd borrowed Bob's truck to move some furniture. After I went to bed, Christina and Elizabeth stole Bob's truck for a little joy ride. Thank God nothing happened, because neither one of them had a license. The only way I knew what they had done, was I found the end of a joint on the floor of the truck the next morning.

"What on earth were you two up to last night?" I asked.

"Not much, why?" Christina asked .

"Not much!" I yelled. "You took Bob's truck out for a little joy ride and weren't smart enough to get rid of the end of your joint before you got out of the truck. I wouldn't call that nothing, would you?"

I was furious with them and couldn't believe they could be so stupid. Funny how our ideas of fun change when we become mothers!

"We're sorry, Mom," Christina said sincerely.

"Yeah me too. We just thought it might be fun to go for a drive, that's all," Elizabeth added.

"Alright, I won't tell Bob, but maybe you should think next time." Think next time. Even that was a new concept for me.

I decided not to tell Bob what they'd done because I didn't

want to add any more stress to my life, and wasn't sure how he'd react. I simply cleaned up the mess and took his truck back.

Between the stress of the girls and my physical health, I eventually had to quit working for Bob. I went to see the Doctor, and after many tests, they said I had borderline Lupus, and toxic poisoning from the cleaners I was using.

I've often wondered if the ammonia they sprayed on me during my wet tee-shirt days had anything to do with the toxic poisoning part. Anyway, I was relieved to find out what was wrong, but it took a year until I started to feel better again.

Things were getting more and more out of hand with the girls. I finally kicked Christina and Elizabeth out because they refused to listen to me, and were drinking and doing drugs. They found a basement suite to live in, which only lasted about a month. Once they realized how expensive it was to live on their own they decided to smarten up so they could move home.

Christina and Elizabeth had no sooner moved back when I noticed Amanda was cutting herself. I was so upset because I had no idea how to help her and felt like a failure as a mother, so I called her dad.

"Kurt, this is Laura."

He could tell by my voice that something was wrong. "What's going on?"

"Amanda is cutting herself," I sobbed, "and I don't know what to do. I am still trying to get myself better, and I need your help. I think you should move in with us for awhile so you can help her out."

"Oh, Laura, what am *I* going to do?" I could tell by his voice that he really didn't know how he could help. "I don't think my moving in is going to make any difference," he said.

"Kurt, we need your help—she needs your help. Be a father

and come and help us out, please. It's the least you could do," I begged.

It was quiet for a moment and then he said, "I'll be there tomorrow."

He moved in, but the stress was too much for me. I couldn't handle what Amanda was doing to herself, and living with Kurt again was hard.

John, my contractor friend, offered me his extra bedroom to stay in until I started feeling better. There were no strings attached; we were just friends and I felt safe there.

Before I left, I could tell Shannon was upset.

"Mom, I don't' know why you have to leave," she said.

"Shannon, you can't fix me this time. I need to fix myself, if I go to John's for a while, it will give me a chance to figure a few things out without having to worry about what's going on around here. I'm only five minutes away and you can come and see me whenever you like, okay my swan?"

That was the nickname I'd given to her and I think by the time we finished talking she sensed I needed to go if I was to get better.

I felt like I was drowning. I was afraid I was going to relapse and hit the bottle again if I didn't get my head on straight.

While I was at John's house, all I did was work on regaining my serenity and calmness. I leaned very heavily on my faith, and God became very personal to me. I knew He was the only one that could help me stay sober and live a fulfilling life.

I continued to go to the meetings and my sponsor told me I'd done the right thing by removing myself from the house. It wasn't an easy decision, yet she kept reassuring me I'd done the right thing, and as time went on, I knew she was right. I was getting strong.

After four months, I moved back home, and Kurt moved

into his own place. I was able to handle the day-to-day stresses because I'd taken the time to work on my own emotional issues and physical health.

The first thing I did when I got home was get my kids back in school. I'll be forever in debt to Bonnie, the youth worker who helped me, as she's a big reason the girls were as successful as they were.

We decided that Christina and Elizabeth should attend different schools until they graduated, and the separation seemed to keep them out of trouble.

Eventually, all five of them graduated, and I cried at every one of their ceremonies. I was so proud of them for graduating, and proud of myself for getting sober so I could be the kind of mother they deserved.

Part of AA is to go through the Twelve-Step program. After a year of sobriety, I finally did the steps with a woman who had a lot in common with me. Her name was Judy, and when she saw how difficult it was for me to read, she used charades. It was hilarious, and I was thankful she was willing to do whatever she needed to in order for me to understand.

One day we were chatting and she said," Did you know it isn't your job to fix everyone's problems? It's God's."

"It is?" I asked.

I wish I had known that before I'd given all our furniture away to someone I thought needed it more than I did.

"Sometimes, Laura, by helping someone, we are only helping them to continue hurting themselves. Consequences are important because they give us an excuse to change," she said.

"My whole life I've tried to run away from consequences," I said thoughtfully.

"For years, Laura, you have let people use you like a doormat and the only one that can stop that from happening is you. "

It sounded like it should be an easy thing to change but it wasn't. I still have trouble standing up for myself, because I feel like my past has defined me and I don't have anything to say worth listening to. About the time I think I have it all figured out, I get blind-sided by something and I want to crawl back under the bed. Thank God I don't stay there as long anymore and am able to handle things in a much better way.

There is one chapter in the "Big Book" I try and read daily. It's on acceptance and it reminds me that I don't need to be a doormat to be loved.

My other sponsor Lynn had a great impact on my life too. She was the one that understood sobriety.

"If you want to stay sober," she said, "you have to let God come first in your life. He's the only one that can give you the strength you need to stay away from the booze. Let him run your life, and you'll succeed, I promise." Her words reminded me of the man who changed the flat tire on Helen's car.

After I'd been sober for a couple of years, I went for counselling to help me deal with my past. Harvey suggested I go see Joan Schultz, a clinical psychologist, and she was a gift from God. I connected with her right away, and found her so easy to talk to.

She never judged me, and helped me to understand that whatever happened to me as a child wasn't my fault. I'd heard that before, but somehow when she told me *it wasn't my fault*, I believed her!

I didn't choose my mother's life, she chose her own. Everything she suffered had nothing to do with me. I wasn't responsible for her happiness or well-being, she was responsible for her own. I hadn't failed, she had. All the guilt I'd held onto for so many years slowly went away because *it wasn't my fault.*

Five years went by before I met my second husband Gary. I'd been going to the gym to keep myself fit when I noticed a man with the nicest looking arms. My self-esteem was at an all time high so I walked over to him and said, "Hi, my name is Laura."

He stopped doing what he was doing and replied, "My name is Gary. Nice to meet you, Laura."

"You might think this is kind of silly, but do you think I could feel the muscles in your arms?" I asked.

I don't know what possessed me to say that in the first place, but he flexed his muscles, and I touched his arms. We both giggled because it was kind of a goofy little gesture, but it broke the ice and we started to talk.

"I think it's important for you to know that I don't drink, smoke or do drugs, and I faithfully attended AA meetings."

I'm not sure what he thought, but he said, "Well, that's good to know, but I bet there's a lot more to you than that," he smiled. "Why don't you give me your phone number and we can get to know one another better," he said.

"Sure, that sounds fantabulous!" I said excitedly.

It had been a long time since I'd been on a date so when I told the girls, we all danced around the kitchen. You'd have thought it was my first date by the way we were acting.

My first date with Gary was on New Year's Day and we went to a very expensive restaurant downtown. We had such a wonderful time together. He told me he worked as a crane operator at a steel refinery, and about his family that lived back east. I loved it when we were together and the kids liked him too.

He told me he drank on the weekends, and called himself a "weekend warrior", but I never dreamed he had a drinking problem.

Some habits are harder to break than others, because I moved in with him after we dated for about a month. Now that sounds familiar, doesn't it? We didn't really know one another, yet we were convinced we were in love.

He started going to AA meetings with me, and at one of them, he stood up and confessed he too was an alcoholic. I thought my heart was going to stop. Out of all the people that day in the gym, I was attracted to someone like me.

After the initial shock, I was convinced that if we both kept going to the meetings we'd be okay, so okay in fact that I asked him to marry me, and six months later we tied the knot.

Joey gave me away, and Gary's son was the best man. It was like a fairy tale. I felt like a real princess, but instead of a horse drawn carriage, we left in a white limousine.

On our honeymoon, we made a trip out east to meet Gary's family. His dad was in a nursing home and everyone loved him because he was a sweet old man with a great sense of humour.

Gary's dad's favourite song was the "Ice Cream" song because it made everyone smile. I was nervous at first to meet him, but the moment he saw his son ,his eyes lit up , and then he gave me a kiss on the cheek.

"Oh," he said to Gary, "I think you caught yourself a good one. I think she'll be a good influence on you if you let her."

His kind words made me smile. I even went to visit him all by myself one day when Gary and his mother went shopping. I wanted to get to know him because I knew it would be awhile before I saw him again.

Gary's mother was one of the sweetest ladies I'd ever met. She was generous, kindhearted and would do anything for her kids. We were alike in many ways, but the craziest thing we had in common was our love for spaghetti! I instantly fell in love with her.

"You know, Laura, I am so pleased Gary chose someone as sweet as you. I think you'll be good for my boy," she said as she held my hands.

No one had ever said that about me before, and her words touched my heart. Finally, I had a mother who was proud of me. When I was married to Kurt I always felt like I'd never be good enough and it was so refreshing to be liked for being me.

We visited for a week and then returned home. Sadly, that was the last time we saw Gary's dad, and I'll bet everyone at the nursing home really missed his sense of humour and the "Ice Cream" song when he passed away. I was so thankful I'd met him. He was a wonderful man.

Although I knew Gary struggled with drinking, he stayed sober for thirteen months before the disease of alcoholism caught up to him. The next few years were full of difficulties for both of us because I wasn't drinking and he was.

I'd always wanted to be a mother, but to become a grandmother was more than I'd ever hoped for. My daughter Amanda had a little boy and called him Matthias, which means "Gift of God," and that he was. I loved every moment we spent together.

There is just something different about being a Grandparent. You are not responsible for the upbringing of this little one, and are free just to love, play, and enjoy this little piece of you.

As soon as Matthias was born, and I held him in my arms, the world seemed at peace. Here was this little boy, brand new and so innocent. I wanted to protect him from anyone or anything that could hurt him even though I knew I couldn't realistically do that.

Each year as he grew, I applauded all his firsts, no matter how small they were. His smile had a way of melting my heart, and if I'd had a rough day, all I needed to do was go see Matthias, and everything looked brighter.

His first year he learned to crawl and explore his world by putting things in his mouth. Then he learned to walk, and those first steps were as exciting as when man first walked on the moon. He was forever tripping and falling on the toys he'd scattered around, yet it never stopped him from running around the house.

Then he turned two, and had to learn what the word "no" meant, use the potty and dress himself. He could run faster than his mother and loved to play hide and seek.

He loved being outside, playing in the dirt just like most little boys. He was full of life, and for the most part was a very happy, content little guy. I, unlike his mother, thought even his naughty side was cute. I loved him. It seemed to me he was the cutest, smartest baby in the whole world.

No one ever expects his or her child to get severely ill, but when Matthias turned three, something changed.

"Mommy, my neck hurts," he said one morning.

"Maybe you slept on it funny," Amanda said, "go play and let me know if you feel any better."

Before the day was finished he went from complaining, to screaming so we took him to a doctor. He thought it was just the flu, or an ear infection, so we took him home. But as time passed, he wasn't getting any better. We were so worried about him, we loaded him into the car, and drove him to Vancouver Children's Hospital.

They could tell by looking at him something was wrong, and after lots of tests, they found he had brain cancer and it had already spread to his spine.

There are no words to describe how our family felt when we got the news. We were stunned. As hard as we tried to stay positive, we couldn't keep our minds from racing into the darkest places.

After the initial shock wore off, the tears came, then the anger arrived, and then we knew we needed to fight to save our Matthias. The Doctors told Amanda and her husband the cancer was quick moving so they could try chemotherapy or just keep him comfortable.

After much soul searching, they chose to try to fight the

cancer. He was on chemotherapy for six months, and even though he was sick from the treatment, he never complained. He always seemed to keep his little smile.

He always seemed so strong, while I was like a bowl of jelly inside, ready to fall apart at any moment. I may have looked strong on the outside, but my heart was breaking on the inside.

I spent as much time as I could at the hospital and Matthias and I danced to his favourite song, "Life is a Highway," from *Cars*. We'd dance and act silly and he loved that. His little laugh filled the room with hope.

He loved his dogs and one day they allowed us to bring them into the hospital so he could see them. He was so excited to see those dogs. His face lit up and brightened the whole room. Every time the dogs licked his face, a little giggle escaped from his lips and for a split second it felt like it did before he got sick.

A few days later the nurses let him go outside in his wheelchair and he held the dog's leashes. It was so cute because when the dogs ran they pulled the wheel chair with them. He thought that was so much fun! His face shone, and he taught us the importance of appreciating each moment.

One day I could tell he was worried about something. "What's the matter Matthias?"

"Gramma, who will look after my dogs until I get better?" he asked.

"Don't worry, love bug, Gramma will take good care of your dogs," I said, as I gently stroked his cheek.

"You will!" he said excitedly. "Thanks, Gramma. I know they will like it at your house."

"And Gramma will like it too, love bug. We'll have a fantabulous time until you get home!"

He smiled and then he closed his eyes and took a nap.

Gary and I moved into a condominium while Matthias was sick, and they only allowed one dog per unit. As hard as I tried to convince the owner to let me keep both dogs, he said he couldn't break the rules. It was hard to decide which one to give away, because of the promise I had made to Matthias, but in the end, a man came along and choose to take Matthias' dog instead of mine, promising to give him a good home.

It was like a death for me. I cried harder than I'd cried in a long time when he took that dog out of my arms. I felt like I was losing not only Matthias, but also the dog he loved. I'd broken my promise.

God is so mindful of our heart's desires. A few weeks after Matthias' dog left the man who'd taken him, called and asked me if I he could bring the dog back because things weren't working.

"Bring him back," I said as I ran to the door. "I'll meet you in the lobby." I was elated. At that point, I didn't care what the rules were. If they kicked us out of the condominium, there were other places for us to live.

I just wanted to keep my promise, and God had answered my prayer so that I could. When the man handed me Matthias' dog I started to cry.

Matthias was progressively getting worse, and as hard as he fought, he was losing the battle. He was so tired all the time that even a smile took effort.

We were outside the last time he saw the dogs, and he held their leashes. The dogs seemed to sense they needed to be gentle with him, and as he sat in his wheelchair, the dogs walked quietly beside him. He giggled and stroked their backs.

The Doctor suggested we take Matthias to Canuck Place where they could look after his medication and keep him comfortable. The poor little guy was so sick, we knew he didn't have much time left.

We moved him over to Canuck Place where he slowly went to sleep, and never woke up. It took four days. Those were the hardest, longest days of my life. How do you say good-bye to your grandson? There are no words.

He passed away with his little "Lightning McQueen" car in one hand, and a frog he'd named "Radar" in the other.

I am sure that God was excited to have him come home, because in Heaven, he could be a healthy little boy. But for us, he left a hole in our lives that will never be filled until we see him again.

Because of what I'd learned over the years, I was able to support Amanda and the rest of my family without running to the bottle for strength. I hung onto God harder than I ever had in my life, and prayed for the strength to help my daughter cope.

I'd been sober for eight years when Matthias passed away, and the night I took my eight year cake at the AA meeting, Amanda stood up, and thanked me for helping her get through the pain of losing her son.

As she spoke, I looked around the room, and was so thankful to those who'd helped me overcome my addiction. If they'd cast me aside, I never could have been the kind of mother Amanda needed in her darkest hour.

When I look in the mirror today, I see a different woman. My eyes are brighter and a sense of calmness reflects back at me.

I am no longer that little girl who used to hide under the bed every time she was afraid. I face my fears and with God's help overcome them one at a time.

I still struggle with acceptance. It is hard for me to say no sometimes, because I want to be liked, but I'm getting better at recognizing that to say no doesn't mean the end of a relationship. Sometimes no is good.

My addiction to drugs and alcohol sucked the life out of me by taking my hopes and dreams away, and sadly not just my life but the lives of many others. Addictions are not fussy, they will attack anyone; rich, poor, any race and age, and no one is exempt from their claws. They are cutting, baffling and powerful, because they're such convincing liars. They let you think you're in control of your life when in fact they are.

I never want to go back to being that drunken woman who was so unhappy that the only way she could cope was to try and kill herself. Thankfully today, I have lots of wonderful friends who help me when my old friend depression begins to whisper in my ear.

As I look back I can see many times where God shot his presence into my life and protected me not only from others, but from myself. The fact I'm alive today truly is a miracle. My spiritual journey has been an exciting part of my life and I look forward to what God has in store for me.

It is my prayer that my story will help those suffering from any kind of addiction. I want you to know there is hope for you, even when you can't see it.

Part Six

God Shots

"For I know the plans I have," declares the Lord. "Plans to prosper you and not to harm you, plans to give you hope and a future. Then you will call upon me and come and pray to me, and I will listen to you. You will seek me and find me when you seek me with all your heart. I will be found by you," declares the Lord "and bring you back from captivity." Jeremiah 29:11-14

"God Shots"

We all take shots in our lives. Some of us have whiskey shots, some of us have beer shots and some of us have God shots. I think God shots are times in our lives where we can look back and see how God shot his presence into our midst. As difficult as my life has been, I can see numerous times where God shot his presence into a circumstance, and saved me from others and myself.

God, and the village of people that surround my life today, continue to teach me that nothing, good or bad, is worth picking up a drink.

I want to thank God for:

- ❖ Allowing me to live. My mother didn't have an abortion because Jesus had a plan for me.
- ❖ All those who threw coins in the fountain on Georgia street. You fed a hungry little girl.
- ❖ The pigeons, because they were there for me when I was lonely and made me feel special because they listened to me.
- ❖ The lady at the Bay who saw a sad, hungry little girl and gave her a free malt.
- ❖ Allowing me to have the wonderful Grandmother I had. She filled my life with love and laughter when we were together.
- ❖ Protecting me from the many dangers I could have encountered while I was wandering the streets in the slums.
- ❖ The man I called Uncle Joe for making my life a little brighter.
- ❖ Ovey, who came at a time when we were so desperate. He took us under his wing and provided food and shelter. He was also very kind to me and tried to be my dad.
- ❖ The work the Salvation Army does for so many. They provided me with my Panda and clothes when I needed them most. They loved and fed me and were angels on earth.
- ❖ Mrs. Swanson and her two children, Kurt and Heather, who willingly took me into their home while Mom was off with Jack. Thank you for opening your hearts and your home to a little girl with nowhere else to go.
- ❖ Shawna and Shelley for befriending me. You will never know how much your friendship meant. You made life more bearable.
- ❖ The Coyne family.
- ❖ Forty some years later I found Sally again and discovered

that Grandpa Tom celebrated twenty-five years of sobriety in AA before he died. He tried to help my mother and encourage her to change her life-style of drinking, but she was not interested. Your Grandfather couldn't help my mother, but he certainly made a difference in my life and many others .Although there were no AA meetings at the time in Princeton, he often took people off the streets, brought them home, and helped them to get sober.

I want you to know that I will always cherish the silver dollar you gave me that belonged to your Grandfather and I carry it with me in my wallet.

* Thank you Sally, your friendship and all the things you gave me meant more to me than I could ever express.
* The "nice lady" who wanted so desperately to look after me and made me feel worthwhile and loved.
* Protecting me from Clive. I believe if I'd slept with him that day I'd ended up selling my body for drugs and alcohol.
* All the people who honestly cared about my welfare when I was put into Foster Care.
* For the social workers who cared about me and helped me as best they could.
* Mrs. Reimer for all her support and love. She never gave up on me and always encouraged me to do my best. As a couple, they were so God-centered in their lives and they helped me in my spiritual journey.
* Royal Oak school and the teachers that taught there. They were caring and saw the potential in me when I couldn't see it myself. Also, without their help I never would have gotten braces for my teeth, and for that I will be eternally grateful.
* Blessing me with four amazing children. They inspire me to be a good mother and their love keeps me going even when times get tough. They show me the value of unconditional love and each of them has amazing qualities. We are a family. They each have their nicknames: Joseph

is Joe "fish sticks", because I thought it suited him and it brings a smile to his face; Shannon is Swan because I see her as graceful and classy. Christina is Slinky because she is so bubbly and bouncy; Amanda is Panda because she's the baby and her hugs remind me of my one eyed panda.

❖ All my grandchildren. They are a constant joy and allow me to be goofy and fun.

❖ Matthias and the way his life touched everyone he met.

❖ The man in the recovery house who opened my ears.

❖ The handful of women that inspired me through Alcoholics Anonymous to be an example to Serve God and help others.

❖ The Founders of AA who had the vision to see the need and come up with an amazing program.

❖ To my AA people, thank you from the bottom of my heart.

❖ For the staff at Children's Hospital and Canuck house.

❖ Creating animals that so often healed my brokenness, right from Ovey's bunny who kept my ears warm, to Stubbs who protected and loved me.

❖ My church family for helping me get the help I needed by paying for my counselling with Joan and teaching me how much Jesus loves me.

❖ Joan, who made me feel like I am a worthwhile person, and showed me that not everything that happened in my life was my fault. She allowed me to see that I deserve good things in my life regardless of my past.

❖ My friend Wendy, who opened up her home to me and honoured me with her presence as we investigated my past. I love the way she is so kind to her children and lovingly looks after her mother who suffers from Alzheimer's disease. As a joke, I always say to her that she's the smartest lady I know. Thank you for all your support.

- ❖ To Diane, who reminds me of Mrs. Reimer because she always sees the good in me.
- ❖ To my husband: I love you and want what's best for you.
- ❖ There are many more, but the main thing I want to point out is we all have things we can be thankful for no matter what our life may look like.

Part Seven
Memories from Sally Coyne

*Sally was the little girl who Laura played with when
she lived in Penticton on the Old Hedly Road.*

I remember her eyes like it was yesterday. There was no Hope in
her eyes. I was young but I knew that look. I had seen hopelessness
in people before and could recognize it in Laura. Her little face
was drawn down and it seemed like she'd given up before she'd
even started to live. She was skinny and had long straight unkept
hair. Often, she wore her mother's clothes. The clothes she had
did not fit her.

I remember her mother's face and everything about her was
dark. Dark eyes, dark hair, white skin. She was the first drug-
addicted person I knew. I wasn't afraid of her, but I didn't like her.
I remember how important it was for me to tell Laura her Mom
was not sad and sick because of her; she was just sad & sick.

I would take Laura away from her mother whenever I could,
just to give her a break. Outside was a fun place for me. I spent
most of each day outside, so that's where I took her. There was
nothing bad out there. Nothing smelled bad, looked bad, or felt
bad. There was just us being little girls. I could show her things
and make her laugh, and quickly learned how easy it was to

make her smile. When she smiled, her eyes lit up, and she was completely different.

You know sometimes when you are with someone who has been oppressed and depressed for such a long time that when they laugh it's like it almost hurts them instead of making them feel good, and sometimes they even cry? That's what it was like with Laura. It was as if all of her emotions were in one bucket and she didn't know which one to let out. When you got her running and playing and she went to laugh, she might cry, or yell, but after awhile she would just giggle like every other little kid.

Stub, Grandpa's dog was not a nice dog. He was a blue healer. Mostly light grey with white, and a bit of black. He bit everyone on the farm but me. That's because I never trusted him. He would sneak up behind people in the grass or in the ditch & bite the backs of their legs, sometimes so badly the person would need stitches. He never did that with Laura. I told her not to trust him, but she did. She used to sit on her steps face to face with him and pet him, and talk to him. About what, I have no idea, but he followed her around like he was her puppy and she loved him. I think if he would have had the opportunity he would have ripped the guy who lived with Laura's Mom apart.

I always got Laura to sit with me on the school bus because the kids would be mean to her if she didn't. Once we got to school, we went in different directions because of our ages, but when we landed up in the schoolyard during recess I would see her alone watching the other kids playing, so I'd go over and we'd play together.

I gave her my coat because that was mostly what the other kids would see everyday. I gave her shoes also; they didn't really fit her, but they were better than her mother's shoes that she used to wear to school. On top of that, she had buck teeth and the kids always pick on anyone with bad teeth.

She used to stay home from school a lot, and when I got off the bus, I would go to her house. I wanted to see if she was still alive. When she came to the door, she would say her Mom was asleep, and she couldn't wake her. She didn't want to leave her for fear she might die or be dead already.

She had the sweetest little heart. I still see her sweet heart, and it is amazing that it is still sweet.

When she came to see me, she told me she was a mother, and a pretty good one, which didn't surprise me, because she's always had a great ability to love.

I have shared my hope with many people over the years, but when Laura came to see me this year and I got to see she is well, and she has hope, I was so encouraged. She shared her story about the God shots in her life and her choice to live a sober life.

She was able to share the same hope with me that I had shared with her years ago, and I don't think she really knew how much she affected me. I was not in a place in life where I had no hope, but I have never had my faith more encouraged than when she shared her story with me.

Hope imparts strength for the day. Hope for the day can grow into faith, and faith can blossom into believing. I told Laura it is time for her to open her heart and receive the blessing that was first intended for her, because it was meant for good.

I believe Psalm 40 is part of Laura's story:

"He brought me up out of the pit of destruction, out of the miry clay and he set my feet upon a rock making my footsteps firm."

The result of her story is:

"And He put a new song in my mouth, a song of praise to our God. Many will see and fear, and will trust in the Lord."

Love, Sally

Part Eight
Letters to Laura

Memories of My mother

Haunted dreams of a troubled past,
Wake me from a dead sleep so fast.

I wish I had a life, that wasn't my own,
Always running away, but the pain has grown.

I bury myself with addiction and sadness,
Trying to tear away, from this destruction and madness.

I will conquer these demons and rise above,
And rip through the earth with passion and love.

As I begin this new journey with worship and praise,
My life is now beautiful, like a rose in a vase.

Love,
Joseph

Dear Mom,

It is with great honor that I am able to write you this letter.

Mother, you have become an incredible role model for us over the past ten years. As a little girl, you faced many obstacles in your childhood growing up. However, for you today to be as patient, loving and beautifully successful as a mother of four grown children and a Grandmother of five is truly an example of loving strength and perseverance.

You have worked hard at rebuilding your life and in your belief that you were and are able to heal. Through your faith, family, friends, and Alcoholics Anonymous, you are a shining example of being restored to sanity. The efforts you display continually in all that you do inspire me as well as all those around you. You are an amazing pillar of strength and I am so proud of you. With the writing of this book, I am certain that if it reaches a single person it will all be worth it to you.

Your journey is just beginning, a journey that is the promise of a brighter tomorrow. May the Lord always be with you and be your strength as you take on new endeavors.

As one of my "heroes" growing up, you have taught me so much about being a woman, and for that I thank you. Keep steadfast on your path and may all your dreams become your reality because you deserve nothing but the best life has to offer.

I love you so much, and congratulations on the writing of your first book.

God Bless,

Shannon

To My Amazing mother,

It has been a crazy journey in life but you have come so far and still continue along a wonderful path.

Growing up with you as my mother, all I remember is a very loving and happy woman. You never let your past bring you down; you just wanted all your kids to have the best life ever, and so we did.

As you and dad went through divorce, things changed and you became sad, but you tried as hard as you could to keep our family together. As the drinking in your life became more unmanageable, your life was slowly falling apart, and so were the rest of us.

As the years went on you met someone who helped change your life: Bob the woodman. He introduced you to AA, and without him who knows how we would be today? He was a true miracle, and that is why you are sober today.

When Matthias died, we all lost a big part of our lives. You lost a grandson, I lost a nephew, and Amanda lost her son. Through that awful time, you kept us all together.

Mom, as I finish my writing, I just want you to know more than anything in the world that I am so proud of you. I can't believe you have finally finished the biggest goal of your life, the book that is going to help inspire other people in life. Congratulations, Mom. I love you from the bottom of my heart.

Love,

Christina (Slinky) The best middle child ever

Xoxoxoxoxo You Really did it!

Dear Mom,

I believe that people who suffer through hard times in their life and come out on top are going to be God's warriors and guiders. Their job will be to save and guide the people that are lost, much like your book.

With all the hardships you've experienced in your life, I'm always surprised that you stay positive. One thing that the unfortunate events have never affected is how wonderful a mother you were and are. Many of your great qualities I hope to pass on to my babies.

When Matthias passed away, you were my warrior trying to save me. When I would feel sad, all I wanted was to hear your voice, because you always had a way to make me feel better and comforted.

If you ever come across any more harsh times, just think about all the positive things you've done for people and are still trying to do. Give yourself some credit.

Thank you for being my Mom. I consider myself lucky.

Love Your Panda Bear,
(Amanda)

Dear Readers,

Laura and I met in the rooms of Alcoholics Anonymous. After we became friends, we realized our paths could have crossed many years earlier.

I had been a police constable in the skid row area of Vancouver during the years that Laura lived there with her Mom. The poverty, alcoholism and addiction in that area are devastating and anyone who spends time there either living or working is deeply affected by the despair.

I later spent two decades trying to protect children from the neglect and abuses Laura suffered as a child. Although our perspectives were different, we nevertheless share an understanding of the darker side of life.

Laura and I both became alcoholics and we both found recovery in Alcoholic Anonymous. We realize a loving God is central to our recoveries.

When Laura asked me to accompany her on her journey to visit the people and places that impacted her childhood and youth I was honoured. What a blessing it has been to witness her encounters with some very difficult memories as well as with a few people who instilled hope for a better life.

On August 27, 2010, we found Sally, the little girl who had been so kind to Laura when she lived on Old Hedley Road. Sally knew Laura immediately. Her face broke into a smile as she commented on the eyes that were imprinted in her memories of some forty years earlier.

As we settled around the kitchen table for what turned out to be a lengthy, heart-warming reunion, Sally said, "Laura, you were the sweetest little girl!" Those words have stayed with me and return every time I try to find the words to describe the journey I am sharing with Laura today.

Why is "sweet" such a perfect description, not only of the little girl Sally remembers but also of the woman Laura is today? Well, she is pleasant, kind, gracious and delightful. A very genuine, innocent love emanates from her being.

She has an angelic demeanour and appearance. It is her history that makes these qualities extraordinary. Laura was born to a single Mom who was already deeply entrenched in severe alcoholism and addiction. As a result, Laura experienced every form of abuse and neglect possible. Basic food and clothing were not provided and she never lived anywhere long enough to make friends. Her buckteeth often made her the victim of cruel teasing and rejection.

She never attended school on a regular basis, so she entered adulthood with less than a basic education. She could not read or write anything beyond three letter words.

She quite predictably sought refuge in drugs, alcohol, and men as her mother had done. Her naïveté and vulnerability attracted many vulturous characters who further victimized her. Somehow she survived it all clinging to a belief that there was a better life available.

The kind people who treated Laura with love and compassion touched her heart and illuminated her darkest moments with hope. I believe God was working through those people.

The most profound observation I have made is that Laura's witness lies in the amazing power of love. Laura's story exemplifies that power. She is not bitter, resentful, or angry. She is filled with love, gratitude and kindness. Laura is a really sweet lady.

Love from Your Friend,
Wendy

A few Words about Laura

There were a few impressions about Laura that stuck with me long after I initially met her. The first was how gently and carefully she spoke of others, with a compassion that often seemed ill deserved.

The second was the amount of resilience she had – even as a little girl she seemed to have tremendous ability to figure out survival strategies to make it through the most difficult circumstances. Even though Laura had little reason to be optimistic and hopeful at times, she appeared consistently to anticipate a more positive future for herself and her family.

It has been my privilege to work with Laura and certain of her family members these last six years. Her story is one of courage and redemption, of pain and perseverance, of failures and moving forward.

I am reminded that it is never my place to judge another human being, and often that each one of us might be in a place to extend a helping hand to another that just might make all the difference to helping them change their world.

I wish you all the best Laura. You have impacted your world for good.

Joan Schultz. PhD,
Registered Psychologist

Dear Laura,

Sometimes, life lets us see a little farther, a little more clearly, and glimpse some of the big picture that allows us to be a little more human.

Most of us bumble along, our noses to the ground, making safe decisions, managing our possessions and comforts; too often success is at the expense of others.

It has been said that when a teacher is needed, one appears. Our challenge is to recognize such a teacher in disguise.

To meet Laura, one would never suspect the repeated setbacks and disappointments she has endured throughout her life. One wonders how someone with her life experiences can be so positive, cheerful, loving and selfless towards all she encounters.

We can all learn a little humanity from a teacher like Laura.

From Your Friend,
John

Dear Laura,

As I begin to write this letter to you, my thoughts go back to the days when we first met in the foyer of our church. As I slowly learned more about you, I felt compelled to get to know you better. My initial thoughts were that I might encourage and support you, but in reality I am the one who has been encouraged and uplifted each time I spend time with you. What a privilege to see what God has done in and through your life.

You are a woman who is beautiful inside and out. You have experienced many hardships, but yet you radiate joy. When I think of you, thoughts come quickly to mind:

- I love how you are so ready to laugh and smile.
- Our common enjoyment of a White Spot Burger:)
- You have a compassionate heart... thinking often of others and their needs.
- You want to talk about God, and not just about your past, but what He is doing in your life today.

As time has gone by, little by little, I have heard your story and I am so very proud of you...such courage and commitment to share your life through written word. I thank you for your friendship; you are a blessing to me.

Love,
Diane

From Lynne L,
One of Laura's Sponsors in AA

In twelve-step recovery programs, an often-heard phrase is "Our stories disclose in a general way what we were like, what happened, and what we are like now." At meetings, members are advised to adhere to the term "General," but are also advised to be more specific with a sponsor.

However, in telling her story, Laura is reaching out beyond the support group, which helped to give the strength to write this book. Her story is intended to be a message of hope to others who may be facing similar extreme life challenges as she has faced.

Her story can't be general. It is specific and hard hitting, and is an inspiration to many as she has left no stone unturned. It's a story of success, and of reclaiming her dignity as a woman and a mother.

Laura is a survivor because her higher power had a plan for her, which she is living and embracing, one day at a time. I'm honored to be considered her friend.

Dear Laura,

What a privilege and honor it has been to write your story. It took great courage for you to open yourself up and share your story with such honesty.

We spent many hours together with you remembering and me writing. Sometimes the memories were so awful we cried together, and other times we would get the giggles because life can be so unexpectedly funny.

I believe your story will touch many lives because it is a story of redemption and hope. It is a story that shows how people can come from the ugliest places and become something beautiful.

When we hold onto the hand of our God, and allow him to lead us, He gives us the power to become the person he intended us to be, renewing our lives with hope and meaning.

Thank you for allowing me to get to know you over this past year, Laura. You have taught me a great deal and I love you as a sister.

Debbie

Photo Album

My Mom

Outfit from
Gramma

Gramma

Memories of
happy moments.

"White Lunch image."
Vancouver Public Library,
Special Collection VPL 81360

Some places called 'home'

Princeton

Penticton

Vancouver

Our precious
Matthias
2005 - 2009

Laura today